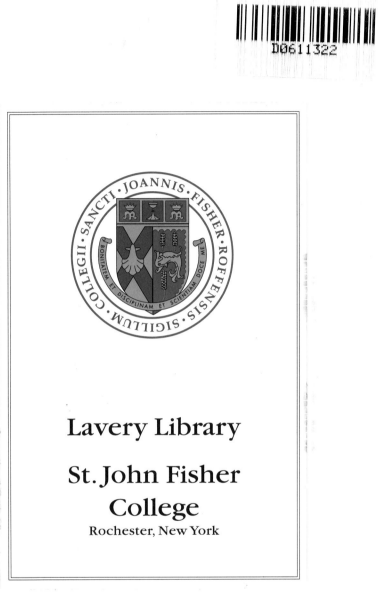

NO ROOM FOR DEMOCRACY

NO ROOM FOR DEMOCRACY

The Triumph of Ego over Common Sense

Richard M. Rosenbaum

RIT Press
Rochester, New York

No Room for Democracy: The Triumph of Ego over Common Sense
Richard M. Rosenbaum

Published by RIT Press
90 Lomb Memorial Drive
Rochester, New York 14623-5604
http://carypress.rit.edu

The views expressed in this book are those of the author and do not necessarily reflect those of Rochester Institute of Technology.
Every reasonable effort has been made to contact copyright holders of materials reproduced in this book. Corrections should be addressed to the publisher.

Cover photograph by RIT/ETC Photo, Elizabeth Lamark
Book and cover design by Marnie Soom / RIT Press
Printed in the United States

ISBN 978-1-933360-32-4 paperback
ISBN 978-1-933360-33-1 cloth

Library of Congress Cataloging-in-Publication Data

Rosenbaum, Richard M., 1931–
    No room for democracy : the triumph of ego over common sense / by Richard M. Rosenbaum.
        p. cm.
    Includes index.
    ISBN 978-1-933360-32-4 (pbk.) — ISBN 978-1-933360-33-1 (cloth)
    1. Rosenbaum, Richard M., 1931– 2. Politicians—New York (State)—Biography.
3. New York (State)—Politics and government—1951– 4. Monroe County (N.Y.)—Politics and government. 5. Republican Party (N.Y.)—Biography. 6. Lawyers—New York (State)—Rochester—Biography. 7. Judges—New York (State)—Biography. 8. New York (State). Supreme Court—Biography. 9. Political candidates—New York (State)—Biography.
10. Jews—New York (State)—Biography. I. Title.
    F125.3.R67A3 2008
    974.7'043092--dc22
    [B]
                                                                2008026151

For my loving wife Judy who has always been there for me;
my children Amy, Jill, Matt, and Julie; and my 12 grandchildren—
all of whom have filled my life with joy and happiness.

and

To my Mom, Sophie Rosenbaum, who taught me the importance of fun;
and in memory of my Dad, Jack Rosenbaum,
who taught me the value of hard work
and the importance of having a good name.

Never stop because you are afraid—you are never so likely to be wrong.
Never keep a line of retreat: it is a wretched invention.
The difficult is what takes a little time;
the impossible is what takes a little longer.

Fridtjof Nansen, 1861–1930
Norwegian polar explorer

Contents

Foreword

I have known and admired Dick Rosenbaum since the mid-1960s, when I took a leave from Harvard to join then-Governor Nelson Rockefeller as his chief foreign policy advisor. Dick was Rockefeller's chief political analyst, the one whom he called his right-hand man. It was impossible not to be swept up by his larger than life personality so like Nelson's own, charged by a powerful intellect and a perceptiveness flavored by wit. Diametric opposites in personality and interests, we became warm friends, which we remain to this day.

Dick Rosenbaum's enormous energy, hearty laugh, and shiny bald pate made him a presence known to thousands in political circles across the country. His rise from humble beginnings, overcoming personal challenges and prejudice to become the ultimate political insider is a story as lively as the man. Dick has always been able to cram more into a day than there are hours. Typical of his hurry to grasp life, he was born precipitously in 1931 in the parking lot of a hospital in Oswego, New York. Richard Merrill Rosenbaum has been on the run ever since. A six-foot dynamo, with a winning sense of humor and a determination that never quits, "Rosie" has challenged life and won through all of his seventy-seven years.

During his half-century spent in the political trenches of city, county, state, and nation, Rosenbaum has applied the grease that kept the gears of government turning, running the Republican machine in New York State in the 1970s, playing an important part in crafting the strategy that won the Vice Presidency for Nelson Rockefeller and working to engineer President Ford's nomination in 1976. He has been involved with many, if not most, of America's important political news-makers. A keen analyst of the political process, no one better understands the workings of government and the minds of those attracted to it. *No Room For Democracy* is a plum pudding of fascinating stories, ranging from Presidents and statesmen to Damon Runyonesque big-city politics, financiers and high-fliers, spiced here and there with high jinks and chicanery.

As Dick's personal story unfolds, we also see the reshaping of American politics, as a tide of conservatism washes over the liberal wing of the Republican Party. We follow him from serious issues of governance to incidents that are uproariously funny. We feel the adrenalin rush that comes from a tough political battle, and the quieter problems of facing personal adversity. We learn from tales of the judiciary to the challenge of balancing a strong family life with his wife of 50 years and four talented children, all of whom have been extremely successful in their fields and to whom Dick has been a devoted father. It is a terrific story, and it will leave you with enhanced respect for the men and women who keep the American political system working, for all its faults still the finest in the world.

Henry A. Kissinger

Preface

Yul Brynner, Kojak, Daddy Warbucks, Michael Jordan, and Dick Rosen-baum—what do we all have in common? Take one look at our shiny bald pates and you win the rubber ducky.

I can't say when my baldness began exactly. I believe I was only eight years old and in the fourth grade when I first noticed spots of bare skin appearing on my head where, until recently, thick hair had grown. Even worse, other kids noticed those bald spots, too. I was mortified. It's called *alopecia areata*.

Soon chunks of my brown locks were falling out all over the place, and my classmates, even so-called friends, began to make fun of me. As I walked up the stairs at Oak Hill School in Oswego, New York, I could hear snide remarks being passed from kid to kid: "Doesn't Rosie look like a plucked chicken?" Believe me, being Jewish in Oswego, New York, in the 1930s *and* going bald was a doozey of a double handicap for a kid.

I became so self-conscious I was ashamed to be seen on the streets. I took to wearing a sailor hat with its brim turned down, and when I saw some kid I knew coming toward me I'd cross the street rather than suffer the taunts I expected to be thrown at me—"Hi, Curly!" or "Hi, baldy!"

Throughout my teen years the situation worsened. By the time I entered law school at Cornell, I was heading toward total baldness—a perfect example of *alopecia totalis*. The good news was that by this time I had done a complete 180 degrees in my thinking. I had learned that the best girls, the intelligent ones, the ones with character and depth, couldn't have cared less about the fact that I had almost no hair, nor could any of the guys I was friends with. I was doing well in law school, was elected president of Cornell's Law Student Association, and was a real BMOC ("Big Man on Campus"). Who cared whether I had any hair? I was instantly recognizable, and I worked that.

A few years later, when I met Judy, my wife-to-be, I asked her if she wanted me to get a "scalp doily." When she told me she loved me just the way I was, I realized she was just what I wanted in a wife and mother for our children.

It had taken me more than ten years to come to grips with what once had seemed an intolerable burden. As I grew in years and confidence, I realized that the alopecia had affected me both physically and mentally. In fact, my sometimes agonizing efforts to overcome related psychological problems, some real and some imagined, had much to do with shaping my life. Along the way I learned to laugh at myself, and in doing so other people became comfortable with me and liked me. What a relief it was to leave that burden behind me!

What had begun as a handicap became a tremendous asset. By the time I entered the legal and political arena, I had learned some important lessons: that persistence, tenacity, and refusing to let things in life get you down can help pave the way to success. Not only had I become cavalier about my appearance, I was actually proud of the way I looked. I had made lemons into lemonade.

Over half a century—as a justice of the Supreme Court of the State of New York, chairman of the state's Republican Party, political guru, entrepreneur, and legal counsel—I've had the good fortune to travel the country. I've dined with presidents in pomp and splendor, eaten a ton of rubber chicken at a thousand political dinners, and polished off more than my share of ice cream and cotton candy at country fairs. Along the way I've had a great time, shed a few tears and had a million laughs.

Wherever I go, someone is sure to recognize my shiny bald head and give me a friendly "hello." And there are other advantages: I never have to waste time washing and drying my hair in the morning or looking for a comb. I haven't been to a barbershop in nearly sixty years, and—even better—I never have to shave. Just think of the time and money I save!

The lessons I've learned made for a large portion of the success

I've achieved. And I do consider my life to date to be a great success—not only because I have four marvelous children (that's attributable to their world-class mother) and twelve terrific grandchildren, but also because of the army of wonderful friends I've made over the years.

As my friends and family know, I have an uncontrollable compulsion to tell stories, and I've had some great experiences over the last half century, both in and out of the political arena. For years, pals have been saying, "Rosie, you've got to get some of this down on paper. It's a real slice of history."

You asked for it, so away we go!

Acknowledgments

This work was encouraged by many friends too numerous to mention by name who never tired of listening to my stories. I am very grateful to all of them.

It has been a special pleasure to see my efforts win acceptance to such an extent that Henry Kissinger, the world's greatest diplomat; Donald Trump, a man of enormous talents; Ed Koch, former congressman and outstanding mayor of New York City; Christine Todd Whitman, who served two noteworthy terms as governor of New Jersey; and Tom Curley, a notable former publisher of *USA Today* and current CEO of the Associated Press, would associate themselves with my work.

I have been assisted along the way by people for whom I have deepest fondness and respect, among them Luann Holtz, who has been absolutely indispensable throughout my professional life in more ways than I can count. Luann insisted I do this work and performed every task to make it happen. Nancy Bolger, who has a way with words. My wife, Judy Rosenbaum, and daughter, Amy Steklof, who discovered editing talents they did not know they had.

Steve Alschuler, a public relations genius; a battery of intellectual property lawyers at Nixon Peabody, led by Michael Orman, who guided me through some difficult problems time and again; Peter Durant and Rich Rochford, who listened and advised, and my partner Bob Bernius, who skillfully vetted the book. Rich Johnson from the firm should also be recognized for his support and superb photographic skills.

The task of editing and publishing this book fell to the more daring imagination of Rochester Institute of Technology's RIT Press. David

Pankow, director of the Press, who loved the book from the start; Amelia Hugill-Fontanel, production editor, whose skill, suggestions, and insights were invaluable; and Marnie Soom, design and marketing specialist, whose skill is quite apparent. Special thanks go to editors Patricia Cost and Jim Memmott, as well as my dear friend, John Castle, of the discerning eye. Thanks also to my friend Arnie Goldman who read the unedited manuscript and offered thoughtful advice.

Finally, thank you to Stacey Sands, my assistant at the Landings in Fort Myers who kept me in touch.

Chapter 1

Let There Be Light

When did I first think of telling this story? The notion came to me one night in October 1974 when I was literally flying high, 22,000 feet over South Dakota. Nelson Rockefeller, then governor of New York State, had taken a few of us out West a few days earlier for a private Republican pow-wow. At the time, I was the GOP chairman for New York State, and as such was very much Rocky's right hand man.

Heading back East, we'd touched down in Minot, North Dakota, for a few hours so the governor could visit a friend. We'd planned to spend the night in Minot, but a phone call from an irate "Happy" Rockefeller cut the visit short. (It wasn't often that Rocky changed his plans to accommodate anyone, even his wife, but this evening was different. Happy wasn't at all happy at that moment, and apparently she meant business.)

As a result, five of us were aboard Rocky's private plane, a luxurious Gulfstream, settling down for the long ride home. In addition to the governor and me, our little group included secretary Ann Whitman (she'd formerly served on President Eisenhower's personal staff); Joe Canzeri, Rocky's chief advance man; and George Hinman, a close friend and advisor and a member of the Republican National Committee, whom I eventually succeeded.

Rocky's plane was the ultimate in airborne comfort, and after a half hour or so we were settling down nicely, glasses in hand, recapping our trip and telling political war stories, when the pilot's voice interrupted our chatter with word that we were about to fly over Mount Rushmore. I'd never seen the Gutzon Borglum wonder, so I leaned over and peered expectantly out of the window; all I could see were pinpricks of light shining out of the darkness from the towns far below.

I suppose Rocky could see by my expression that I really was disappointed. I'm a sucker for patriotic symbols, and I knew this is one of America's most spectacular—a monument that had been attracting visitors since work began in 1927. I hardly noticed when Rocky got up from his seat and disappeared toward the back of the plane. A few minutes later, we all were thunderstruck when the landscape below suddenly was flooded with blazing light. All conversation stopped as the plane dipped and circled the great granite mountain. There, almost so close we could touch them, were the monumental faces that every school kid knows by heart (or used to, anyway)—Washington, Jefferson, Lincoln and Teddy Roosevelt—carved out of the mountain in images sixty feet high, each face the height of a six-story building and all shining as brightly as if it were noon, not midnight. It was a breathtaking moment.

Three times the plane circled the monument. Then, in an instant, just as suddenly as they had appeared, the lights were gone and the vision faded. Quietly, its engines humming, the plane lifted up into its flight pattern and moved eastward over the Black Hills into the starry night beyond.

The magic was over. As my critical faculties slowly returned, I realized that Rocky must have phoned the National Park Service from the plane and called in a favor. "Let there be light," I could imagine him saying, and then there was light. (Until that night, I thought only God could accomplish that.)

Taking up my glass again and settling back into my seat, I realized the conversation among us, usually animated, had become desultory. We'd all been affected by the strange and wonderful experience. How in the world, I began to wonder, did I ever come to be sitting here in this plane with Nelson Rockefeller, one of the most powerful men in the country, a man who had just worked a miracle of sorts for my pleasure? How did it happen that this kid from Oswego, New York, had come to travel the corridors of power, on a first-name basis with governors and statesmen, even presidents?

It was then, I think, that I realized my story might be worth telling.

Chapter 2

The Road to Kansas City and "The Last Great Convention"

L ittle did those of us who went to Kansas City for the Republican National Convention in August 1976 realize, we soon would be embroiled in an epochal event, a watershed in American political history. We knew there was trouble ahead—and that we might face an internecine war between the moderate/liberal wing of the party, headed by President Ford and Vice President Rockefeller, and the powerful conservative block backing California's governor Ronald Reagan.

What we didn't know was that we would be actors in the drama surrounding the last really great political nominating convention, that every day would be a cliffhanger, and that the outcome would remain unresolved until the final tumultuous floor vote. Nor did we realize, as we struggled to hold the party together, how close we would come to losing this not-so-civil war.

Behind each GOP candidate for the presidency that year stood his chief strategist: for Ford, it was election campaign chair Rogers C. B. Morton, and for Reagan, John P. Sears. As chairman of the party in New York, head of the state's delegation, policy architect for the Northeast, and chairman of all those Republican National Committee chairmen, I was both standard-bearer and gladiator. The job was a heady one: I led a delegation that represented nearly fifteen percent of the electoral votes needed to capture the presidential nomination. In the months before the convention, both camps were working feverishly to secure the 1,130 votes needed to assure success.

In New York we won a critical skirmish just weeks before the convention. At the heart of the matter was our uncommitted delegation, a

154-vote powerhouse. For months, John Sears had been wooing me on Reagan's behalf. I refused to budge, for very good reasons: if our delegation committed—even to Ford, our clear first choice—we would lose any leverage to obtain much-needed economic help for the Northeast, and in particular for my own New York State.

To tell the truth, I had been dangling our delegate votes just out of the president's reach for five months, a painful fact for Ford because for much of that time he was trailing in the polls. Some of our delegates had, in fact, threatened to bolt and publicly commit for Ford. I was able to hold them in check due to my reputation as a strict and unforgiving disciplinarian, a reputation that had earned me "The Iron Chancellor" nickname. I was helped by Rockefeller supporters, angry because they felt Rocky had been shoved off the ticket. (Rockefeller and I always suspected that Donald Rumsfeld, then Ford's chief of staff, was the perpetrator of the conspiracy to jettison him from the ticket—an act that arguably cost Ford the election.)

The Vice Presidential Question: Round One

As the first weeks and months of 1976 ticked away, the battle between the Ford and Reagan camps intensified, and still neither side seemed to be gaining ground. It was becoming clearer every day that conflicting ideologies would have to soften if delegates were to be lured away from their original positions; both sides began offering tempting inducements to change. When Reagan's man John Sears met with me, I told him that any attempt at delegate-stealing on his part would be considered a hostile act and would be met with severe retaliation.

Each wing of the party grew increasingly desperate to enroll as yet uncommitted delegates—and I myself was beginning to feel the pressure. Ford's loss to Reagan in the Indiana primary hit us hard; he became the first incumbent president in more than ninety years to trail in numbers of committed delegates for the nomination of his own party. The realization that Ford—president by appointment, not election—faced a public confidence problem didn't help.

If I was troubled, Reagan's strategists clearly were desperate. Two

No Room for Democracy

weeks before the convention, they made a move that sent shock waves through the political ether. Reagan announced on July 26 that he had picked Pennsylvania senator Richard Schweiker as his running mate. The *New York Times* called it "surely the most startling pick since John F. Kennedy chose Lyndon Johnson," and suggested that Reagan may have just "committed hari-kari." For the conservative Reagan to move to the far left in forging an alliance with Schweiker, one of the country's most liberal senators, seemed both a high-stakes gamble and clear evidence of desperation. How many of his wealthy right-wing backers would Reagan lose? On the other hand, how many liberal-leaning delegates in the Northeast could he lure away from Ford? In fact, within a week, John Sears was reporting that twelve delegates suddenly had committed to Reagan, ten of them from Schweiker's own Pennsylvania. The gamble seemed to be working.

The Reagan camp then began a daily drumbeat of increasing intensity: the president should announce his running mate now, before the convention. The strategy was clear—if Ford's choice could be smoked out, he would become fair game, a potentially vulnerable pawn in the political chess match. That would be especially true if Ford's last-minute choice turned out to be Rockefeller, the incumbent (and perceived liberal) vice president. Fear of Rockefeller lingered among conservatives, even though he had announced publicly that he would refuse a spot on the ticket. All Ford would say, in answer to a storm of questions from the press, was that he wanted a middle-of-the-road running mate. Rumors raged over possible favorites, a list that included Howard Baker, Bob Dole, and Bill Scranton; the latter, like the defecting Schweiker, was a Pennsylvanian. (For a while, John Connally of Texas was thought to head the list, until it became clear that his name had been scratched for fear of reopening Nixon-era scandals.)

Clearly, the next move in this war of nerves had to be ours. The matter of selecting a vice president had been carefully considered when I chaired the Rules Committee of the National Republican Committee. In committee, we took the position that the vice presidential choice should never be identified before the presidential nomination was secure. To do otherwise might undermine the power of the chief executive while giving his second an inordinate position of power. I have a letter from Vice President Rockefeller addressing that very issue, a letter that is an important piece of American political history. In it, he thoroughly discusses the vice presidential role and makes a strong plea not to change the method by which the VP is selected. (A copy of the letter is included in Appendix A, Rockefeller to Rosenbaum Letter, June 10, 1975.)

Reagan's continued insistence that President Ford announce the name of his running mate would become a major issue at the convention, as we shall see.

New York's "Operation Rescue"

I knew that New York's delegation could play the role of "white knight" in this, or any other, political chess game, and for months I'd worked my tail off to keep our delegates uncommitted. In May, a Rochester political writer dubbed me "The Paderewski of Politics" and suggested I was the featured soloist in the "Uncommitted Concerto." He must have been working late that night and drinking too much coffee.

In fact, I was the guy burning the midnight oil, making late-night phone calls to our delegates three or four times a week. I knew the first names of their wives and children and used them often. But in the ever-changing world of politics, I had learned early never to say "never." And so it was that, sitting at my desk in Albany one morning in May (just before "Super Tuesday") when many primaries would take place the following week, I realized events were forcing me to rethink our strategy.

Mulling over the possible effects of the upcoming national primaries, I saw the danger in keeping New York's delegates neutral. I knew Ford's slight lead in the delegate count nationwide was both slim and precarious. It could easily be dissolved on "Super Tuesday" only one week away when primaries would be held in Kentucky, Tennessee, Arkansas, Nevada, Idaho, and Oregon. Reagan was the overwhelming favorite in all these states except Oregon, where voters were reported to favor Ford. Crossover voting in primaries, authorized in some states, further clouded the issue and helped account for Reagan's pre-convention lead.

I saw clearly the possible disaster that lay ahead if we could not control what I labeled "the lemming effect"—a skewing of voting results directly linked to television coverage of the primaries. Statistics had shown that politically unsophisticated boob-tube watchers (including many delegates) tended to vote for the apparent front-runner—and the numbers of TV sets in American households had proliferated during the sixties and seventies. We had to get the New York delegation committed to Ford, fast—and we had to make that commitment clear on national network news.

My urgent call that morning to Vice President Rockefeller sounded the alarm. He must call an emergency meeting of his top strategists in Washington that very night. That evening, five of us gathered in the meeting room at the Rockefellers' Foxhall Road home in Georgetown. In addition to Rockefeller and me, there were Hugh Morrow, the governor's spokesman; George Hinman, my predecessor on the Republican National Committee; and Bill Ronan, a political science professor whom the governor considered an astute analyst. For several hours we discussed the pros and cons of committing the New York delegation to President Ford, chewing over the fine points like bulldogs.

One of these fine points loomed large. If the convention ended in a Ford-Reagan deadlock, wouldn't that open the door for a "Draft Rockefeller" movement? Even though Rockefeller had made it clear from the beginning that he would not be a candidate for any office, it was an interesting possibility. In fact, one of my reasons for trying to keep the New York delegation uncommitted was the possibility that Rockefeller eventually might change his mind about running.

Still, in the face of Rockefeller's reluctance, we would have to become Ford's gladiators. I voiced my opinion: If New York did not commit and Ford lost the nomination, we—including Rockefeller—would be blamed. By four in the morning our plan of attack had been hatched and I headed to my usual room at the top of the stairs. (In those days, I was a frequent guest at Foxhall Road. If I arrived late I could always expect a note saying, "You know where your room is. Cookies and milk are in the kitchen. Make yourself at home.") About ten the next morning the phone rang at the mansion; it was Rockefeller, calling from the White House with news that the president liked our plan very much. I should fly back to Albany immediately and start the ball rolling.

At once, telegrams flew from my office, urging every New York delegate to come to Albany for an important meeting on the day before "Super Tuesday."

The newspapers got wind that something was up and anticipated a big breaking news story. They suspected that finally New York was going to move out of the uncommitted column. That Monday, more than 150 delegates and their support staff gathered at the Americana Inn near the airport and our meeting began. As state chairman, I ran the meeting. Sitting on the dais behind me were Governor Rockefeller, Senator Jake Javitz and State Attorney General Louie Lefkowitz.

I anticipated fireworks (for reasons at that point unknown to the delegates), so before I officially opened the meeting I asked, "Are there any reporters in the room?" Silence. I countered: "Now, I know there are some and I'm asking you to leave. If you don't, I'll have you removed." At that point both Micky Carroll and Frank Lynn of the *New York Times* slinked out of the room. My next words nearly caused a riot. I asked the party secretary to have the clerk begin the roll call of delegates beginning alphabetically, because I knew Albany would vote for Ford. This was a dramatic break from protocol, since traditionally districts were polled in strict numerical order, beginning with the first congressional district from Suffolk County. Fortunately for our strategy, I knew ahead of time that the Suffolk county delegates were planning to abstain from the polling; they were afraid to offend the Conservative Party leadership and, by doing so, possibly lose cross-endorsements for their local candidates. I feared a possible chain reaction of abstentions by other districts (again, the "lemming effect").

I expected an uproar from this surprise move, and I got it. As soon as the clerk called out "Albany," the leader of the Reagan delegation, George Clark, from Brooklyn, jumped on his chair and yelled, "You can't do that!" I said, "George, I'm the chairman. I make the rules. Sit down." That was the end of that revolt. By the end of the roll call, Ford had won overwhelmingly; my best recollection is that he got commitments from 119 delegates, about fourteen backed Reagan, and the rest remained uncommitted. (Rocky loved the whole brouhaha, especially my forceful leadership.)

As it turned out, my strategy worked perfectly. On "Super Tuesday" Ford and Reagan split the delegations just about evenly, with Ford surging ahead by about 125 votes, almost the same number he'd polled at the time of our Albany meeting—and a number almost identical to his eventual margin of success at the national convention. If the New York delegation had gone uncommitted to Kansas City, any "lemmings" among them could easily have been drawn into the Reagan camp.

* * *

That's the story of what came to be called "Operation Rescue." As usual, there's a story-behind-the-story. Here it is:

That pre-"Super Tuesday" meeting in Albany highlights one of the great ironies of my career. The fact that, with my help, Nelson Rockefeller should suddenly find himself in the position of Ford-saver was bizarre in the extreme. While Rockefeller and Ford were personally friendly, there was little love lost between the governor and some of the president's staff. In fact, the White House's manhandling of Rockefeller during the ascendant days of chief of staff Donald Rumsfeld was what prompted Nelson to declare himself *hors de combat* for the vice presidential nomination. Obviously, if the president had been leading Reagan by a solid margin in the delegate count we could have remained uncommitted.

In hindsight, I think now that the governor may have been waiting for me to take off the gloves and try to carve out a national constituency for him. To this day I regret that I didn't fight harder with Rocky to support my position that our delegates should remain uncommitted. As a result of the shift to Ford, the influence of the moderate/liberal Northeastern wing of the party was dissipated. It's always been my thinking that Ford would have won the November election if he'd had the guts to tell the conservatives to lay off Rockefeller. A Ford/Rockefeller ticket would have carried New York State (which we lost) and in all likelihood Ford would have won the presidency.

At a personal level, I felt a Reagan nomination would be a disaster for our ticket in New York, that it would threaten our control not only of the state senate, but also of party leaders throughout the Northeast. At particular risk would be Ford supporter and Pennsylvania state chairman Richard Frame, who had lost Schweiker to the Reagan camp in the weeks before the convention. (Sadly, Frame, who was mortally afraid of flying, died in a plane crash shortly after the convention.)

On to Kansas City

"The Queen of the Cow Towns" had seen political conventions before, the first in 1900 when cowboys watched in amusement as city-slicker Democrats rode their carriages through the dusty streets of Kansas City, and men who'd only eaten beef, never raised or slaughtered it, marched carrying banners promoting William Jennings Bryan. Twenty-eight years later, on the eve of the Great Depression, when silent Cal Coolidge, who said, "If you don't say anything you won't be called on to repeat it," did not choose to run, a rowdy GOP crowd came to nominate former Secretary of Commerce Herbert Hoover, on the first ballot. What they found was that the town had moved with the times. (As the booster in the musical "Oklahoma" boasted, "Everything's Up to Date in Kansas City.") That same year saw the Democrats nominate Al Smith in Houston—the first Catholic to be nominated for president.

By 1976, the Queen of the Cow Towns had become something of a Midwest wonder. The Crown Center Plaza was a source of civic pride—bringing together a grand hotel, deluxe apartments, and upscale shops. The ultra-modern $23 million Kemper Arena, the site chosen for the convention (described by its fans as "a 21st century coliseum" and by its detractors as "a snow-white sardine can on stilts") had lifted Kansas City out of its architectural parochialism. This was now a city, according to the *New York Times,* where "women wear Halstons and Bill Blass [and] the men put their Gucci loafers to the accelerators of Ferraris and

Rolls-Royces." Kansas City's legendary barbecue spot, Arthur Bryant's, was about to be overrun. So was the convention's favorite watering hole, the mahogany bar at the venerable Radisson Muehlebach Hotel (once dubbed "Harry Truman's Midwest White House"), where the martinis were cold and peanut shells covered the floor. Across the Kansas state line, caterers for affluent Mission Hills dinner parties were placing orders for mountains of shrimp, oysters, tenderloins, gin and whiskey.

Hot, humid weather blanketed the city as advance teams rolled in for this thirty-first national Republican National Convention. It was August at its below-the-Mason-Dixon-line worst, and 20,000 Republicans were about to descend on the city in hundred-degree-plus heat. An in-your-face insult to KC's upscale image came from the crowd of Yippie protestors camping out in the city's largest park, waving their "Nobody for President" placards and threatening to force their way into the elegant Crown Center Plaza to avail themselves of its fancy restrooms and drinking fountains. The eight-year memory of angry crowds of anti-war demonstrators was very much in the collective psyche, and the KC police were stockpiling teargas grenades and canisters.

After all, these were still uneasy times in America. Ford had stepped into the presidency after Nixon's humiliating resignation, and Watergate scandals still clouded the White House. Jimmy Carter, the Democratic nominee for president, seemed to be on a roll. Within the Republican Party, Ford supporters claimed Reagan was inexperienced; detractors from both parties called him a warmonger. Meanwhile, Reagan's backers promoted his conservative views and claimed that his position as a "Washington outsider" would appeal to Democratic crossover voters. Not even experienced pollsters could call the convention's outcome with any certainty.

* * *

Lightning had struck on August 11, the week before the convention opened, when New York senator James L. Buckley announced to the press that he had been urged to become a compromise candidate in the event of a roll call deadlock between Ford and Reagan, and that he was available for the nomination. Would Buckley pull enough delegates away to deny Ford a first-ballot majority at the convention?

When a *New York Times* reporter asked me about the news, I was quick to respond. I was quoted in a page 1 story as saying, "This is nothing more than a thrashing about by the Reagan forces in an attempt to establish a beach-head. It isn't going to work." Four days later in the *Times*, New York Attorney General Louie Lefkowitz voiced his scorn over Buckley's move: "The Senator is either naïve or uninformed if he believes that he is not being used by Ronald Reagan's supporters. [He] must know he cannot be nominated." This, coupled with my thinly-veiled threats, caused Buckley to withdraw his name from consideration on the second day of the convention.

* * *

The Sunday before the convention opened, President Ford's team flew into the Kansas City airport and headed for the Crown Center Hotel, where two floors had been sealed off for our use. There were almost a hundred of us—59 staff people, Secret Service men, three staffers from the National Security Council, and military aides. Speculation was rife about the reasons for Ford's early arrival, a highly unusual departure from the norm. Most reporters, of course, claimed the president was there to do some last-minute arm-twisting because the delegate count was so close. Questioned about Ford's motives in arriving early, press secretary Ron Nessen simply said, "You know the president's interest in politics. He's been at every Republican National Convention since 1952. It would be hard to keep him away." Why shouldn't he make the most of this one?

When I think back to the months, weeks and days before the opening of the convention, I am amazed at the amount of time and effort that went into corralling delegate votes. Toward the end, convincing uncommitted delegates to come on board for Ford was like pulling teeth. Every vote was worth its weight in gold, and the media trumpeted the news whenever we garnered even one vote.

Working assiduously with me to gain delegate strength were Jim

Baker, then Ford's campaign manager, later secretary of the treasury under President George H. W. Bush, chief of staff under President Reagan, and finally secretary of state; Dick Cheney, then White House chief of staff, and later vice president under President George W. Bush; and Stuart Spencer, a California political consultant. (Baker often shortened my "Iron Chancellor" sobriquet to "Chancey," which I countered by calling him "Magnolia" since he was from Texas.)

* * *

The air was electric as the opening day of the convention drew near. We Ford supporters controlled the machinery of the convention, but just barely. The *New York Times* alerted its readers: "[This] will be unlike any Republican convention you ever watched. It will be full of passions, conflict, gamesmanship and suspense. It will be untidy. It will be fascinating." It certainly was all of that.

With the candidates in a near dead heat, the Reagan camp looked ahead to floor fights over potentially divisive issues to win over uncommitted delegates, issues such as the Equal Rights Amendment, busing, abortion, and, above all, Rule 16-C, a proposed requirement that a presidential nominee identify his running mate before the final roll call. The fight we had waged weeks and months before the convention over the vice presidential selection was still far from over.

Most of New York's delegates had publicly committed to the president (thanks to "Operation Rescue") before the opening of the convention. By mid-August, it seemed that Ford had won enough commitments from other delegates to assure him of a majority, although doubt still lingered over the ultimate outcome of the nominating rollcall. Now it was Mississippi's 30-delegate vote that held a significant hand. Reagan had counted on this support from the Deep South, but two weeks before the convention the Mississippians switched their support to Ford. Would they continue to hold their so-called "unit vote," or would they split? On August 18, Mississippi voted 30-0 against the resolution to force an early VP announcement, an act that signaled a Ford bandwagon in the making. The next day uncommitted delegates by the dozens broke ranks and moved toward Ford.

I came into the convention as an influential power broker, but power is not always as golden as it seems. Here's what the *Times*' Frank Lynn had to say: "A national convention floor is probably the only scene where political giants in a state are treated just like everyone else— seated on hard chairs in a cramped space, sweating, having soft drinks spilled on them, trying to make themselves heard even to their own neighbors amidst the constant din on the convention floor." Lynn was right: national political conventions are messy. (Just my kind of game.)

Mary Louise Smith had asked me to speak as Nelson's representative, but to my chagrin Rocky begged me not to praise his leadership in New York State, fearing to raise a ruckus from the conservatives. As a result, my hands were tied—and so was my tongue; I was left with only platitudes to offer from the podium.

Confusion and conflict were often rampant in Kansas City that week, as the following anecdote from its early hours suggests. Each Ford-supporting state chairman sat behind a table equipped with three phones: a red hotline connecting us to an off-site "nerve center" trailer; a white phone linking us to other delegations; and a gray phone connected to the outside world.

My red phone suddenly rang; when I picked it up I was warned by staff at the nerve center that some Iowa delegates were wavering in their support for Ford. I turned to Rocky, who was sitting next to me, and said, "You know, Governor, the Iowa people are very fond of you. Would you mind going over and talking to their delegates? Let's get the ones who are wavering back in line." He said he'd be glad to talk with them and went off down the aisle.

We were in a rather awkward spot as far as seating was concerned. Right in front of us was the North Carolina delegation—very pro-Reagan, lots of "Reagan for President" signs in evidence. To our right was Utah, also highly pro-Reagan, and to our left was Texas, about as pro-Reagan as you could get (Texas's own senator John Tower was considered too liberal to be allowed into the delegation). Our backs were literally to the amphitheater wall.

No Room for Democracy

Half an hour later, the vice president returned from the Iowa contingent having corralled the mavericks, but as he walked past the North Carolina delegation, one of the delegates rudely shoved a "Reagan" sign in his face. Rockefeller grabbed the sign, stormed ahead and threw it under my chair. Within minutes I was facing not only the angry North Carolina delegate, J. A. Dalpiaz, who'd had his sign lifted, but one of the Utah delegates, a big six-foot-four guy named Doug Bischoff. Bischoff said, "If you don't give him his sign back, I'm going to pull your telephone out." Never one to avoid a fight, I jumped right up and said, "If you touch my phone, I'm going to punch you in the mouth." Whereupon Bischoff grabbed the receiver and started running down the aisle, with me in hot pursuit. I was just about to grab him when the Secret Service descended on us, grabbed Bischoff under the arms and dragged him off the floor. The place was bedlam! People were screaming and yelling and I could barely get back to my seat, the aisle was so jammed.

Of course, I immediately reported the event to the trailer and a repairman had the phone fixed in short order. I asked him to give me the torn-out telephone receiver and cord as memento; later I had it framed in a glass case and I presented it to Vice President Rockefeller as a souvenir of the convention. (When Rocky passed away, the famous phone returned to me and now hangs on my office wall, along with other mementoes of our long partnership.) The episode itself has become part of historical convention lore.

∗ ∗ ∗

Describing the chaos that overcomes any national political convention on the final days is difficult, but especially this one. Reagan's supporters came to Kansas City to be heard—and they were. Thousands of horns blared, thousands of voices yelled and screamed, creating a din so overpowering that no two people could communicate with each other, no matter how close together they were. Speeches were delayed for as long as half an hour while Reaganites hollered and snake-danced around the floor.

Of course, we contributed our own noisy support for our candidate.

We achieved one particularly effective tactic by modifying a Reagan mantra. Our neighbors in the Texas delegation, courting the Hispanic vote, greeted Reagan's every entrance with a yell, "Viva!" Their alternates sitting in the mezzanine would respond, "Ole!" On the second day, I passed the word among the New York delegation that we also would greet Reagan with a loud "Viva!"—but *our* alternates should holler back with a good loud Yiddish "Oy vey!" They did—and *that* made national news.

The roll call of delegates took place on Wednesday, and the suspense before and during the polling was almost unbearable. Not until the last two states called out their responses was there a sure winner. Ford had won, 1,187 to 1,070. Pandemonium broke out again, with the convention floor awash with cheering delegates, posters, banners, standards, flags, and balloons—while amidst and above the frenzy bounced colorful lightweight beach balls bearing the name of the new Republican nominee for president—Gerald R. Ford.

***

Success at last, and yet the night was far from over. Party unity had been badly strained. In an effort to heal the wounds, President Ford met with Ronald Reagan at 1:30 in the morning to discuss the biggest of the still-unanswered questions. Who would be the presidential running mate? The local newspaper, the *Kansas City Star*, already had reported that I'd suggested that Dole would be a good pick. At 3 a.m., the president asked for my opinion; I told him that both Rockefeller and I agreed that, as president, he should make his own choice. By morning, the answer was clear: Ford's pick was Senator Robert Dole.

With the president's bow to party harmony, Vice President Rockefeller said goodbye to the private political hopes he had long harbored. If the convention had been painful for him, the pain was not yet over. He himself would make the speech nominating Dole as his successor— and a graceful speech it was.

We had won our fight for President Ford, but, in the onrush of conservative sentiment within the Republican Party, I had lost the battle to keep Rockefeller at the president's side. Still, I'd relished almost

No Room for Democracy

every moment of the challenge, and I had made a difference. Frankly, I enjoyed wielding the power that came from representing my own great New York State, power that is both real and strong. At the convention's close, the *Times'* Frank Lynn wrote: "It doesn't happen often, but at this convention, a party leader, Richard M. Rosenbaum, the Republican state chairman and head of the New York delegation, proved to be the dominant figure, overshadowing such heavyweights as the Vice President and the state's two Republican senators."

It was a good fight. I'll always remember that Bicentennial year, and the event that will go down in history as "the last great political convention."

It is interesting to consider why this was called the "Last Great Republican National Convention." I attribute that description to the fact that starting with the 1980 convention, primaries began to proliferate so rapidly that now the nominees are selected before they ever get to a convention. Interestingly, primaries are the political leaders' answer to the media's early criticism of the method employed to select candidates. It was thought by the so-called "do gooders" that the electorate should have the real say in the candidate selection process. The irony is that the primaries almost always have given party leaders excellent cover to pick whomever they want to run for office. Primaries normally involve fifteen percent of the voters and the political leaders simply get the organization vote out that amounts to at least ten percent. So unless twenty to twenty-five percent of voters participate, the political leaders now not only have control, they have cover to do what they want. Keep in mind, however, that the party organizations are barred by law from participating in a primary. A law that is usually ignored.

In an article published in the *New York Times* in April 1979, I extolled the virtues of regional primaries that would distill the primary process into a more abbreviated and efficient system. A copy of this article is contained in Appendix B, "Toward Regional Presidential Primaries," *New York Times,* April 19, 1979.

Chapter 3

Scenes from Childhood—A Bad Boy's Tale

My first recollections are of the second-story flat over my grandparents' clothing store in Oswego, New York, where I spent my first years. That flat was a tight little island, safe and warm (even in that often-frozen northland), and rich with the flavor of a traditional Jewish household. One daydream and I'm back there again with *Bubbe* and *Zayde,* two old people talking together in Yiddish as they sit near the big kitchen range. Suddenly, I'm flooded with sensations. The aroma of fresh-baked bread and simmering brisket fills the air, my shoes are tucked near the stove for warmth, and Mother is saying, "Dickie, I want you to listen. You laugh at this Yiddish now, but you're going to remember it with love all your life."

In 1931, the year I was born, Oswego was in many ways a typical upstate New York town, population about 20,000. An accident of geography makes the city unique—especially for the kind of active, inquisitive kid I was. Oswego is a small port city on Lake Ontario, and the waves of this eastern-most Great Lake lap (and sometimes rage) over the waterfront, lending the town a nautical flavor, very appealing to small boys. Nestled in New York's northern Snow Belt, the region's bone-chilling winters are legendary. From January to March giant snowfalls threaten to bury cars and mailboxes, and temperatures of 20 below zero are common. Almost every year, some unfortunate would be found frozen to death in a snow bank...Is there a boy who wouldn't love meeting the challenges of water, snow, and ice? I certainly did.

The fact that we were in Oswego was due entirely to my maternal grandparents, Max and Bessie Karch Gover. Oswego was the end of a long journey for Max and Bessie; each had emigrated from Russia to America in the early years of the twentieth century. Grandpa Max was an extraordinary fellow, small in stature but built like a little Cossack, strong as an ox. A man of unforgettable good humor, he chose for his tombstone's epitaph the words, "He laughed at life." Max had been an actor with a traveling troupe back in the homeland until the growing threat of pogroms forced him to pack up his bags and join the throngs traveling westward toward Ellis Island and America. He, like so many others in that tide of refugees, was struggling for a little happiness after a very difficult childhood, years filled with physical abuse, name-calling, no educational opportunities for him or his progeny, and no hopes for a decent job of any kind.

Once in New York City, Max found a job in a factory where he toiled with other newcomers for a weekly paycheck of three dollars. The work may have been hard, dull, and poorly paid, but it had one benefit: In that factory he met my wonderful grandmother, Bessie; they fell in love and married, a match that lasted all their lives. But the crowded tenements of the teeming city soon became dispiriting for the lively ex-actor and his bride. Investing some of his meager savings in a horse and wagon, Max took up the life of the traveling peddler, riding northwards with his wares through western New York and eventually into Ohio, before turning back eastward and settling in Oswego. I've always thought that the North Country's raw weather may have reminded him of the winters he spent in his Russian village. (What perversity makes us cling to the memory of the hardships in our lives?)

Grandpa had put together enough money to start a little dry-goods store on the edge of town, topped with a second-floor flat where the Gover family could live. For a while that family expanded to include two great-grandmothers and an aunt. That flat!—it always seemed to be full of women! My grandmother's Russian mother, Esther Rosenberg Karchevsky, was an integral part of the household until her death of cancer when I was five. I was rather frightened of this big woman, who spoke no English, only Russian or Yiddish. A perennial fixture in the kitchen, she always sat warming herself by the kitchen stove, muttering strange words I couldn't understand.

Aunt Frieda arrived from Russia to join us several years after my grandparents had started their little store. Aunt Frieda's hand was a magnet for me—why was it missing one finger? She said it had been amputated when it became infected (a hazard of her trade as a seamstress). But an overheard whisper suggested a more ominous reason for that missing finger. Was it really true that Aunt Frieda was fleeing from a husband who beat her? Could that terrible Rasputin of a husband have cut off Aunt Frieda's finger in a rage? This was powerful stuff to ponder for a four-year-old with an active imagination.

For a while, still another woman shared the Gover household: my grandfather's mother, Rachel Sass Gover, who also came over from Russia to join the family. Too many women, apparently, led to a bad mix. After a few years, that great-grandmother went back to Russia, and all I ever really knew of her was the photograph Grandpa Max carried in his wallet.

Max and Bessie turned the former dry-goods store into a family-run clothing emporium, Govers' Department Store. Their one full-time employee was Agnes Murray, a lovely little Irish lady, a seamstress with no children of her own who was a whiz at using an old-fashioned treadle-operated sewing machine to make alterations on the customers' purchases. (When my sister Elise and I were too young to fast during Yom Kippur, my parents would take us to Agnes' house, around the corner from the synagogue. There we would sit at her kitchen table and eat peanut butter sandwiches until the holiday ended at nightfall. Often that holiday would coincide with the Notre Dame-Michigan football game, and I could be found avidly listening to the game on the radio. The advent of television wasn't even a dream in those years.)

Grandpa and Grandma Gover were very loving, but because they were so busy trying to scrape out a living, there was little time for them to spend with their grandchildren. My grandma worked very, very hard, both in the store and in the little home upstairs. In my memory, she is always running downstairs to the shop to wait on a customer or running back upstairs to pick up an interrupted chore—plucking chickens, baking bread, keeping an eye on my sister and me during one of our many visits. A generous woman, Bessie tried to do everything she could for her children and grandchildren. While the Govers were certainly frugal, they were far from poor. I once asked Aunt Frieda what her favorite memory was of arriving at Oswego from Russia; she said it was the thrill she felt when my grandparents picked her up at the train station in a car. She couldn't believe someone in her family actually owned an automobile!

I have fond memories of my years with my grandparents. About two blocks to the west of their store was an area called "Forks in the Road," marked by a huge metal trough where horses could drink. Children, of course, loved to play there, too, although strict warnings from my parents and grandparents kept me from joining the neighborhood kids who would slake their thirst there on a hot summer day. Even more intriguing than the horse trough was the nearby gas station, where I discovered a nickel slot machine hidden in the back room; I lost many a hard-earned nickel there. At Guy Jones' grocery store, about a block east of my grandparents' store, you could buy a big bag of candy for a nickel; he too had a tempting "one-armed bandit."

A special memory of those years with my grandparents is that of the fleet of horse-drawn wagons and trucks that serviced the town. Horse-drawn wagons were common in those days. Farmers would load up their wagons with vegetables and fruit, roll through neighborhood streets shouting out their wares and sell to their customers right at curbside.

Of course, there were no refrigerators in those days (at least, we didn't have one), but an icebox was indispensable. Every few days a truck would lumber down the streets, stopping house-to-house delivering huge blocks of ice, twenty-five pounds or fifty pounds, depending on the amount ordered, as shown on the cardboard sign in a window facing the street. On hot summer days, we neighborhood kids would chase that ice truck down the street, hop on the back, grab the ice pick we knew was stashed there, and chip off hunks of ice to suck on.

My cousin Harry Lasky managed Oswego's Netherlands Dairy, whose horse-drawn wagon delivered milk products throughout the town. Of special interest to us kids was the manure pile behind the dairy—a huge, steaming pyramid filled with worms, a great resource for my pal Pat Kelly and me when we ran out of the nightcrawlers we needed for our fishing excursions.

Winter brought a different kind of fun. A barn was attached to the back of my grandparents' store, and I recall winters so fierce that snow piled up to the barn's second floor. Bundled up from head to toe in hats, coats, scarves, mittens, and galoshes, my friends and I would struggle through the drifts to the shelter of the big barn doors. Once inside, we would climb the ladder to the loft, then hurl ourselves like snowbirds out the window into the soft, fluffy banks below. Over and over again, we would fly out that window, until at last we were exhausted.

Those winters were something! I remember the January when three of my father's friends came over one night to play pinochle. By the time the game was over, all of Oswego was snowbound. The card players stayed with us for three days.

* * *

My mother, Sophie, was sixteen when she married my father, Jacob, a young lad of eighteen studying at the University of Buffalo to become a pharmacist. Sophie was stunning, very beautiful, and Jacob was handsome; together they made a striking couple. The young people met at a party in Rochester, Jacob's hometown. Almost immediately he began courting, driving up to Oswego as often as he could—and whenever he could find money for gas. (Often on the return trip the gas tank would be nearly empty. At the bottom of a hill near home, he would turn the car around and back up the hill, hoping the gas would flow into the carburetor so he could cover the last couple of miles.)

When it became clear that this young man was intent on marrying his daughter, Grandpa Gover offered Jacob a job at the store. Even though my father was a straight-A student at the pharmacy school in Buffalo, he accepted the offer and soon became the store manager. (He later told me that, at the time, he considered Grandfather Gover's offer a wonderful opportunity, but confessed that he once dreamed of becoming a lawyer. I think he was more naturally suited to the profession than I am. I say this because he was always calm, analytical and inspired confidence in others.)

Because they were so young, my parents often seemed to me like an older brother and sister; the fact that they had Americanized their names to "Jack" and "Shirley" (from "Jacob" and "Sophie") somehow made them seem even closer to my age. For hours, my mother would sit with me in our breakfast nook playing an electric football game. I always wanted to win and would do almost anything to make it happen. If the game was close and she was ahead, I'd find reasons to extend the game until I captured the lead. In later years I came to appreciate her inexhaustible patience.

Early on, my mother taught me a valuable lesson about the importance of standing up for your own rights. Here's the story: When I was about ten or eleven, I had a job at a carnival that came each summer to Oswego. The boss gave me a stick with a nail on the end and told me to pick up the paper trash that littered the grounds around the stands. He promised to pay me a quarter if I did a good job. I did the work well, but I didn't get the quarter. As a result, the boss and I got into a big argument; it was a case of "Someone else promised the quarter," and "No, you did." When I got home, angry and disappointed, I told my mother what had happened. She marched right back to the carnival with me, approached the boss at top speed with blood in her eye, and said, "Give my son the quarter you owe him or I'm calling the police." That got me not only the quarter, but an important life lesson: Never back off if you know you are in the right.

* * *

My sister Elise, who is two years older than I am, early on evidenced a musical aptitude that my parents nourished. When Elise was four years old, my mother drove her to Syracuse University once a week for harp lessons, where her teacher, Grace Wymer, considered her a child prodigy. After high school, she continued at Syracuse University and became a concert harpist, with an extensive schedule of recitals, including an appearance at Carnegie Hall. Years later, I found out that she had a national reputation. Several years ago when my wife and I were in Calgary, heading for the Canadian Rockies, we were having breakfast in a hotel where a harpist was playing. When I complimented her on her playing and told her we were from Rochester, she asked if we knew Elise Lestin, with whom she had studied.

My sister's personality is similar to my father's—laid-back, sweet, quiet, and kindly. Like my mother, Elise married young, at 18, as soon as her beau, Chuck Lestin, finished his military service. Later, Elise would complete a Ph.D. in education. Today she and Chuck live in both Rochester and Fort Lauderdale.

***

When I was about four, we moved to a two-family side-by-side house on the eastern outskirts of Oswego. I recall good times riding my Roadmaster bicycle (of which I was very proud) and having fun with fireworks, which in those days were legal. The Oak Hill grammar school was about five or six blocks away, and I would hike up the hill to school every day.

To say that I was a model student would be a mistake; I was, in fact, a hyper and disruptive little kid. Often my mother would come to school to get me, only to find me standing behind the piano, banished to that spot because I had—once again—upset the teacher by jumping around and making a lot of noise. I was so mischievous in grammar school that the principal eventually made a blanket decision: *every* day after school, I would have to go to his office for an hour's detention.

Even my beloved Zayde often tired of my antics. One day he taught me a lesson I'll always remember. We were visiting his good friend Sam Rosenberg, the two men sitting on the porch talking, I jumping around and causing as much distraction as I could. All of a sudden my grandfather, the little Cossack, had had enough of my nonsense. He reached out, grabbed me by the legs, turned me upside down and carried me home, shaking me all the way. I was terrified, and never again would I act up around Grandpa Gover.

In those days there were only about ten Jewish families in Oswego.

Our synagogue was so small that it was often difficult on Friday nights to gather together a *minyan*, the ten men needed for a formal prayer session. My grandpa and I would go around knocking on doors where Jewish families lived, trying to round up enough men for prayers to begin. Our rabbi lived upstairs over the temple and we worshipped downstairs.

Of course I went to Hebrew school, but frankly, I hated it. I was easily the most disruptive kid in the class. Often the rabbi would call my father in and threaten to expel me. I was always fighting, throwing erasers around the room, and doing all kinds of crazy antics, like hiding in the temple kitchen's dumbwaiter and jumping out to scare the rabbi's wife and her visitors when she raised it to the residence above. I didn't want to sit in the synagogue; I wanted to go out and play football or baseball. Hebrew school represented an intrusion, and I spent as little time there as possible. After school I would ride my bicycle to the synagogue (a distance of about three miles), put in an obligatory appearance, slip out as soon as I could, hop back on my bike and ride the ten miles back home.

Those early years of the thirties saw the rise of Nazism in Germany. Anti-Semitism was on the rise in this country, too, and often took a virulent form. As the threat of war came closer, Congressional debates raged between "America first" isolationists and those who urged support for the threatened countries of Europe. Those opposed to war looked for a scapegoat; as usual it was the Jews. One day when I was about five, our doorbell rang; a few minutes later, I was surprised to hear my usually mild-mannered father shouting, "Get off my porch! You ought to be ashamed of yourself!" Curious and a bit scared, I asked my father what the trouble was. The doorbell-ringer was raising money for Father Coughlin, the Catholic priest who used his radio program to support his isolationist, anti-Semitic views. The solicitor certainly had rung the wrong doorbell when he called on Jacob Rosenbaum.

I knew first-hand what Nazism could mean. In 1944, when I was a young teenager, President Roosevelt created a "safe haven" in Oswego for a remnant of war refugees, most of them Jews. Roosevelt may have felt guilty for refusing entry to the Jews fleeing Germany on the ship

St. Louis that was sent back to Hamburg. Whatever the reason, Roosevelt subverted the immigration quotas by identifying the foreigners as "guests." He turned nearby Fort Ontario into a free port, creating a temporary home for 982 men, women and children from eighteen different countries, the only refuge of its kind in this country.

I was about ten when America entered the war. I remember sitting at the dining room table playing with my Erector set on December 7, 1941, when the announcement came on the radio that the Japanese had bombed Pearl Harbor. At the time, we had a young college student staying with us, Ben Rosenzweig, whose mother wanted him to live in a kosher home. Mrs. Rosenzweig had seen my mother's recipe for soup cakes in a Jewish cookbook published in New York City where she and her family lived. She contacted us to see if we would give her son room and board while he was studying at the state teachers' college in Oswego.

One day Ben saw a notice on the college bulletin board that part-time groundskeepers and helpers were being hired at Fort Ontario in preparation for the arrival of the refugees. He got a job, and so did I; because I was tall, no one realized I was under-age. I will never forget my first sight of those families, carrying their cardboard suitcases, exhausted, confused, frightened, half-starved, their eyes haunted by past terrors.

In those days there was a constant hum of anti-Semitism. I was the only Jewish child in my elementary school, and I first experienced its bitter taste when I was about seven. As I grew older, the taunts grew worse. Often as I walked to and from school, I had to endure name-calling—"Kike!" "Dirty Jew!"—and sometimes I'd be attacked by kids who would jump me. One Polish kid in particular, Andrew Swiacki, was always calling me names and punching me, an approach that only taught me to be more aggressive. By the time I was in seventh grade, I finally corked the kid on the nose; he never came near me again.

I'm still puzzled by the relationship between my admittedly aggressive nature and that early ugly heckling. Which came first—this stubborn desire to excel or my defiant response to anti-Semitism? There were other Jewish kids in town, and none of them ever complained to me about being taunted. Why was I different? To this day, I feel the sting of that early prejudice. In fact, years later, when I was the Republican state chairman and invited back to Oswego to speak to a large gathering at the Pontiac Hotel, now long gone, I couldn't resist mentioning, in an understated way, how much my so-called friends in Oswego had hurt me during my childhood days. (On that occasion, news of my love for peanut butter, on which I practically was raised, preceded me, and I was presented with a case of the Ox Heart product, processed in Oswego.)

As a boy, I was very tall, strong, and athletic, while most of my friends were not. When our public grammar school teacher set up contests to see who could jump the farthest, I was always the winner—but after I'd jump, all the boys would swarm on me, whack me, and hit me. I soon got used to the ritual. By the time I was thirteen or fourteen, I was six feet tall (a giant compared to most of my classmates) and I may have been something of a threat. I admit it: I wanted to be in charge, to run everything.

Because of my height—six foot two inches by the time I was 13—it's perhaps no surprise that I was the star of our basketball team. But while I was always the highest scorer, I never was made captain. (It would have been unthinkable then in upstate New York to have a Jewish kid as captain.) My rival—the boy who *was* captain—couldn't stand the idea that I outscored him, so when he reported the game scores to the newspaper he always docked my total number of points and increased his. I remember that very, very well, and I continue to link it with the anti-Semitism that seems to color so much of my early life.

Here's another example: I remember going to play basketball against St. Mary's, a parochial school in Oswego. After the game, we were all in the shower when a priest came in. Immediately the boys called out, "Look at this guy, Father! He's a Jew!" The priest said not a word, either in reprimand or in my defense. I never forgot that. Silence can have a terrible power.

* * *

By the time I was eight or nine, my father had enough money to buy us a house on Draper Street, on the outskirts of town—the first house we

No Room for Democracy

ever owned. He paid $500 down and the bank held a $4,500 mortgage; this was the depths of the Great Depression, and banks were happy for any business. I thought the house was wonderful; it was a Dutch colonial, with a detached single-car garage, and an open field where I could play. (More "true confession" time: Sometimes when I was bored, I would set that dry field on fire, then run and hide when the firemen came to put out the blaze, a conflagration that sometimes grew to cover several acres. I don't think the identity of the juvenile arsonist ever was discovered.)

Almost from the beginning, I had a penchant for getting into trouble, as the following anecdote makes clear. I knew that in the office of the Netherlands Dairy (run by my cousin Harry Lasky) there was a locker containing ice cream goodies. Some packages contained a model airplane and some specially marked boxes of Eskimo Pies had valuable coupons inside. At age eight I fashioned a tiny lock pick, broke into the office, and was handing out the prizes to a friend when the office's secret alarm went off without my realizing it. I looked up to see two grown men standing in the doorway, looking down incredulously at two very small thieves. My father was pacifist by nature, but did I ever get it that day!

Although I liked that neighborhood, I spent a lot of my time alone. The family next door had a brick garage that bordered our property line. Hour after hour I hurled a baseball at that garage wall as hard as I could, trying to develop accuracy. I made a game of this solitary exercise: If I caught the ball in the air when it bounced off the wall, that was an "out"; if the ball hit the ground first, that was a "single," or whatever I wanted it to be (since I was the king of the game). I threw the ball at that wall so hard I actually dislodged some of the bricks. I also practiced drop-kicking a football over that garage until I got very, very good at it. (Unfortunately, that skill became outdated before I reached high school.)

Even though I loved athletics, I did have other interests. I loved reading newspapers. When I was about ten, I started my own penny-a-copy neighborhood paper, a one- or two-page sheet I called *The Oswego Daily Cub* (despite the fact that it came out only once a week). I bought a mimeograph machine from a friend for five dollars and became the the *Cub*'s publisher, editor, typist, machine operator, and newsboy. I tried to report on everything that was going on in the neighborhood and wrote a column (title stolen from another newspaper) called "Predictions of Things to Come," in which I forecast the coming of war a week before the attack on Pearl Harbor. The paper flourished until the day I divulged some private family news. Shortly thereafter, my parents pulled my license.

Mostly, I played alone. Across the road from our house was the Oswego Normal School, whose campus included a nice woodlot, a little jungle where I could disappear and build my own private hideouts. If desperate, I might play with my cousin Joel Lasky. Joel was a different kind of boy than I was; he was quiet and well-behaved while I was admittedly overbearing—to say the least! Looking back on those years, I'm not sure either Joel or I really enjoyed our playtimes together.

Of course, there were other children in the neighborhood—the Dashners, the Kellys, and the Chetnies—but we didn't get along very well. When they saw me coming down the street after school they'd line up and call me all kinds of nasty anti-Semitic names, even when I was in the car with my father at the wheel. How I longed to play in their pick-up baseball games! Somehow, I was never invited. I always had to bribe my way in by giving them comic books. It's painful for me now to remember how I would sneak those comics out of the house under my sweater. I was both ashamed, knowing that I had to bribe my way into the game, and fearful my parents would discover me giving away something I valued just to get into the game.

Perhaps those neighborhood kids resented my sister and me because we always had nice clothes and a car. Often my father would drive me to school on his way to work, and I remember how the kids would crowd around the car, looking at it and touching it. That car was a luxury, but it was also a business necessity. Things were rough in those days, and, as store manager, my father used the car to collect from customers who would "put a dollar down" on merchandise they couldn't afford to pay for in full. I recall my grandparents saying to me,

"If we don't work hard, or if we spend too much money, we're all going to be working in the match factory," a reference to the Diamond Match factory a few blocks away. Just as the young Charles Dickens dreaded being near the blacking factory where he had worked as a child, I felt uneasy every time I walked near the match plant's front door. This was a feeling I couldn't understand, since often I was fearless to a fault.

* * *

I'm grateful that none of my four children were as difficult to raise as I was. I was always getting into trouble; I had a fearless nature and would never shrink from confrontation. Frequently a doorbell would ring during dinner announcing a mother come to complain that I had given her son a bloody nose or hit him on the head. I wasn't afraid of tackling a bigger, older kid if I thought he had "done me wrong."

Maybe I also wanted to show off. I know that when I was about ten I was friendly with Kathy Swetman, daughter of the chancellor of Oswego State Teachers College (the new name for the old Normal School). The college owned a dozen or so little cottages on the lakeshore where faculty could spend time in the summer. One day, no doubt bored, maybe angry, I knocked out all the windows in those cottages and then told the daughter of the chancellor what I had done. Of course, she told her father and I was promptly and summarily expelled from school. The principal told my parents that I needed discipline, and that the school's laissez-faire, progressive nature was inappropriate for me.

My mother tried very hard to handle this difficult son she was raising, but I often must have driven her to distraction. I remember the time she ran out of the house in despair after I had done something particularly mischievous. She once said she wouldn't give up on me until I got sent to reform school; fortunately, I managed to avoid that fate. In that, I may have been lucky.

Sex arrived in the form of my grandparents' boarder, Bella, a young Teachers College student. Whenever I was upstairs in the apartment over the store, Bella always seemed to be in her bedroom, a mystery and a magnet to a twelve-year-old boy. Bella took to calling me in to play cards with her, her bed our improvised card table. One day, I realized she had more in mind than "Go Fish." Embarrassed, bewildered, aroused, and afraid, I threw down the cards, jumped up and went home. Even though nothing happened, I felt guilty for weeks afterwards and was glad when Bella—and the temptation she offered—left town.

★ ★ ★

There were, of course, plenty of happy times in those early years. Lake Ontario was full of wonderful beaches, like Lakeside and Sheldon's, where I would go skinny-dipping with my pals. (When my mother found out about that, she'd bawl me out; my father was always more understanding about boys and the things they like to do.) When I was twelve, I joined the Boy Scouts, Troop 5, which met in a church on the other side of town. In no time, I became the patrol leader and the highest-ranking member of the troop. (Unfortunately, we left Oswego before I could reach Eagle rank). In those days, I walked to Scout meetings, a good six miles, which seemed like nothing to me. I am amazed now to think of how much walking we did. On school days, for example, I'd spend my lunch hour rushing to my grandparents' store, have lunch, and then trot back to the classroom, cutting it close, but always getting there on time.

One of my favorite diversions was fishing. The Oswego River teemed with bass, perch, and pike. In summer I'd get an early morning start, arrive at the river about seven a.m. and by ten o'clock I'd have a stringer full of fish, so heavy I could hardly carry it. Sometimes I'd sell the fish to the local fish market for a nickel apiece. More often, I'd stop by the synagogue and offer several of the fish to the rabbi. We all knew the Jewish community in Oswego was so small that his salary was minimal, and donations of food were considered a mitzvah, a blessing. Often I'd stop to sit on the temple's cellar steps and watch while the rabbi ritually slaughtered chickens brought to him by all the Jewish families who kept kosher kitchens. As a result, I have never enjoyed eating chicken. Somewhere in the back of my mind is the smell of the slaughter and the sight of those birds running around with their heads chopped off and disgorging their bladders.

One of the best things about those Oswego days was my wonderful dog, Wager, a beautiful Norwegian elkhound. We were inseparable. My parents acquired Wager when they visited a cousin in Brooklyn who had won the dog on a bet. (A good thing, too; Wager was far too big for any apartment.) Wager knew exactly when I would be coming home from school and he would trot down the half-mile of hillside to greet me and we would go home together. Unfortunately, our neighbors, the Durfees (Mr. Durfee owned a drug store in town), owned a mean Irish setter they treated like the child they'd never had. The dog was a cat-killer, and he hated Wager; he was always trying to steal his food or bite behind his ears. In those days I was absolutely fearless (or maybe just plain stupid), and whenever I saw this happening I would jump the dog, ignoring his bared teeth and menacing growls. Wager died when he was seventeen years old, just after I'd started college. For almost all those years, he was really my best friend.

Throughout those years, my father encouraged me to work. Like many other boys, that meant a variety of jobs—mowing lawns with a hand-mower (for a dollar a week), picking beans, working on the carnival grounds, setting pins in a bowling alley, and selling the fish I caught. In addition to providing me with some pin money, work helped channel some of that energy of which I seem to have an overabundance.

In thinking back over my years in Oswego, I realize I did have some good friends and many good times. Perhaps I was overly sensitive to the nastiness around me (itself a factor of those troubled times) since the experience certainly did have a silver lining. As I came to understand my confrontational personality, I learned to make an extra effort to get along with people. That habit, I'm sure, stood me in good stead later in the world of politics and government.

Chapter 4

To Rochester...and on to "The Halls of Ivy"

I was fourteen when Mom, Dad, Elise and I (and Wager, the dog) moved seventy-five miles southwest to Rochester, leaving my maternal grandparents and the rest of Oswego behind. When I first heard the news that we were moving, I was devastated. How could they do this to me? Now I could never be the star football player at Oswego High School. That old gymnasium would never rock with cheers as I bucketed the basketball in the final seconds of the traditional game with Fulton, our perennial rival. What pleasure could the future possibly hold? What would kids in Rochester think of me, this tall, gangly kid with bald spots on his head?

To tell the truth, I was carrying a big chip on my shoulder. I viewed the world as a place where Jews were not only unwelcome but often the subject of taunts, abuse and outright discrimination. A week after the move to Laburnam Crescent, a middle-class enclave on the city's east side, I thought I had died and gone to heaven. I could scarcely believe it: nearly all the kids on my block were Jewish and I instantly had dozens of friends. Most of the houses on the street were two-story; we lived in the upstairs flat at Number 140 and my Rosenbaum grandparents lived in the downstairs flat.

Next door lived Les Hurwitz and his family. Les was a pitcher on the Monroe High School baseball team; a fine musician, he was headed for Boston Conservatory of Music and a career as a concert pianist. Les's younger brother Ernie was much more fun, in my opinion, because he was less serious. We had a lot of laughs together. Across the street lived another pal, Harry Nagin (formerly Naganavitsky), and further down

35

the street lived Hiram Paley, a very sweet mathematical genius who later joined the math faculty at the University of Illinois. On Laburnam Crescent, we called Hiram by his Hebrew name, Chai Mer, because that's what his parents called him.

We kids were outside all the time, playing "against the steps," our favorite made-up game. We would hurl a ball against the cement risers of the stairs in front of our houses, then catch it on the bounce for points. We tried to avoid the gaze of Don Sloat, a strapping, handsome guy who had had the bad luck to contract polio which left both his legs paralyzed. Don would sit on his porch for hours, watching us guys running around in the street. He made us realize how lucky we were to be young and healthy.

A few Gentile kids lived in the neighborhood and I was friendly with most of them. One day, however, I couldn't resist the opportunity to become the tormenter, rather than the victim. Hanging on the porch rail, I watched an Irish boy (I knew he was Catholic) sauntering down the street toward our house. As soon as he was within earshot, I gave him the business, taunting him and calling out every slur I could think of. I knew I was doing wrong, but I harbored a lot of resentment. My father was on me in one minute, calling me into the house for a real tongue-lashing. Just because people had tormented me in the past didn't give me the right to act that way. Why should I stoop to their level? It was a good lesson and I never did it again.

In Rochester, as in Oswego, grandparents played a major role in my life. Grandpa and Grandma Rosenbaum had come over from Russia with my father (then six years old) before the 1917 revolution, crawling on the ground to escape the notice of border guards. (My father remembered his mother whispering a warning in Yiddish for silence: "Sha! Jake. Sha!") In Rochester, Grandpa Max found work in one of the city's many clothing factories. A foreman, he made a good salary for those days and he was a clever investor, putting much of his money in real estate. When he died, we were surprised at the size of his estate, even after the devastation of the Great Crash of 1929. Years later, my grandmother recalled those fearful days when telegrams from brokers

No Room for Democracy

would arrive, demanding immediate funds to cover the margin calls on Grandpa's accounts. Somehow the family survived, and my grandfather became highly respected in the business community.

People still tell me that Max Rosenbaum was a man whose word you could count on, a man so prompt "you could set your watch by him." He, my father, and I would often go to baseball games together, always sitting in the low-priced bleacher seats; I loved those summer afternoons, and could almost always count on coming home with an errant baseball. I had so much respect for Grandpa Rosenbaum, probably because I rarely saw him, that I never even considered acting up around him, as I had with Grandpa Gover.

During the Oswego years, I had always enjoyed Sunday trips with my father, mother, and sister to visit his parents in Rochester. In those days a drive of almost three hours separated the cities, but as twilight approached, there was still time on the way home to stop in the little lakeside town of Sodus, where my father and sister would have a beer. If somehow I could manage to behave in the back seat of the car, I might be rewarded with an ice-cream sandwich, three scoops, three flavors, and all for a dime. When we arrived home, Mom was always thankful that we'd returned safely.

It wasn't until years later that I realized that some of those visits had involved tense talks about our future, family conferences prompted by my father's growing unease with the situation at his in-laws' store. Grandpa and Grandma Gover had a son fifteen years younger than my mother; Uncle Norman was a spoiled young man with no head for business. My father saw trouble coming, so he pulled up stakes and moved us all back to his own family turf. For the first six months in Rochester, Dad had no job. I remember how he cried tears of relief when he finally was hired as head of the men's department at Sears Roebuck. Later he acquired a franchise for women's foundation garments and made a decent living, although I'm sure he always regretted leaving pharmacy school prematurely. Once someone tried to sell Dad a pharmacy, telling him that even if he got caught selling drugs without a license it would be no big deal; he'd only be assessed a small fine. Dad, of course, would have none of it. My dad was the most honest man I've ever known, and he made it very clear that he expected my sister Elise and me to be the same.

With money in short supply, I learned to earn my own. Winters in the "Snow Belt" provided a perfect opportunity for a young entrepreneur who craved a little spending money. On days when the snow was so deep that no traffic could move and schools were closed, I would charge out first thing in the morning with my snow shovel and spend the day clearing sidewalks for fifty cents or more a shot. My goal was to make ten bucks a day, the equivalent of at least twenty sidewalks cleared. That was big money back in the 1940s, and I always reached my goal. (Often, however, when school reopened the next morning, I was too sore to get out of bed.)

My delight with our new life in Rochester grew even greater the first day I entered Monroe High School. Here was a school where I knew I could thrive! It was a big school—almost a thousand kids—and many of them were Jewish, so I no longer felt like an outsider. Academically, the school was tops, which meant that I had real competition and could no longer breeze through classes. (In Oswego, in those days, if you scored 100 on an algebra test or if you were accepted at a college, it made the front page of the newspaper, the Palladium-Times.) I knew I had to do well academically so that I could get into a good college. For most lower-middle class Jewish families in Rochester, as everywhere else, sending the kids to college was a necessity. My father, who knew first-hand about the diaspora, used to say, "Education is the most important thing you can get because it's portable. Wherever you go, you can take it with you."

But at that point in my life, athletics trumped studying. I knew I was strong, I knew I was determined, most of all I knew I wanted to be a high school star. At Monroe, I would learn a few painful lessons, and their sting remains with me to this day. The first shadow was cast on the football field. At 15, I was tall, strong, and aggressive by nature. I was also the only Jewish kid playing high school football in the city (others may have been too smart to get banged up). In my dreams of glory, I was in the backfield on a sunny Saturday afternoon, the bleachers full and screaming as I caught an impossible pass, then streaked

No Room for Democracy

down the field and between the goalposts. Unfortunately for me, the coach had other ideas; he stuck me in the line. Somehow being a punching bag didn't square with my inflated vision of myself as hero. Halfway through the second season, I quit.

A few weeks later, at basketball tryouts, I found that I had been identified as "a problem." If the basketball coach didn't actually say the words "I won't have a quitter on my team," he must have come pretty close. Basketball was my best sport; I was really good at it, I was dying to play—but the door was barred. I'd become my own worst enemy, and the knowledge hurt.

Dejected but undaunted, I turned to the third sport in which I'd shown promise: track. Determined to rise to the top, I ran and ran, and then ran some more. It was on the running track that I learned another one of life's great lessons—and I learned it a painful, heart-searing way. My goal in that last year at Monroe was to win a victor's sectional shield in track, more important and impressive to me than a varsity letter because it rewarded individual performance. To improve my race time, I literally ran my butt off. I lost 25 pounds and steadily moved up in the ranks of the city's quarter-milers, placing second or third in most races, and finally qualifying as one of the eight fastest runners in the county. I knew I could never take the top spot; that belonged to my friend, Sonny Belucci (who would soon be recruited to Oklahoma University on a track scholarship). But I did think I could make the four-man relay team in the county sectionals; all I had to do was be one of seven runners out of a field of eight to qualify in speed trials.

The day of the trials, I drew the third spot, a position that seemed to me so advantageous that in a burst of generosity I offered to switch places with Belucci, who was after the city championship that day and who had had the bad luck to draw the eighth slot. In my effort to convince Belucci to trade positions, I totally lost my edge. By the time the starter's pistol sounded, my concentration was shot, my running was sloppy, and when the runner behind me shouldered ahead in the last second, I became the last to cross the tape. Of those eight runners, I was the one eliminated—and the loss was truly traumatic.

A week or two later, sitting forlornly in the bleachers at the University of Rochester's Fauver Stadium on the day of the sectional meet, I was miserable, knowing that by giving up I'd lost my chance to be with those guys on that field. Belucci, who broke the county record that day, understood the depth of my misery and gave me his sectional shield, a gesture of friendship I'll never forget. Since then, whenever I've been in a tough spot, I tell myself: "Dick, run as hard as you can—and be sure to run through the tape."

It's odd for me to look back at the boy I was then. Like every adolescent, I was a bundle of contradictions—aggressive one day, uncertain the next; self-confident, yet wary; driven, but often distracted. Unlike most teenagers, however, I had a special problem—I was going bald. As I described in the Preface, my hair had begun to fall out when I was about eight. During high school the loss accelerated, and great hanks of it filled my comb in the morning. I grew up hearing the taunts of grammar school kids making fun of me, and by the time I was a teenager I was pretty sensitive. At an age when appearance often seems all-important, I looked pretty strange.

At that time, my parents didn't know much about alopecia, the condition in which hair follicles starve because of a minor circulatory malfunction. In spite of years of medical consultations and the occasional helpful remedy, my hair just kept disappearing. At Monroe, I took to wearing a hat when I went out on a date. By my mid-teens I thought I had come to terms with my growing baldness, but the psychological effects apparently were still strong; for a long time, if a girl turned me down for a date, I was sure she thought I looked funny; if she said "yes," it was only because she felt sorry for me. Clearly, I was an example of adolescent angst ratcheted up to the max.

One thing that helped boost my confidence was being invited to join a high-school fraternity; among the Adelphians, I found a bunch of Jewish brothers who made me feel at home. To top it off, we put together a basketball team that won the Jewish Young Men's Association city championship in a hard fought three-game series—and I was the captain! What a thrill, after my painful Oswego experiences.

College Days

Deciding on a college was relatively easy. Hobart College is an hour's drive from Rochester, in Geneva, at the head of beautiful Seneca Lake, the largest and some think the most beautiful of New York's Finger Lakes. As a family, we'd visited Hobart when Elise's husband Chuck was studying there on the GI bill after his stint in the Navy. I liked the place a lot, and am still devoted to it. (I later became the college's first Jewish trustee and have served on its board for thirty years.) A small Episcopal college founded in 1822, Hobart had (and has) a fine reputation. Sports were important, the town was attractive—and there was a "sister college," William Smith, with its own campus nearby. That meant there were four hundred girls around, a strong new interest for me!

In the spring of 1948, I was accepted at Hobart as an incoming freshman with a scholarship that promised to pay full board and half tuition. Once again, I nearly blew it. At Monroe, I'd been so involved in track and other sports—while becoming the star ad salesman for our yearbook—that I'd sloughed off studying; "Who needs history anyway?" I'd thought. The college admissions office thought differently. When word came through that I'd scored a dismal 68 on the Regents history exam, Hobart had serious second thoughts about young Richard Rosenbaum and his qualifications as a scholar.

A letter to my parents made the admissions committee's doubts quite clear. My father and I drove down to Geneva and together we pled my case. The director of admissions decided to admit me when I promised to make up the work in summer school; I did (scoring 98 on the Regents exam the second time around), and added typing to my list of skills. In September, I resigned from my weekend job as freight elevator boy at Rochester's Temple Building and headed for the next adventure—college! Once again, I was full of steam and raring to go.

And once again, sports preoccupied me. At seventeen, I was the only kid on the freshman football team whose parents had to send a letter of permission before I could play. I was bigger than most of my classmates, and fast for my size. In my freshman year, when Hobart used the single wing formation (using an unbalanced line that slowed down the offense), I played fullback. A year later, the coach switched to a split-T formation (using a balanced line to achieve more speed). As a result, during my four years on the football team I often played both offense and defense on the line.

Lacrosse has been the premier sport at Hobart since it was introduced in the 1920s; the schedule for its Division 1 team includes matches against Army, Cornell, Syracuse, and Penn State, all much larger schools. The game's speed and toughness appealed to me, as did the opportunity to be on a team that could play the role of "David" against a "Goliath." I played attack during my freshman year, then varsity defense, and finally turned to boxing. In boxing, I believe I found my true métier: during my last two years at Hobart, I was the college heavyweight champion. (Some time later that honor would lead to an amusing—and rather painful—encounter with world heavyweight champion Floyd Patterson. More about that later.)

I desperately wanted to be in a fraternity, but I'd brought my anxieties with me and was afraid I wouldn't get a pledge bid. Of the eight Greek houses on campus, I knew most had "an understanding" about taking in Jewish members. Fortunately for me, I was pledged by the best of them—Phi Phi Delta, the oldest local college fraternity in the country, one that attracted both jocks and scholars. During each of my years at Hobart, the fraternity was awarded the Blessing Trophy, emblematic of superiority in athletics and scholastics. (Of the sixteen members of Hobart's boxing team, for example, thirteen were Phi Phi Deltas; we fought each other. So were eighteen of the twenty-two men on the first two strings of the football team.)

Many of Hobart's Greek societies are housed in handsome nineteenth century landmarks. Our house was the most modest, but our membership fees were the lowest, and—from my point of view—we had the best time. When I think of Phi Phi Delta in those days, I think of a bunch of lunatics, wreaking havoc in a style that was just what I was looking for. Think "Animal House"—and you're only half way to that crazy scene. At the time, I was deep in a delayed adolescence, homesick one moment, eager to break away the next.

Faced with a son who seemed hell-bent on swearing, drinking, partying down, and general mayhem, my mother—probably like many others—reacted like a cloistered nun; if she'd had worry beads, she would have worn them out. Fortunately, half of the Phi Phi Delts were returning war veterans, rough-and-tumble guys who became older brothers in both senses of the word. They really helped raise this big, naïve kid who'd been hatched in a strict little nest, a gangly kid who was eager to break out of his shell.

Life in the fraternity house on Hamilton Street was a circus from morning until night. Coming close on the end of a world war, the period encompassing the late forties and fifties was in some ways a mindless era. No protests, little political involvement—maybe in Manhattan, but not in upstate New York. Partying *was* the program. I managed to get to German class at eight every morning, but studying for any class was almost impossible. The house bar always had beer on tap, a party was always underway somewhere on campus, and the challenge of how to brew up the next rude, crude mischief was always on my mind. Every night was New Year's Eve.

Early in my freshman year, I discovered one of the advantages of fraternity living. Facing an imminent Psychology class test for which I was egregiously unprepared, I moaned my plight to a brother. "Rosie," he said compassionately, "Don't worry!" Putting his arm around my shoulder, he showed me to an upstairs room where a library of past exam copies was stored. "Take a few of these and study them. You'll do fine." I took them, stayed up all night, and I did indeed do fine.

The brothers were a surprisingly diverse group. Several were Jewish, including Horace Bernstein ("Harold Burns, for business purposes," we'd joke when we talked about him—a jibe that cracked up my father every time he heard it). Poor Horace was the butt of what were probably too many slams. When we learned he was paying secret nightly visits to Geneva's off-limits woman of easy virtue, we made him eat meals by himself at a card table set up in the hall. We were merciless, not just to Horace, but to everyone. One warm evening, when a group of William Smith girls came to serenade us, we stripped one poor brother down to the bone and shoved him out the front door, then locked it after him. Constantly in motion, constantly in trouble, most of us were pigs to a degree that now almost (almost!) embarrasses me.

Not all the brothers fit the mold. Several had come to Hobart from prestigious New England prep schools, and their aura of old wealth and quiet savoir faire fascinated me. Wes Rich was one of these. Wes was a product of St. George School in Newport, and came from a very wealthy family in Andover, Massachusetts. Somehow, in spite of (perhaps because of) our differences, we became very good friends and fraternity brothers. Soon after we met, Wes told me he was delighted to know me, because he'd never talked to a Jew before and didn't know what to expect.

The first time I visited Wes's family in Andover I was bowled over; their home, a Colonial-era landmark, seemed huge—and it hugely impressed me with its comfortable library and 200-year-old hand-blown window glass. I was even more amazed to see that the Rich family had a full staff of servants. At dinner, I was completely flummoxed by the array of forks and knives at each table setting; only by watching what others did was I able to get through that first meal. Wes knew, of course, that in my family one fork generally did the job.

I certainly didn't hide the fact that their life-style was a revelation to me. For example, I often heard Mrs. Rich calling Filene's in Boston (a twenty-cent call from Andover in those days), and each call impressed me; at my house, long-distance phone calls were considered an extravagance, only to be resorted to in an emergency. The Rich family's laundress and Wes had a cordial, kidding kind of relationship. One day he complained to her: "You're always losing my socks." Turning to me, she said (in front of the family), "I'll bet you don't talk to your laundress this way." "No," I said, "we treat my mother pretty good." They thought that was one of the funniest things they'd ever heard, and from that moment Mrs. Rich practically adopted me.

Through Wes, I met Sy Dow, one of the heirs to the Dow Chemical Company fortune. We hung around in Boston, going to hockey games and to Sy's private club. Through Wes and Sy and their friends, I learned a lot about how to act among people of wealth. But even though I was hobnobbing, I wasn't truly impressed, and never had the feeling that this was "real life." It was just very interesting.

Adventure on the Cheap: A Trip to "The Big Easy"

It was the winter of 1951 and I mean it was cold! No doubt the upstate New York weather had sunk us into the doldrums. Whatever the reason, my fraternity brother Jerry Williams and I knew we had to get out of Geneva for a while and have some "fun in the sun." Our destination: The Big Easy. These were the happy-go-lucky days when you could stick out your thumb and hope the next driver would take pity and pick you up.

This would be our second attempt to reach New Orleans on a budget that would make even Frommer blanche. A few months earlier, dressed only in khakis and sweaters, we managed to make it to Penn Yan, a town fifteen miles away, before we realized that if we stayed out any longer we would surely freeze to death. Now, in February, we were once again heading south, dressed more warmly and ready to rock and roll.

At Carlisle, Pennsylvania, another college town, we considered bunking at a fraternity house, but we were eager and time was short, so we decided to push on. Where would we sleep that night? We hadn't a clue; when you're twenty, you just don't focus on unimportant things like that. At dusk, after a couple of good lifts, we found ourselves in Martinsburg, West Virginia, just north of Winchester, Virginia. A small diner beckoned, and so did its sign: "25 cents for a bowl of chili and all the bread you can eat." (The folks working there probably got rid of that sign the minute we left; I think we each chowed down a whole loaf.)

Our next ride left us on the road outside a small country church. Five hours later and no ride in sight, I suggested we jimmy the church door and spend the night sleeping on the pews. Jerry didn't much like the idea, but it was getting chilly and there were no streetlights. We were seriously considering the break-in when a car shot past us in the pitch dark, braked with a squeal and backed up. The driver beckoned us into the car and not only drove us to Winchester but took us to an all-night diner, fed us, and invited us to spend the night in his apartment. I was wary, but Jerry enthusiastically accepted his invitation. That night we flipped a coin to see whether Jerry would get the couch and I the chair, or vice versa; I lost and spent the night sitting up. Sometime during the night our host got up to pee and I, who had slept fitfully, woke up expecting nothing short of murder. When dawn came up, much to our surprise the guy drove us to another diner, fed us, and deposited us on the outskirts of Winchester. That night we checked into a cheap motel in Knoxville, Tennessee, and slept like the dead.

The following day we were hitchhiking through Chattanooga when we were picked up by an attractive young couple on their way to visit their daughter at a college whose name meant nothing to us. As soon as we got in the car, the woman reached into the glove compartment and brought out a pint of moonshine; every few miles they'd each take another slug. As we drove through the mountains, the driver suddenly lost control of the car and crashed into a guardrail. That barrier probably saved our lives, preventing us from careening off the road and into a deep ravine. Bloodied but unbowed, we crawled out of the car which had been badly damaged, and headed off on foot.

After hoofing it for about a mile, we were picked up by a couple of rednecks who showed us a fine example of Southern culture. As we drove past a couple of black kids on a motorcycle, our good ol' boys let out a string of vituperation, threatening lynching and other mayhem. (Remember, this was 1951, before any civil rights legislation and only three years after Jackie Robinson, with the help of Branch Rickey, broke major league baseball's color bar.) Our experience with the rednecks left us disgusted, but that was far from the only evidence of ugly racism we encountered on our trip. At a gas station in Georgia one cold night, we noticed a black man waiting for a bus try to step inside the station to get out of the cold. We watched horrified as a white man with a club chased the black man away every time he approached the door. When the bus finally came we watched a large group of white people line up, forcing the black man to go to the rear of the line.

In Meridian, Mississippi, our driver left us on the curb and told us that, if we were still there the next morning, he'd pick us up and drive us to New Orleans. We were, and he did. Those Deep South accents really amused us, and this guy was the real thing. He drove with one arm out the window and kept saying over and over, with a drawl you could cut with a knife, "Somethin' like to bite the shit raaght out o' me." I could hardly keep from laughing out loud. When he inquired about our respective religions and learned that Jerry was a Catholic and I was Jewish, I thought he was going to throw us out of the car and leave us among the wild pigs we could see foraging along the roadside.

Once in New Orleans, we found that the Big Easy really was easy— at least, for a couple guys like us with empty pockets. Lucky for us, you could buy hamburgers for a nickel each, six for a quarter. (No Antoine's or Galatoire's for us.) At least we had a decent place to sleep, thanks to the hospitality of Joe Dara, a fraternity brother who was now selling insurance in New Orleans. At night, we explored the city, especially the jazz joints on Bourbon Street. My favorite was a place called the "Famous Door" (unforgettable as the place where I saw a giant guy fully eight feet tall).

At last, it was time to hit the road again, this time for home. Our first ride took us to Birmingham, Alabama, where once again we found ourselves outside a gas station. Our last hamburger meal was well behind us, and hunger struck. Picking up a couple of candy bars from a rack inside the gas station, we asked the proprietor, "How much?" "Take all you want," he said. "I'm going out of business tomorrow." The resulting sugar surge kept us awake through our next ride, a lucky one—several hundred miles in a huge semi, with us dozing fitfully on the hard floor of the trailer. The driver left us off on the outskirts of Penn Yan, and we hitchhiked back to Geneva. Our fraternity house was empty because of spring break and we sacked out, peacefully, for twenty-four hours straight.

Perhaps the most remarkable thing about that adventure was its price tag: $19 each for the whole trip.

★ ★ ★

My four years at Hobart were full of the usual high jinks (like damaging my mother's brand-new car while on a date with a neighboring Keuka

College girl, a minor crash that resulted from one too many brews). Yet somehow, I managed to make the dean's list every quarter, tutored the brothers on Sunday afternoons during my senior year, and graduated with the school's highest average in History, my major. (Ironic, when you consider my earlier experience in high school when I bombed the History Regents exam with a 68.)

Two regrets linger. The first was my dropping out of a challenge to win Hobart's Herbert Bayard Swope Prize in History. I was one of three students hand-picked by our history professor to compete for the prestigious prize, which included a hundred-dollar stipend. Halfway through senior year, my high marks ensured that I was the leading contender, but somehow I never bothered to write the required essay. I was having too much fun elsewhere. On Graduation Day, when the Swope Prize was awarded to someone else, I couldn't meet my father's eye. Even though he never knew I'd been a contender for the prize, I knew, and I felt I'd let him down.

My second regret comes from knowing that I easily could have made Phi Beta Kappa, if I'd applied myself. I saw my years at Hobart as a chance to be carefree, to find myself. "These are my 'salad days,'" I told myself. "I can do this work without half trying." News that I'd won a scholarship to Cornell Law School only made me more self-confident.

"Mr. Smart Guy" was about to get his comeuppance.

No Room for Democracy

Chapter 5

The Paper Chase

Upstate New York's Finger Lakes are spread out like digits on a hand, their glacial beds separated by gently rolling hills, patch-worked with vineyards and dairy farms, their glens spangled with waterfalls. Only about fifty as-the-crow-flies miles separate Hobart College, at the head of Seneca Lake, and Cornell University, crowning its hill "far above Cayuga's waters," to quote the chorus of its alma mater. Intellectually and physically, however, the two are worlds apart. I had just spent four sequestered years with 800 other male undergraduates who shared "separate but equal" space with the 400 women on the adjacent William Smith College campus. In September 1952, I suddenly found myself thrust into the academic Big Time.

Cornell, like every great university, is a world unto itself, a sprawling cosmopolitan island where every culture, every intellectual discipline jostles for time and space. When I arrived in Ithaca, Vladimir Nabokov was there, along with Nobel Prize-winners, Buddhists, Moslems, Black activists, artists, star athletes—a rich and yeasty mélange that had my head spinning. At its summit was Cornell Law School, lofty domain of some of the world's greatest legal scholars. How in the world had I ever managed to win a scholarship to this pinnacle of learning? As I eagerly paced the quadrangle, looking up at Myron Taylor Hall, the school's physical focus, I wondered what I could make of the next three years—or what those years would make of me.

I found a place to share with other first-year students in a rooming house on Williams Street, the steepest of the streets just off campus. Most of that first year we would survive on peanut butter sandwiches and milk, which we bought in great quantities and immediately consumed, since we had no refrigerator; as a result, I bulked up rather too well that year, and had to face the dietary consequences later.

The first week, armed with fifty pounds of new and second-hand law books, and energized by the golden glories of September in the Finger Lakes, I prepared to make my first charge on Cornell's legal bastions. The force of its first repulse was shocking, and came in the form of John MacDonald, preeminent scholar, head of the state's Law Revision Commission, and professor of Constitutional Law.

We were introduced to the master at eight in the morning in one of the law school's amphitheater-style classrooms, a space admirably designed to amplify MacDonald's voice, an organ of such power that it easily could be heard four rooms away. I was transfixed by that voice for an entire hour, and then was paralyzed when he handed out six major cases and ordered us to prepare briefs of all of them by class the next morning. (The smallest—a case involving U.S. Steel—was over 80 pages.) A few among our class of 125 already knew something about the law and its arcane language; they'd had a father or grandfather in the profession, or they'd taken pre-law as an undergraduate. I knew *nothing*—and I felt overwhelmed and terrified.

I hustled back to my room to begin work on the briefs; by midmorning, my eyes had glazed over and I was only two-thirds through the first case. Desperately needing a break, I headed up the hill and across the bridge over the gorge to "college town" for coffee and sustenance. Along the way, I fell into step with another newcomer, a fellow I'd seen in MacDonald's class. Hoping to find a sympathetic sufferer, I asked, "How are you doing with those briefs? Tough, aren't they?" His response came with supreme nonchalance: "I've finished them." (If empathy was what I was looking for that morning, I wouldn't find it in C. Addison Keeler, Jr., scion of a family of legal eagles in Binghamton, a guy who would breeze through law school with straight A's and leave a record as one of the smartest graduates ever to come out of Cornell.) As "Sonny" Keeler and I walked along (in silence now), I remember thinking, "Let me out of here. Maybe I should just go into plumbing."

No Room for Democracy

I tried to study. I really did try, but I'd brought with me bad habits, like expecting that a burst of concentrated last-minute study would enable me to bull my way through most exams. Things were complicated further by the fact that I had a girlfriend; Jean would drive to Ithaca from Watertown, up in the North Country, every weekend, and we'd disappear together. This exercise went on for several months; I'd knock myself out studying and writing papers during the week, and then goof off with Jean at the end of the week.

It didn't take long before I was caught up short. This time, my nemesis was Professor Rudolf Schlesinger, a brilliant refugee who taught the course in Quasi-Contracts. (Actually, Schlesinger did something far more important than lecture; he taught us how to *think*.) One particular morning, he arrived in class bearing a briefcase full of our completed homework. Fumbling through the contents of the bag, he isolated one paper, raised it aloft and shook it like a banner, riveting everyone's attention. Then, in his inimitable, high and nasal voice, he shouted. "You see this paper? When I read this paper, I didn't know whether I was a man or a woman! I want to tell you one thing: Whoever wrote this paper will not be here at the end of the year, unless he shapes up!" With that, and with the whole class watching, he handed the offending paper to me, its big "D-minus" written large in red for all to see. Never in my life had I had a D-minus! What humiliation! I was shaken to the core. Almost immediately, I went to the phone booth and called Watertown. "Look, Jean," I said. "I really like you, but if I'm ever going to get out of this place without flunking, we've got to call a moratorium." And so we did, forever.

At midterms, I packed all my books into the back seat of my old jalopy and went home to Rochester. There, I moved my bed into our pine-paneled basement and went into seclusion for fourteen days, coming out only for meals. I swallowed those books whole! The first day back in class, I was called on and surprised everyone with my answer. I went from being the class dunce to the class genius...at least for a while.

Cornell's law faculty was impressive and imperious; we saw them as world-class intellects standing at the loftiest heights of the profession. There was George Jarvis Thompson, who literally wrote the book on contracts, and, even more important, wrote it in a way we could understand. A fine old gentleman, Professor Thompson commanded a rhetorical style that, like a river, often was unstoppable. Seeing my raised and questioning hand one morning, at a moment when the stream was in full flood, he rebuffed me with the words, "Mr. Rosenbaum, don't stop me now! I'm glory-bound!"

Perhaps even more picturesque (and picaresque) was Horace Whiteside, who wrote the book on future interests. A giant of a man, six foot eight and weighing three hundred pounds, Whiteside had a big face topped with a shock of grey hair. He also seemed to have something of a drinking problem; perhaps it was a genetic flaw, since he often would refer to a grandfather "who was addicted to the bottle." In spite of Ithaca's bitterly cold winters, Whiteside always seemed to be sweating; on entering the classroom, he would shuffle down toward the lectern, wiping his big brow with a giant white handkerchief and bark out the order in stentorian tones, "Somebody open the windows!" We would sit there for the next hour shivering while Whiteside continued to mop his brow.

A sense of decorum, almost entirely absent these days, was prevalent on campus during the fifties. Peter Ward, who taught torts, might cancel his class if he looked up and saw a student without a jacket and tie. Since I've mentioned my general rejection of any level of control not self-imposed, you might think I would have considered this attitude both stuffy and repressive. Not so; I understood that, for Professor Ward, it was imperative that we learn not only discipline, but respect for our profession, our peers, and ourselves.

At that time, Cornell's law school was the only professional graduate school on the Ithaca campus. As a result, law students, like athletes, were BMOC ("Big Men on Campus"). My own self-esteem grew when I was visited one day by an older law student who surprised and pleased me by asking my opinion on who among my classmates should be considered for election to Phi Delta Phi, the law school's honorary fraternity. Imagine how pleased I was to be brought into the inner circle. Contrasting this with the disappointments of my Oswego experience left me with a sense of wonderment that I still harbor.

My status was elevated further during my second year when I was elected president of Cornell's Law Student Association. I campaigned hard for the post, and won by a runaway margin, garnering 121 of 126 possible votes, and swept two friends into office with me, John Considine, Jr. as vice president, and Jerry Williams as secretary. John was another Rochesterian, and Jerry was from Batavia; as a result, the election was seen by some as "an upstate takeover." This was my first taste of politics, and the beginning, I believe, of my life as a political animal.

As president of the association, I was also a member of the school's Honor Court, the body responsible for adjudicating cases involving serious misdemeanors and malfeasance. Fortunately, the Honor Court rarely met; unfortunately, it was called into session during my tenure. One day, a British student came to my room to report a case of cheating. Brad Walls told me he had watched someone leave an exam and take a textbook into a stall in the men's room where he had remained for what seemed to Walls, his observer, as an inordinate amount of time. "Doesn't this suggest cheating to you?" Walls asked; I agreed.

The next day I contacted the student in question, told him he'd been reported on a serious charge, and that the Honor Court would have to be convened to examine the case. As was pro forma, I also asked to meet with the dean of the law school, to alert him to the situation. To my astonishment, Dean Stevens said, "I really don't think I should get involved in this." When I learned later that the father of the accused was head of a powerful faculty union, I lost a lot of respect for the dean. As for the young man, he continued in class until the end of the term and then dropped out. Before leaving Ithaca, he looked me up. "You know," he said, "it's really all right. I never wanted to be a lawyer; my father insisted I come here. I'm glad to be leaving." Even though he seemed to have acted shamefully, I admired the guy's guts in being ready to face up to his father and his sensitivity in recognizing that I felt badly about the whole episode.

As for Dean Stevens, he'd taken my measure early on. At the end of my admissions interview with him, he said: "I'm going to recommend that you be accepted. I look at your record and see that you'll be a success here. But, given your personality, you are in danger of being only a C-minus success." (Looking back at my time at Cornell, I'm afraid I have to say that Dean Stevens was right. It took me a while to take his warning seriously.)

Perhaps it was my status as a big man on campus that enabled me to attract the attention of one of the most beautiful undergraduates, a self-centered Jewish girl from downstate who seemed to really like me. This girl could bend a man around her little finger without even trying. After a few dates, I was hopelessly enchanted. Our romance was the talk of the campus and I spent entirely too much time with her. At the end of the year, we broke up. I could see that I needed a girl who was not only beautiful but smart; a girl with character, someone who could center me, check my impulsiveness, be a loyal friend, as well as a lover. (Five years later, I would get one—beautiful Judy, my wife of fifty years—and a Cornell girl, at that!)

Older and wiser, I entered my third year determined to concentrate on my studies; I had a lot of catching up to do. By that time, my scholarship had been expanded to include a large room and bath near the law library, its leaded windows looking out onto a pleasant courtyard. This was wonderful, because I could study in peace at any hour of the day or night. A fringe benefit was getting to know the professor who headed the library, Lew Morris, a brilliant guy and a great squash player (who also admired the brownies my mother sent from Rochester).

I loved that library; I loved the whole atmosphere of the law school, even though it often seemed intimidating. For example, there was the great table, longer than any I'd ever seen, that enhanced the foyer of the main classroom building where we would gather on the day that grades for the previous semester were reported. Our anticipation and nervousness were unbounded as we approached that formidable table. Its surface would be covered with neat rows of white envelopes, each marked with a student's name and each bearing within it the hoped for (or dreaded) result. I always picked up my envelope and quietly slipped away to ecumenical Annabel Taylor Chapel, where I said a few silent prayers before opening it.

No Room for Democracy

Law students then (and probably now) learned early to benefit from the work of students who preceded them. I refer here in particular to the common practice of selling lecture notes; these study guides were also a hedge against the occasional missed class (skipped or slept through). As incoming students, my friend John Considine and I had bought our own set of notes from the Real Property course. After looking them over, John and I thought we could do better, so over the summer we streamlined and improved them. In September, we made a point of returning to campus early to market them to the first-year law students during their orientation week. Our plan worked like a charm, and we each netted $300 from the enterprise. (When a colleague complained that he'd had the idea first and that we had undercut him by not giving him notice of our sales plan, I coached John in the authentic New York way to say, "Does Macy's tell Gimbels?")

As the end of my third year approached, I was eager to get out of academia and into the real world. Not even the idea of a graduation ceremony could interest most of us. (In fact, there was no official ceremony for graduating law students; those who elected to stay on acted as marshals in Cornell's June graduation exercises.) Our mind was focused on the real challenge: passing the bar exam. To that end, I returned to Rochester, unpacked my bags and reconnected with family and old friends. A week later, I drove to Buffalo and took a room at the local YMCA; there, with other nervous legal neophytes, I spent the next four weeks cramming for the exam.

Finally, the dreaded examination day arrived. For what seemed like endless hours, I tried to first remember and then record what I'd learned about the law over the past three years. Putting down my paper at last, I left the room with a sick feeling in my stomach. I sensed that Dr. Stevens had seen the writing on the wall when, at my admissions interview, he'd warned me about distractions, of how I was in danger of being "only a C-minus student."

Two months later, Dean Steven's prediction seemed confirmed: word came that I'd flunked the bar exam.

Chapter 6

Enter "R. Rosenbaum, Esq."

Have you ever felt truly sick at heart? If you have (and I think it happens to most of us, at least once), you'll understand the terrible end-of-the-world feeling I experienced on opening the letter that told me I'd flunked the bar exam. Let me tell you, failure and I are not good partners. To put it mildly, I suffered.

Forty-eight hours later, I put a stopper on the self-pity, pulled myself together, looked at the facts head on, and knew the worst: I'd deserved to fail. Cornell had done its best by me, but I hadn't returned the favor. I wasn't fully grounded even in the basics of law practice. Too many good times, too much romancing, too much politicking. Now it was up to me to fix the situation.

In the two months since graduation, I'd tramped the streets of downtown Rochester looking for a clerk's job and had been turned down by the local "big" firm—Nixon, Hargrave, Devans & Doyle. This firm which was—and still is—the pinnacle, had strong connections to the city's business elite and represented the corporate giants Kodak, Xerox, and Bausch & Lomb. In retrospect, I realize that I came to that first interview with a lack of confidence that is uncharacteristic.

At twenty-four, I really thought the big firms were beyond my reach. In particular, I saw Nixon, Hargrave as a "silk-stocking" law firm, which, in fact, it was and is. As for myself, I knew only too well who I was: a poor kid who went through law school on a scholarship and who was currently living in a second-floor walk-up. I told myself, "They don't want me and I don't really belong with them." (Much later, I would join the firm as a full partner, and my years with the firm, now Nixon

Peabody, have been among the most enjoyable of my legal career. I truly love the firm.)

Undaunted, I continued to tramp until I found a welcome at a small firm of journeymen lawyers, Wilson, Trinker & Gilbert. In their offices in the Wilder Building at 8 Exchange Street in downtown Rochester, I officially began my legal career—at the munificent sum of $40 a week, plus half of whatever business I could bring to the firm. The partners seemed to like both my style and my law school record, which was in fact promising. They also were impressed when I secured my first business, an estate case, on my first day at work. The local newspaper had reported that morning that I'd joined the firm, and I got a call right away. (Actually, the new client was the mother of a friend, but what's the difference? A client's a client, right?—and this was a good one.)

There's nothing like a good start in a job, but late in July, I had to confess to the partners that I'd just learned the bad news: I'd flunked the bar exam. That scarcely bothered Wilson (or Trinker or Gilbert), since none of the three had ever even sat for the exam. In those early post-war days (this was 1955), war veterans like these guys, who had been called up for military service after their first year in law school, were allowed to practice without taking the bar exam, as soon as they successfully completed three full years of course work.

The partners knew there was a lot I could do for the firm, even without being a member of the bar. In fact, as a clerk, I was a godsend. I was full of beans and raring to go, and they threw everything on my desk, every little thing. In turn, they became a godsend to me. In their office, working all kinds of hours—and loving it— I learned the practical aspects of the practice of law, and learned the hard way.

Even my size (six feet two, two hundred and forty pounds) often helped. A big part of the firm's business was with the Household Finance Company, and I turned the business of bill collecting into a fine art. Serving summonses in the inner city at two dollars a pop, I could supplement my paycheck by about eighteen dollars a week. (Now it seems foolish to me that I sometimes took my life in my hands just for a couple of bucks, but at that age, we males think we're invulnerable.)

Unlike my mentors at Wilson, Trinker & Gilbert, who'd coasted on the GI bill provision, I was not going to let the bar exam business stay unsettled for long. When I told the partners I'd been researching "cram programs" and had pinpointed a very good one in New York City, they generously gave me a month's leave of absence.

Once again I packed a suitcase and my law books into the jalopy, and this time headed downstate where I found a room in the St. George Hotel in Brooklyn. The next morning, at a nearby branch of the YMCA, I met the incomparable Charles Sparacio, L.L.D., member of the faculty of St. John's University Law School. Sparacio was a born actor, a one-man show. He strutted, he gestured, he was often vulgar, but what he taught, you would never forget. (Sparacio had a penchant for describing a case as occurring in "the County of Pantygirdaloon." Each time he finished demonstrating how to demolish an opponent's case, he'd shout, "Chapeau, ya' little bastard!"—his shorthand for the act of filling his opponent's hat with his excrement.)

I spent those four weeks shuttling on the subway between the St. George and the YMCA, living on pizza, beer and bananas, burning the midnight oil in my tiny closet of a room, and soaking up what Sparacio was drilling into me. Later that summer, I took the bar exam over again in Brooklyn—this time a particularly tough one judging from the percentage of failures—and passed with flying colors.

Two things about that second bar exam seem significant to me now. The first is this: one of the reasons it was considered so tough (only forty-two percent of us passed) was a series of thirty questions based on a complicated tax case. I read through the case—and began to sweat bullets. I didn't know much tax law and this was a corker. But I had one thing going for me: when faced with a situation that seems impossible (and this one did), I can become totally focused and completely energized. That's what I did with that tax question, and I beat it.

The second factor in my favor that day was this: unlike those in the cohort who were fresh out of law school, I'd been in the trenches at Wilson, Trinker & Gilbert for the better part of a year. Several questions that day were right on the money, involving situations I knew well from first-hand experience. As I have said, my first year at that law firm was a godsend to me, pedestrian as much of the work was. Working for the firm was my practicum, my true introduction to the legal profession.

Fast forward several months. The night before the results were to be announced, I stood on the front lawn of my house looking up at the stars in the dark night sky and saying my prayers. I remember feeling as though I was falling into an abyss.

When I walked into the office the next morning, our secretary said, "Mr. Rosenbaum, you had a call from Les Fanning in the Appellate Division. He wants you to call him." I knew what the call was about; he had the results from the bar exam. I was so excited I didn't bother to phone; I ran out the door, down three flights of stairs, raced two blocks over to the County Court House, dashed up three flights of stairs to Les's office and burst in. "You called me?" I asked. "Yes, Mr. Rosenbaum. You passed the bar exam," he said quietly. With a great cry of glee, I dashed back to the office and announced my new status with a series of whoops and shouts, "I passed! I passed!" Poking his head out of his office, Wilson, the senior partner, said dryly, "Give him the day off. He won't be any good around here today."

He was right. That night, the Rosenbaum family and friends celebrated until well into the morning.

On the Loose in Europe

If the law was occupying all my working hours, my nights at that time were unraveling. I followed the age-old pattern that characterizes the young, unattached male animal: I traveled in a gang of card-playing, beer-drinking guys. Each morning, one of us would call to say, "What'll we do tonight?" I call it "the 'Marty' Syndrome"; any reader who remembers the Ernest Borgnine character from the 1955 movie will know what I mean. Here I was, a recently minted law school graduate in the year 1956, clerking for a small law firm in Rochester and feeling pretty lonely. I found myself scrounging around for dates with girls much younger than I—and in spite of some success I felt, well, just plain left out.

One day, a girl I was dating invited me to join the Genesee Valley

No Room for Democracy

Ski Council, a group of avid skiers, and I decided, what the hell, let's give it a try. It was a great move for a variety of reasons. We all got together once a month and shared information on the best slopes and the best equipment. Best of all, there were plenty of cute girls to date.

At one of our meetings John Lazor, then the council's president, announced that he had a great deal for a European ski trip. If we could get sixty people to sign up, we could charter a plane from Rochester to Munich and back for only three hundred dollars a person. Sixty-two of us jumped at the chance, and on a cold and windy day in February a KLM Royal Dutch Airlines plane arrived to ferry us to Germany via Goose Bay, Labrador; Reykjavik, Iceland; Amsterdam, Holland; and into Germany. It was "wheels up" for a three-week adventure in Europe. Everyone lucky enough to have a European adventure when he or she is young treasures the memories, including the inevitable misadventures; in this I am no different.

What a trip that turned out to be! The era of the jet engine was yet to come, and we were flying in a four-engine DC4, one of the old Berlin airlift planes used to bring troops back to the States. The weather was so bad the day we left that we never did get to Goose Bay, which was socked in; we landed in Greenland instead. How well I remember the sound of the near gale-force winds that we heard when the crew opened the door to make a delivery.

In spite of the dark and stormy night, the captain decided to take off for Reykjavik shortly after our arrival. On landing in 20 below zero weather, we were met by a bus whose driver had the wit to be playing Hawaiian music on the radio. After a quick supper at a mess hall, we reboarded the plane and headed out over the North Atlantic. The snow was thick, and even though the partying on the plane was lively to say the least, we were aware that we were flying through heavy weather. We sobered up fast when we learned that something had gone wrong with the plane's de-icers and that we were losing altitude. When the captain turned on the wing lights, I could see the ice build-up from my seat opposite the right wing. Two flight attendants were running back and forth from the cockpit trying to give us instructions should we have to ditch.

Was I scared? No, I was terrified! My legs were shaking uncontrollably and I thought we were goners. An eerie quiet settled over the plane as it continued to drop down through the skies. Then a miracle occurred. I must have passed out, either from fright or alcohol (or a combination of both), but the next thing I remember is waking up to see sun shining in the windows and hearing the plane humming along smoothly. (Later the captain told us we had dropped to 4,500 feet before the de-icers finally kicked in and saved our lives.) At last we saw the English coastline, and a short time later our plane landed at the new Schiphol airport near Amsterdam. A decent breakfast did a lot to restore our good spirits and we were soon back on the plane heading for Munich.

After stowing my suitcase at our hotel, the Koenigshof, I headed for the nearest *hofbrauhaus* and some *Gemutlichkeit.* The Germans I met seemed friendly, but I found it very hard to warm up to them, realizing what many of them had done only twelve years earlier. The next morning, sitting in the hotel restaurant, I made a decision. Originally I had planned to stick with the ski group, but after twenty-seven hours of togetherness I decided that he who travels alone travels fastest and farthest, and experiences more. (Would you believe that I felt a wave of homesickness for the plane once I left it behind in Munich?)

Impulsively, I boarded the train for Lucerne, Switzerland, and for the next several hours gazed out the window at towns and rolling farmland. I arrived at my destination in a snowstorm, hurried to my hotel and stowed my bags. My room was small but pleasant, and the bathroom was huge. The view from my balcony was a mystery; the night was so dark and snowy that nothing could be seen. After checking things out, I headed for a good restaurant recommended by the concierge. When dinner was over, I came back to the hotel. There, alone and lonely on this, my second night in Europe, I spent the evening writing postcards home.

The next morning I awoke at dawn and opened the French doors to the balcony. I will never forget the breathtaking sight that awaited me. My eyes filled with tears as I watched the sun come up over the Pilatus and Riggi mountains beyond Lake Lucerne. I quickly showered, dressed, and hit the street—my first stop was at a candy store for a breakfast of

Swiss chocolates. (Boy, were they good!) After wandering around the city for a while, I headed once again for the train station.

This time, my destination was the Jungfrau Region and Interlaken, a resort town high in the mountains. It was freezing cold, of course, and my boots crunched on the hard-packed snow as I walked through the village, admiring the lights and the fancy shops. The next day I took a ride up the mountain in the tram to 12,000 feet; along the way the conductor pointed out three bodies dangling on ropes, unfortunate climbers who had made a fatal misstep and whose bodies couldn't yet be rescued from the sheer walls of the mountain called The Eiger ("the Killer"). The mountain air was so thin that even without much physical exertion, I found it painful to walk and hard to breathe, a "first" in my experience. With the exuberance of youth (or just plain foolishness) I walked beyond a "Danger! Go no further!" sign. To this day I wonder if I was close to stepping off the mountain.

Back at the base of the mountain, I hurriedly packed my bags and hopped on the train, eager for my next destination: Milan where I would catch the train to Venice. Just as the train approached the Italian border at Domodossola, someone burst into my compartment and asked if I would carry a package into Italy with me. I refused, of course, but have always wondered what was inside that package.

A word about European trains as they were in the fifties: A second-class ticket entitled you to ride in a glassed-in private compartment which accommodated up to six people. The car was clean, the seats comfortable, and the large windows made it seem even more spacious than its dimensions might suggest. First-class ticket holders had access to more amenities, but no more room. Trains were crowded, because autos were expensive and few could afford them. (I found this out in Milan when I boarded the train for Venice with a second-class ticket and saw people already hanging out the window, eating bread and drinking from bottles of Chianti that you could buy from vendors at the station for the equivalent of twenty-five cents.)

My car to Venice was so full that I managed to insinuate myself into first-class, where I sat with a couple of well-dressed guys a little older than I. When the conductor saw my second-class ticket, he tried to send me packing, but my new friends came to my defense and he left me alone. My fellow travelers seemed pretty ignorant about United States geography, although they knew something about Montana, probably from cowboy movies. When I told them I was from New York, they were impressed. (Of course, I was pretty ignorant of Italy. Like a rube, I managed to get off the train one stop too early and found myself in the middle of the railroad yards.)

Finally I got to my hotel on the Grand Canal. What a stink! I hired a gondola and a guide who directed me to an excellent restaurant, Taverna La Fenice, named for the famous opera house nearby. While I was having dinner a large, well-groomed cat jumped into my lap and sat there, hoping for a handout. After dinner I strolled across the street to the opera house and, even though the evening's performance was sold out, I managed to get a center orchestra seat for *Turandot*, thanks to a ticket that had been turned in at the last minute.

The next day it was off to Bologna to visit my old college friend John "Dorky" Dwyer, who was enrolled in medical school there. Coincidentally I had arrived on Dorky's birthday and he took me to his favorite restaurant, a hangout so popular with university students that each had his own special apron hanging on a peg and which he wore when dining. I also met Dorky's fiancé (whom he later married and then divorced). After dinner we stayed up half the night at his place, drinking copious amounts of cheap *vino* and laughing ourselves silly. The next morning, off to Florence, where I made a whirlwind tour of the famous art and sculpture masterpieces.

Next stop: Rome. I took the night train from *Firenze* and shared the compartment with a well-dressed older *avvocato,* a lawyer who gave me a quick course in Italian during our journey; half a century later, I still use some of the phrases he taught me. After a few days of sightseeing in Rome, I was so annoyed by pestering street vendors that I'd had quite enough. (One guy wanted six thousand lira—about ten dollars— for a pen. I negotiated him down to a dollar, but later when I tried the pen it broke in half in my hand. So who won?)

No Room for Democracy

Sorrento beckoned. It was nearly midnight when I arrived and, to my dismay, I found my *pensione* locked up. After fifteen minutes of pounding on the door, the landlord appeared in his pajamas, handed me a key, and went back to bed. I was too wound up to follow his example, so I headed for the town square. I had no money in my pocket, just travelers' checks, and I knew they wouldn't be much good at a local tavern. That's where I wanted to be, hobnobbing with the locals, something I've always loved. A young *carbonieri* patrolling the town square listened to my tale of woe and without hesitation handed me about three thousand lira (then about six dollars, a week's pay), not knowing whether he would ever see me again. Talk about hospitality. At a neighboring bar, much to my surprise, I met a bunch of American sailors whose ship was in port. They were partying and I got right in with them. The next day I went to the police station and paid back the officer, including a big box of candy.

Even though I was on a really tight budget, I found ways to make my money go far—such as the huge cheese sandwich I bought that noon from a farmer's wife for five cents, a monster meal so large I couldn't finish it. That afternoon found me in the fabled Blue Lagoon on the Mediterranean Sea, where the guide knew just the moment to pull on a rope that would thrust our boat into the hidden lagoon before rising waters could block the entrance.

The following day I rented a little Vespa motor scooter and took the Amalfi Drive through the village of Positano, high in the mountains, a trip that can only be described as precarious, since breathtaking views of the blue waters below threaten to distract the driver from oncoming traffic that appears suddenly around a curve. That night I boarded a train back to France, heading for Nice where the annual *carnaval* was about to begin. There the streets were crowded with people in costume, tossing handfuls of confetti, singing, dancing and partying all night. I wouldn't have missed it!

A few hours later, another rented Vespa scooter took me to Monte Carlo. No sooner had I entered the great gambling casino when I had the dubious honor of attracting the attention of an elderly lady who tried to pick me up. She was one of many women "of a certain age" there that day accompanied by younger men, clearly gigolos.

Finally my time was running out, and I needed to get back to Paris. Hopping a crowded train, I arrived in the "City of Light" several hours later, with enough time left (several days, in fact) to explore the most famous of the famous landmarks. When I saw the Arc de Triomphe, the Eiffel Tower, the busy boulevards, and the fabulous shops, I realized that Paris is a city best shared, and I regretted being alone. The aura lingered, as I took the funicular up to artsy Montmartre and traveled beyond the city to once-royal Versailles with its spectacular palace and gardens.

Just before leaving Paris I found myself in the front row at the Folies Bergere. I was laughing and really enjoying the show when suddenly one of the dancing girls descended on me and dragged me on stage, along with a Dane and a German from the audience. On stage with us were three big wooden horses on springs, each with a balloon in its mouth. We were each to ride our horse, an up-and-down action that would force air into the balloons. Whoever broke the balloon first would be the winner. To me, nothing less than the honor of my country was at stake, so I rode furiously—and won a small bottle of cognac and the audience's applause.

At last I linked up with my friends from Rochester, who had had great skiing adventures while I was in the sunny South, and we boarded our plane at Orly field. Our flight home was uneventful, a short stop at the Shannon airport in Ireland and another in Goose Bay, Labrador. We arrived home to find that the back of winter had been broken. It was mid-March and the weather was greatly improved.

My whirlwind tour of Europe was over. I'd had three weeks of non-stop adventuring—and an experience I will never forget.

Time to Get Serious

One of my pals in Rochester in those years was Malcolm Glazer, the guy who now owns the Tampa Bay Buccaneers, as well as a big chunk of Britain's legendary Manchester United football team. Malcolm is a very interesting character. He never went to college himself (although

No Room for Democracy

he financed his younger siblings' education), but his genius for business has made him one of the wealthiest guys in the country. One day Malcolm called me and said, "You know, I had a date last night with a girl I think you'd like. She's way too smart for me, but I think she's just right for you. You should call her. Her name is Judy Kanthor. She's a bacteriologist working at Strong Memorial Hospital. By the way, she's a Cornellian, too."

I called Judy right away, but she was busy. I called her a week later, busy again. Even though she said each time, "Please call me back," I thought to myself, "What a brush-off!" It wasn't until we met at a New Year's party a few months later that we really had a chance to get together and talk. That, as they say, is history.

Judy and I were married in her temple on June 1, 1958; she was 24, I was 27. That day, Dick Rosenbaum (tough bill collector, occasional scourge of the courtroom) was the typically nervous bridegroom, scared of the enormous step I was taking, worried about how well I would face up to the responsibilities of marriage. Then I saw Judy walking down the aisle, so beautiful in her wedding gown, and I realized, once again, that she was everything I'd been looking for in a wife.

Now, after fifty years of marriage, four wonderful offspring and twelve beautiful grandkids, I know that she's the best thing that every happened to me. When I think of some of the marriages I've seen over the years, I can't believe I've been so lucky. Judy is the quintessential Jewish wife and mother: she keeps kosher (and what a cook and baker!), she lights the candles on Friday nights, she likes to go to temple. Above all, she has always set a terrific example for me, our children, and now our grandchildren.

***

By the time of our marriage, my days at Wilson, Trinker & Gilbert were over. The parting of the ways probably was inevitable, but I'd had a burr under my blanket for several months before the relationship ended. Probably most guys writing about their life would let this story pass, but since it relates to the *real* Dick Rosenbaum, I'll tell you about it.

The kid from Oswego will never tolerate a personal slur against him. This one occurred on the golf course at the Irondequoit Country Club in Rochester, where I was playing one afternoon in a foursome with the firm's senior partner, John Wilson. We were on the eighteenth green when Al Gilbert, another of the three partners, who happened to be standing nearby, accused me of changing my ball position to my advantage. When I protested with some vigor, Gilbert shot back, "You're nothing but a clerk, so just shut up." That day, I knew my tenure at Wilson, Trinker, & Gilbert soon would be over.

Sometimes painful jibes serve as a useful prod. Certainly this one helped propel me into my own practice. I was doing well at Wilson, Trinker & Gilbert, well enough so that I had to think twice before making the break. By that time, I was thinking about getting married; so leaping into the void was something I had to consider carefully. Then, through a friend, a big personal injury case came my way. Still uncertain, I called Judy and asked what she thought about my going out on my own. "What are you afraid of?" she said. "You're a good lawyer. You should do it now." That was very inspirational, and told me a lot about my Judy. She wasn't afraid of the future, and we were going to meet it together.

In Art Agnello, I found a good partner. He was a young lawyer too, looking to share space and expenses; his former partner had moved on to a larger local firm. We had modest offices in the once handsome Elwanger & Barry building, which at that time was looking a little stodgy. Our suite was simplicity itself: one office for Art, one for me, and a reception room with a desk, a couple of chairs and two telephones, one for each of us. Since the firm had just doubled in size (from one lawyer to two), we advertised for a part-time secretary.

I'll never forget the day Eleanor Burke arrived in answer to our ad. The door creaked open and in came this little elderly woman in a white dress carrying a purple umbrella; she looked like she'd stepped right out of Mary Poppins. Unfortunately, Eleanor got off to a bad start. We'd shown her the ropes, explained the filing system, discussed her hours, and retired to our own offices. Soon, I heard a ring on the phone that connected to my office. Listening at the doorjamb, I was both appalled

No Room for Democracy

and amused to hear her response: "This is Mr. Shapiro's office...I mean, Mr. Goldstein's office...I mean, Mr. Rosenberg's office..." She seemed to run through any Jewish name that came into her head. Finally, I ran out of the door, grabbed the phone, and barked, "Hello! This is Dick Rosenbaum. What can I do for you?"

Poor Ms. Burke was only the first of a number of secretaries who probably thought they'd hooked up with a madman. The fact of the matter is, I was driven. Talk about intense! From the beginning, I was out there to be a success; my attitude generally (then and now) has been, either get with me or get out of my way. I was a working fool; hours meant nothing to me, and fortunately Judy was sympathetic. My first year out, in the early fifties, I made $35,000, an achievement that was almost unheard of for a new lawyer with a small firm. Art and I worked out a neat division of labor: I tried the cases and he handled the "desk work"—real estate closings, wills, divorces, and research.

During the sixties, the legal scene in most mid-size cities was far different from what we know today. For one thing, lawyers didn't advertise, at least openly. The phenomenon of the big-time "ambulance chasers," firms whose marketing budgets now total millions of dollars a year, was unknown. Curiously, most lawyers in those years did not try cases. But at Rosenbaum & Agnello, I developed a reputation as being a success with juries; as a result other firms often sent me cases to take to trial for a split fee. I loved trial law, it was like catnip to me. I'm a real kosher ham; some of the skill comes naturally, some I've worked to develop. For example, I made it a practice at the start of a case to learn all the jurors' names and to use them frequently.

Even my baldness became a useful *shtick;* joking about my shiny head helped create a relaxed atmosphere in the courtroom that often worked in my favor. At the opening of a jury trial, a lawyer often asks, in the interest of fairness, if any juror knows him (or her) personally. I would often add (rubbing my bald head conspicuously), "Now, I don't want you to mistake me for Telly Savalas or Yul Brynner," two actors with shiny domes who were then media stars.

Above all, I worked hard at the law; I was compulsive. I discovered that practicing law was easy for me. No matter how complicated the case, how crazy, I could find a way to beat my opponent, and I especially loved the strategizing that led to success. My focus was laser-like, and my goal was always to get the best result for my client. I remember one case involving a $300 settlement on which I'd worked countless hours; at the conclusion of the pre-trial, the elderly presiding judge said to me, "You really give your clients' their money's worth, don't you?"

But by 1969 I was getting bored with life in a law firm, even though it was my own. I was making a lot of money, but fifteen and a half years of trying cases, of working like a lunatic, was getting to me. Then too, things were changing around me. Judy and I had bought our dream home in the neighboring town of Penfield, in a secluded area we called "Shangri-la"; we had three kids and we were planning to have another. I told myself that life should get less complicated now.

But any idea that I could adapt to "the simple life" was a delusion. During the past fifteen years, I'd been seduced by a powerful agent: politics. From 1960 on, my need to become a major player in the Republican Party moved front and center.

Chapter 7

"All Politics Is Local"

Tip O'Neill, the late and legendary Speaker of the House, often told this story, one of my favorites. Early in his political career, the O'Neills lived next door to a widow for whom Tip (good Irishman that he was) often did favors. He'd pick up a few groceries for her when he was in town, keep an eye on her house when she was away—and all summer long he mowed her lawn. In 1936 he ran in his first bid for office. A few days after the election, Tip learned from the widow that she had voted for his opponent.

"Why didn't you vote for me?" Tip asked her, perhaps more puzzled than annoyed. "I thought we were good friends." "We are good friends," said the widow. "But he rang the bell and asked me to vote for him. You didn't."

This anecdote supports the truism that all politics is local. I understood that early, and I've made the most of it in my career. I caught the political bug when I was a teenager; certainly in both college and law school I spent energy campaigning that might better have been spent on my studies. But I've always needed to be in the middle of the action— and if I can't find some, I'll generate it. Competition of any sort fuels me, and I relish the rough-and-tumble that has always been at the heart of the political process.

Because I'm such a bulldog, so eager to go all-out to reach the goal, my rise in local Republican politics was meteoric. In less than six years, I rose from a beginner's role on the little town of Penfield's GOP committee to become chairman of the party in Monroe County, an indus- trial-suburban region encompassing the city of Rochester and environs, then home to three-quarters of a million people. At 36, I was the youngest county chairman ever, and the first of my faith chosen to lead this largely Protestant constituency.

But because "all politics is local," I had to prove myself at every step of the way up the ladder. I knew nothing would be given to me—quite the opposite, I had to pay my dues, win my way in. Somewhat to my dismay, my first efforts to break into the party were rebuffed. In 1958 we lived in Brighton, a suburb of Rochester then solidly Republican and run by an "old boy" network that wanted no part of a brash newcomer. Try as I might, the Brighton supervisor, Len Boniface, wouldn't let me in. (It was satisfying later on to have him come to me for favors and "kiss my ring," or my ass, as the case may be.) Fortunately, Judy and I found our dream house later that year in the neighboring town of Penfield, and so in the summer of 1959, that's where I began to cut my political teeth. I was a brash 28-year-old, and I was ready to make my move.

As soon as we'd settled into our new house, I called on the town's GOP leader, Joe Trau, and told him I'd like to get involved. "Nothing open now," he told me, but he passed me along the line to Tom Farrell, my district leader. I told Tom I'd be glad to help in any way I could, and he jumped at the offer. A year later, after I'd worked hard at the routine campaign work (such as ringing doorbells) that keeps a party strong, Tom called and said, "We're going to have an opening on the committee. Are you still interested?" I was delighted.

"The Committee," whether district, state, or national, is where the real power lies; it functions in the same way a board of directors does in the corporate world. For a relative youngster, it's a great training ground. Here's where you get to know the folks who call the shots, where you find mentors. Here's where you learn to deconstruct complex political relationships, and here's where you learn the power of patronage. Above all, here's where you learn to know your constituents—how to keep the "party faithful" loyal, and how to convert the unbelievers.

Penfield in those days was a sleepy little Republican town, its eastern half almost entirely agricultural and its western half increasingly suburbanized. Town Hall, at the village four corners, was back then a

No Room for Democracy

converted residence. The night of my first meeting as a committeeman, one of the old-timers, Henry DeRoo, took me aside; he'd heard I was ambitious and he took me under his wing (even though he represented a district different than mine). "Look," he said. "Penfield is growing. Right now, Penfield is a second-class town, and the justice can serve as both councilman and justice. Soon we'll be big enough to qualify as a first-class town. When that happens, Dick Connors [then the town's justice of the peace] will have to give up his post in order to stay on the town board. You can become the justice." DeRoo was right. Shortly thereafter, Penfield became a first-class town, Connors went on the town council and I had a shot at becoming justice of the peace.

I was immediately informed that the town fathers, GOP leader Joe Trau and town supervisor Howard Frank, had offered the position to local patent attorney George Shaw. George is a fine fellow, but he knew nothing about politics. In addition to Shaw, four other candidates for the position had declared. Forty-eight votes were to be cast by the party's various committeemen. I was a newcomer, and I wanted to prove to the old-timers that I was the right man. I invited my fellow committeemen to our house to get to know me and my family, and I spent night after night calling on them to talk over town issues. (Several were farmers, and more than once I barely escaped the jaws of their suspicious dogs.)

When the votes finally were counted, I had garnered forty-two of them, with the four other candidates splitting the remaining six votes. I was appointed, elected, elated, and launched! Judy was amazed; she thought that since I was Jewish I wouldn't have a chance in what was then hidebound, Waspy Penfield.

Every other week I dispensed justice, sitting at a table in the JP's makeshift courtroom in the town hall. No robes, no fancy business; but in that little courtroom, I got a great post-graduate education. Town court is at the very heart of the American judicial system; this is the court that's closest to the people. Every session dealt with real-life problems, small perhaps, but important both to those directly involved and to the safety of the community at large—traffic violations, drunken driving, petty larceny, domestic violence, breaking-and-entering, assault.

During my first months in office, the townspeople learned that I ran a tight ship, and that I could be counted on to be compassionate and fair.

At that time, the state police wielded a lot of power; most justices would take the word of a trooper over a defendant; half the justices had no legal credentials and often let the troopers run their court. As a result, the citizenry had developed a sense that the police could be overbearing. I set about to change that. At the beginning of every court session, I would tell those who had been charged, "Let me tell you something: This is your court. Your taxes pay my salary, so in fact I work for you. You're going to get a fair shake in here." (And they would.) With these words, you could feel the atmosphere go from tense to relaxed. To the troopers, I'd say, "Look, it's your job to arrest them. It's my job to dispose of the case. After you've given us the facts, your job is done and mine starts."

I cut my judicial teeth, so to speak, during those first months. Then came the moment of truth—I had to campaign for the office at the next election. This was a moment I'd been looking forward to. I knew party leaders had promised the post to George Shaw and that he had the backing of the "graybeards." I sensed that the entrenched were waiting to see me fall on my face. The situation was made for me—I had a fight on my hands! I campaigned like a madman. Calling my shiny bald pate into play (and being sure never to wear a hat!), I went door to door, passing out combs printed with the words "Vote for Richard Rosenbaum." The effort seemed to amuse everyone.

On election day, with the town judgeship coming up to a vote, my biggest coup came in the form of support from an unusual constituency: the two thousand or so residents of Penfield's four mobile home communities, almost all of them registered Democrats. For weeks before the election, I hung out at the parks, setting up weekend *kaffee klatsches* at their on-premises social clubs, talking, listening, asking about their concerns. This was something different—nobody in politics had ever paid attention to these people; consequently, they believed they were voiceless and insignificant. On meeting days, I'd arrive at the park loaded down with donuts; if I learned that someone was working the night shift and couldn't be there, I'd deliver a bag of crullers—and my card—to his or her door. The residents of the parks saw that—finally!—someone was paying attention.

Most of the residents believed that park owners were overcharging them for fuel oil. Here was a way I could really help: I knew one of the owners, Malcolm Glazer (the friend who had introduced me to my wife). Malcolm had a monopoly on the fuel oil being delivered to his park; if residents didn't buy from him (and pay his price), they got a thirty-day notice, after which they were out. Not without some difficulty, I persuaded Malcolm to cut the price enough to make a noticeable difference in the residents' monthly fuel bills. Did they ever love me for that! They ended up thinking I could do anything. I even got a call at two o'clock one morning asking me to come and rescue a cat stuck in a tree! (I admit, in this I failed them).

As a result of my efforts, I won the mobile home parks district six to one, led the ticket, and attracted the attention of the county's political leadership. The odds against my leading the ticket should have been overwhelming; I was, after all, still a rank outsider. But I was the candidate with "the fire in the belly," and that's often what it takes.

* * *

Most of the cases I dealt with as town justice were routine. One, however, still casts a terrible shadow. The town was horrified one morning to learn that the body of a little girl from one of our own neighborhoods had been discovered; thirteen-year-old Pamela Moss had been raped and murdered (by the gardener who worked next door to her home, as it turned out). For a week or more, the story made headline news on television and in newspapers. Soon, carloads of sightseers were coming out to Penfield to have a look at the scene of the crime. Naturally, the parents and neighbors were distraught at the ghoulish attention; so was I. Calling a press conference, I announced that any non-resident found driving on the street in question without a valid reason would be arrested; I asked troopers on the block to back up my threat. The legality of the move may have been questionable, but I saw my job as justice as protector of my community—and the people of Penfield supported me.

The murderer, James Moore, had followed poor Pamela and attacked her in a wooded area that served as a short cut to the local shopping mall. For two weeks fear reigned in the town, until a smart investigator checked Moore's past, discovered his previous conviction for raping a young girl, put two and two together, and arrested him. The night he was caught, I was awakened at two a.m. by a knock on the door from Rochester sheriff Al Skinner, district attorney Jack Conway, sheriff's lieutenant Jim Wiesner and others. I hastily dressed and arraigned Moore at the town hall. (Moore remains in prison to this day, and I, among others, continue to resist his applications for parole.)

* * *

Early in 1963, I made my next move. My target: leadership of the Republican Party in Penfield, a step encouraged by most of the district's leaders. This was an important move; if I won, I would automatically have a seat on the county GOP's executive committee. Fortunately for me, the Penfield party was ready for new leadership, but I had to play my cards carefully because I was bucking the old guard. This was a situation that called for all my diplomatic skills, all the force of my personality, and more. When I got calls from several committee leaders asking me to run, I told them I'd like to, but that I didn't want to raise a civil war within the party. After all, the present leader, Joe Trau, had supported me as a newcomer (although sometimes reluctantly).

The fact of the matter is, the party's leadership had no idea how to handle this tornado, this guy who'd burst on the scene only two years ago, and who now was taking over everything. Note to young Machiavellis: If I'd been in their position, I would have shut me down fast. I would have threatened with whatever it took—that's what leadership means to me. But in this case, I had the backing of the rank and file, and Trau was afraid to put the question to a vote for fear he'd lose. Ultimately, he resigned.

In retrospect, I think I overwhelmed them, both with the force of my personality and with my hard work. Trau apparently sensed that I had so much support from the committee that he threw in the towel. Shortly after the election, the GOP's county leader, Don Foote, called me in and asked, "How in hell did you ever get those people in Penfield to support you?" (What he *really* meant was, "How can a Jew become a leader in a German Lutheran town?") I had an answer for him: "Don, I was born and raised in Oswego. I know how to handle people who think they don't like me—I just go to work and win them over!"

Winning the job as town leader meant giving up my post as justice of the peace, this was mandated to avoid any semblance of conflict of interest. I knew just the guy I wanted to fill my unexpired term: Don Mark. Don was a good friend and a dedicated, hard-working lawyer who had always responded when I asked for political help. The night arrived for the town's GOP committee meeting at which I planned to nominate Don; with it came another example of the kind of prejudice that rankles me so deeply. A few hours before the meeting I got a phone call from the town supervisor, Howard Frank, asking me to hold back the nomination. "You know," he said, "Don's Italian. We've never had an Italian office-holder in Penfield." I said, "You know, you never had a Jewish town justice or a Jewish GOP leader either, until I came on the scene. I'm telling you this: If you do anything to stop Don Mark, I'll see you don't get the nomination for supervisor next time out." (He later apologized, saying he'd been tired from working all day on his farm and withdrew his opposition.)

In 1966, I took one more big step forward and ran for the Monroe County Legislature. For this campaign, our neighbor, high-school student, and former babysitter Sylvia Vernarelli, was an ideal leader. She would bring her friends (often more than sixty of them) to the town hall on Saturday mornings, I'd bring donuts and cider and we'd plan a course of action. For weeks, they showed up at town events wearing "Vote for Rosenbaum" sweatshirts. Those girls were everywhere! (Their parents loved this exercise in civic responsibility, and they supported my campaign, too.)

The day after the election, the local newspaper referred to my campaign as "a stunning run"—I had amassed about eighty percent of the votes and became an instant prospect for higher office. Because of my powerful showing, I was appointed the legislature's majority whip (assistant majority leader), unheard of for a freshman legislator.

★ ★ ★

At that time, the Republican Party in Monroe County was in the hands of a powerful triumvirate: Vince Tofany (the past county chairman); Gordon Howe, the county manager; and sheriff Al Skinner. Tofany was splitting his time between Rochester and Albany, having been appointed by Governor Rockefeller to serve as commissioner of the Department of Motor Vehicles. Howe for many years had led the Town of Greece, the county's largest town. "The Silver Fox," as he was called, became a mentor to me, as well as other young politicos.

As for Sheriff Skinner, he already had become something of a legend. Al's life was being sheriff and his religion was the Republican Party. A bachelor, he lived in an apartment within the jail. There, at least three times a week, he hosted euchre games for the enlightenment of party leaders; I frequently was in attendance. The fare at these games was milk and cookies, the latter made by the sheriff's housekeeper.

At that moment in 1967, the local GOP was in a holding pattern. Tofany had followed his fortunes to Albany, and filling in for him in Rochester was the avuncular Ralph Murphy, a party regular who was serving as caretaker, rather than leader. Tofany still held power in the party locally, since he held the chair of its "executive committee," a position he created when he elevated Murphy. Everyone realized, however, that the party needed a strong, full-time leader in place.

Once again, after only thirteen months in the county legislature, I got the call. Tofany, Howe, and Skinner all wanted me as the party's leader. On February 8, 1968, I was elected Republican chairman for Monroe County by the county's GOP committee. I was 36 years old, the youngest in the history of the local party, and the first Jewish chairman. The local newspaper broke the news with a headline that trumpeted: "Rosenbaum: Flare and Pizzazz." The article praised my "infectious enthusiasm," and "shrewd political insights," but warned that I could be "a tough operator."

How could a freshman legislator jump over so many heads to the party's top county post? In my case, there were at least three reasons. First, the party chiefs knew I'd built a powerful base in the affluent districts of Brighton and Penfield, two bellwether GOP towns. Second, I'd proven myself a powerful vote-getter, having scored higher in the recent election than any other legislator in the county. Third, I was seen as representing an important cadre of bright, energetic "young Turks," and the party was looking to this group for much-needed new blood.

The first test of my strength as county chairman came early, when it was time to pick my successor as assistant majority leader on the legislature. I knew the man I wanted to fill my seat; others felt differently. My candidate won, and Henry Williams, a smart local lawyer and loyal friend, was elected. (After considerable maneuvering on my part, Williams actually was nominated for the post by his rival, Peter Vandertang from the Town of Ogden!) The fact that I could pull off that feat of diplomacy helped solidify my position as party leader.

A second challenge came fast on the heels of the first. This one taught me something about myself that I hadn't fully appreciated. Here's what happened. That year, 1968, the Republican National Convention was scheduled for Miami. Three men were in contention for the presidential nomination: Richard Nixon, Nelson Rockefeller, and Ronald Reagan. As party chair in the county, one of my jobs was to pick four delegates to represent our district at the convention. From the east side of the city I picked former county judge John Lomenzo and myself; from the west side of the city I chose party leaders Gordon Howe and Vince Tofany.

As soon as I announced that we were going to the convention as a "Rockefeller delegation," we immediately had a fight on our hands. Rockefeller, our governor, was a moderate, but many considered him a liberal. Among the challengers was Fred Eckert, a conservative activist and Nixon supporter who put together his own slate of proposed delegates and forced a primary. This challenge was like a tonic for me! I'd only been in the post for a couple of months and already the routine bored me. The minute I had a fight on my hands, I found myself totally energized. All during that period I went to work early and worked late, whistling all the way!

Eckert won the draw for ballot position and his slate was listed on Row A. His luck of the draw made me furious; I'm not used to second place. I was eager for a fight, totally energized, and I worked my fanny off to win that primary. I spent a couple of hundred dollars and hired a plane to fly over the city trailing a banner emblazoned with the words, "Vote for the *Real* Republicans. Vote Row B." At a party that afternoon, I jokingly countered a question about the plane flying overhead by saying, "Yes, that's our plane. I borrowed it from the Israeli Air Force." I made such a thing about voting for Row B that Eckert, in a television interview, blurted out that "Row B" stood for "bullshit." I was amused. Of course, my slate won the primary and Lomenzo and I led the ticket.

We went to Miami in August to support Rocky. Even though the city was hotter than Hades, it was exciting for me to be at a national convention with delegates from all over the country, including legendary figures like Strom Thurmond, the senator from South Carolina, and others.

Those first victories, while satisfying, were relatively small potatoes. I had a *really* big fish to fry: my next goal seemed to many an impossible dream—to bring the Democrat-controlled city of Rochester back into the Republican camp, after an absence of ten years. Such a feat would run against the rapidly increasing trend in New York State to make the urban areas Democratic strongholds.

Chapter 8

They Said It Couldn't Be Done:
Rochester Goes Republican

As my mother often says, "A new broom sweeps clean." As soon as
I became GOP county leader in 1968, I announced my Number
One goal for this election year: to sweep away ten years of domi-
nance by the Democrats and bring the city of Rochester back into the
Republican fold.

This would be no small task, since simultaneously we had to mount
and win both a city and a county election—and, as county chairman, I
was still a relative newcomer. Local Democrats, the press, even some
Republicans said it couldn't be done. To win back the city, we had to
elect four of the five city council seats at the next at-large election. The
Republicans were in charge of Monroe County, and recent county-wide
property tax hikes would complicate my job. The electorate was sullen,
their pocketbooks bleeding; it seemed we might even have difficulty
holding offices then under Republican control.

I determined that winning those four city council seats was all-
important; that's where we needed to spend most of our money and
our effort. A decisive win in the city could have a ripple effect, helping
us pick up seats in those county legislature districts that crossed city
boundaries, perhaps even altering the political balance on the Democrat-controlled city school board.

By targeting a win in the city as our first priority, I raised a big
question: What about GOP candidates in the towns? Would we alienate them by investing most of our campaign money in the city? This
was an issue that must be addressed by the chairman; as usual, I was
frank. When speaking to candidates in towns that had long been GOP

strongholds, I emphasized their favorable position. If they'd been doing their work, I told them, they already were well known and well funded; this year, they would have to finance the greater part of their own campaigns. I promised, however, that we would come to their rescue if a race promised to be close. Winning back the city, I insisted, was our major target.

The campaign to win back the city began immediately with a search for qualified candidates who were willing to work hard—and who were electable. In a move that was considered both startling and innovative, I advertised for candidates in the newspaper; from about forty responses, I picked eight likely prospects and grilled each intensively; all eight met my qualifications. "The new broom" metaphor fit the group perfectly: we promoted our candidates as bright, youthful, and vigorous, and we effectively compared their average age, 33, to that of their Democratic opponents, which was almost 50.

We kept a tight hold on where our money was going. GOP city council candidates each received the same amount of party funding, but all bills for campaign expenses were to be sent to headquarters where a weekly accounting would be made. If we saw that a candidate's campaign was faltering, we sweetened the pot and upped his advertising budget.

Over several months, we worked with a research team to draw up a thirty-two page platform that presented the Republican agenda for improving conditions within the city, including specifics on "how," "why," and "how much." The platform reflected what we learned from several thousand questionnaires and telephone calls, asking independent voters what they liked and didn't like about the city government.

Several months before the election, when the platform was at last finely tuned, we scheduled a major press conference, in conjunction with a luncheon at which media representatives could meet and question our candidates. A similar luncheon brought together the city's union leaders. The months devoted to developing our platform was time and money well spent. The entire GOP team knew our game plan by heart, our positions were clearly defined, and our slate featured

No Room for Democracy

attractive, articulate candidates. The Democrats were left at the starting line, fumbling for an effective response.

Cries of "too high taxes!" seemed to meet us at every turn, and we reacted creatively. We launched "Operation Tax Cut" and chartered a bus to take GOP legislators and selected news media to Washington. As we traveled I talked with each Republican legislator on the bus, asked how his or her campaign was progressing, and insisted that every candidate have a sound plan for winning.

At the Capitol, we met with Congressional leaders, including Wilbur Mills, the powerful chairman of the House Ways and Means Committee. We told them that Monroe County was facing real trouble—an increasingly stiff tax burden and high welfare costs—and asked for their support. Daily press releases were fired back to Rochester from Washington, and meetings with cabinet officials were filmed for future use back home.

Shortly after our return, we learned that President Nixon was about to recommend that uniform welfare standards be adopted. We were not above implying that our consultations with government leaders had influenced the president's thinking on this issue. Immediately after the president's speech, we gave each of our city council candidates a thousand petitions to recruit support for the president's welfare reform program. Each petition-signer was presented with a button bearing the slogan "Keep Cutting Costs" and a pamphlet printed with two photographs—one of the president and one of the candidate—and excerpts from the president's speech.

If voters were going to the polls with high taxes on their mind, we would be on the right side of that issue.

* * *

We were like circus jugglers that year, balancing several slippery balls in the air as we coordinated campaigns to win seats on the city council, county legislature, assembly, and city school board.

Occasionally, we ran into trouble. One near-disaster happened in May, on the eve of our major election-year campaign dinner. Well over a thousand supporters were expected to gather at Rochester's War Memorial to hear George Romney, then secretary of the U.S. Department of Housing and Urban Development. Urban development was a hot topic here, and we'd sold out the house. So, when I learned just before the dinner that Romney had been dispatched to India to attend a state funeral, I was fit to be tied. I fired off an angry telegram to President Nixon, asking, in effect, "How could you do this to us?" and demanding a good replacement speaker. Nixon had his honcho at the National Republican Committee call me with several suggestions, all of which I vetoed. I told them I wanted Rogers C. B. Morton, then GOP national chairman. I got him. When I met Morton at the airport the afternoon of the dinner, he gave me a funny look and then said, "You know, Rosie, that telegram you sent the president is tattooed on my ass." Morton had a very earthy sense of humor. He once told me that in certain cases he had as much value as teats on a boar hog.

What helped keep us on track during those harried months was a detailed communications plan that kept everyone on the same page, whether they were working for us in the city or the county. A comprehensive campaign chart was drawn up, and I appointed a trusted captain to direct each of the various fronts— cities, towns, and county legislators in all twenty-nine districts. As county chairman (I was re-elected to that post in July), I was very definitely the commander-in-chief. Four times a week we held strategy meetings with our city council candidates, our media team, campaign advisors, and GOP school board candidates. Once a week, candidates for the legislature in at-risk districts met with me and my staff to work out strategies designed to improve our odds of winning.

In the towns, I had to play hardball. Early in September, I announced a vote quota for each town, and told the leaders that those who met their quotas would be favored with patronage, if and when we won the city election. Throughout the campaign, I continually called on ward leaders and town officials, prepping them on the issues and building enthusiasm for our candidates. A big smile and an encouraging word proved to be effective; one town leader told the press, "I always feel

No Room for Democracy

better after talking to Dick;" others said the same thing to me.

A highly experienced events coordinator did yeoman service. Every day, our candidates received a calendar that listed "campaign happenings" scheduled throughout the city and towns, with a note to tell them where they were expected to appear. Phone calls alerted key residents in the targeted areas to upcoming events. Always and everywhere we stressed the importance of "maximum exposure."

Nothing could be left to chance. To that end, an all-day "school for candidates" was held, during which PR professionals explained how to run an effective campaign, how best to interact with the media, and how to meet and greet voters to best advantage. So that the candidates' time could be used most effectively, west side GOP leaders were ordered to schedule fall campaign rallies and dinners on odd evenings of the week; even-numbered nights were to be filled by events scheduled on the city's east side.

As September approached, we were very decidedly on the move.

★ ★ ★

In the weeks before the election, our already-frenetic pace increased.

We began bombarding the media with commercials promoting our city council candidates as a team. Our billboards and commercials were built around short, hard-hitting messages, featuring average citizens voicing their concerns: "I've had it with violence in our schools," or, "Somebody's got to stop crime on our streets."

All candidates had been told, at the time of their selection, to prepare for grueling schedules. They were expected to greet workers arriving for the 6 a.m. shifts at local factories. Often they arrived at the plant gate to find the county leader already there, busy shaking hands—and checking to make sure the vote-seeker showed up. (They all did.)

In September, the five GOP candidates for city council challenged their opponents to a debate. We hired a hall and pumped up the event to the media every day for a week. When the Democrats failed to show on time, we reaped a media bonanza. You can imagine the remarks that flew when TV screens across the county showed our five guys holding down the stage—and next to them, five empty chairs! I loved it!

As election day approached, teams of "shock troops" were formed, with orders to move at a moment's notice into areas where GOP reinforcement was needed, to ring doorbells, distribute literature, and generally to be everywhere in evidence. Earlier in the year, the women's division had poured over voter enrollment books, furnishing phone numbers for every Republican listed. These would prove invaluable in getting out the vote on election day. So did our "special ride service:" any town or ward leader who needed help transporting voters to the polls could call Republican headquarters on election day and a car and driver would be on the way.

Our experienced and talented public relations team set up a "GOP newsroom" in the city. Candidates visited the newsroom on schedule for briefings on specific issues. Their coached and carefully rehearsed comments were recorded on site and released to radio stations, to be aired throughout the next few days beginning at six each morning. If a candidate's campaign was lagging, we bought additional airtime for him or her, often running the ads for several days in a row.

Three weeks before the election, a facsimile of the Republican row on the election ballot was reproduced and distributed throughout the city and the county with town and ward workers doing the legwork. This visual aid made a real difference, as we were drawing to the polls new voters, unfamiliar with what they would find behind the voting booth curtain.

A "victory headquarters" was set up downtown and some hundred thousand pieces of mail went out the last week of the campaign to special interest groups—seniors, veterans, naturalized citizens, police, firemen, even parents of students at our community college. Each letter highlighted an action taken by the Democrats that adversely affected the community or, conversely, quoted from newspaper articles that supported the Republican position on a given issue. The weekend before the election we printed and distributed a four-page newspaper filled with articles from the past two years that cast the Democrats in a bad light.

A poll taken in October revealed that a substantial number of city residents still were undecided. To meet this challenge, we played our ace in the hole. We knew we had a hot ticket in young Steve May—bright, energetic, and the scion of a local family famously linked to the University of Rochester. In every way Steve was a favorable contrast to the incumbent mayor, by then middle-aged Frank Lamb. Taking advantage of the fact that at that time Rochester's mayor was elected not by the people, but by a majority vote of the city council, we made our big announcement a week before the election: If Republicans won control of the city council, Steve May would become mayor. That announcement, I'm sure, won us votes.

★ ★ ★

On Monday, November 3, the day before the election, I flatly predicted that the Republicans would win four of five seats in the city council, that we would maintain our twenty-four to five majority in the county legislature, and that we would take control of the city school board. It had taken months of working 25-hour days, but I could smell success in the air.

Some election districts in the city were susceptible to voter fraud, a sobering fact revealed by a study we'd conducted early in the campaign. To ensure a fair election, we put together a security team made up of fifty young attorneys and representatives of area businesses and industries; a respected retired police captain was recruited to manage the team. On election day, after a 5 a.m. breakfast at GOP victory headquarters, two-man teams of poll monitors fanned out into the twenty-five districts where voting irregularities were feared. Each monitor wore a lapel tag marked with an American flag and the words "Ballot Security" in bold print. Not only did the teams effectively discourage voting fraud, but they became magnets for media attention.

Late that night, as election returns were being counted, a Democrat "party faithful" was seen entering an elevator at the Sheraton Hotel. "Going down," the man intoned soberly. "That's the way we've been going all night," came the glum reply from a fellow passenger.

Both were right—and so was my prediction. On Wednesday morning, the local newspaper trumpeted the news: "Strong Republican Tide Rolls into City and County." One lone Democrat was left on the city council, we had won twenty-four out of twenty-nine seats in the county legislature, and we'd captured the city school board four to one. Of the many congratulatory telegrams I received, I particularly enjoyed one that said, "Now we have bald Jewish power!"

It was called "a brilliant campaign" that had produced "astonishing results," especially since elsewhere across the state Democrats had prevailed. Others may have been astonished, but not I. Months before, I had told Governor Rockefeller that we were going to win. A headline that appeared two days after the election captured the real reason for our success: "Republicans: Had Issues, Tried Harder."

Chapter 9

His Honor, the Judge

In those post-election weeks of 1969, we Republicans in Monroe County were ecstatic. Our overwhelming success at the polls had surprised everyone, it seemed, except me. Writing about the GOP tidal wave in Rochester, UPI correspondent Clay Richards described it this way: "The reaction ranged from shock among Democrats, to disbelief among newsmen who were caught off guard. No one had predicted the Republican sweep and it went counter to most other areas in the state where Democrats rolled up impressive margins to either retain control or kick Republicans out of office."

Hard work, strong issues, and an attractive slate of candidates had won the day for the Republicans. The press, I must say, made much of my role in our success. Bill O'Brien, political reporter for Rochester's morning newspaper, got it about right when, in an election summary that appeared the following Sunday, he described me as "an ebullient sort who punctuates his sentences with laughter," and "the architect of the Republicans' Election Day domination and the takeover of City Hall. He didn't win it by laughing his way through the campaign. A hard-nosed taskmaster, Rosenbaum was constantly herding his candidates for 5 a.m. appearances at plant gates and demanding that they follow through their campaign into the night."

I was a hard-driver, and I know that over the years I've pissed off a lot of people because of it. Rochester's John Parinello, a prominent criminal attorney and friend, once told local bank CEO Art Richardson, "Every time I want to go up and tell that son-of-a-bitch off, I get as far as the elevator and I lose my nerve." (That amuses me, because Johnny is a great criminal attorney and he has a lot of nerve.)

Another local political reporter, Christy Bulkeley, filed this post-election critique of my leadership role: "Rosenbaum is careful to check with ward and town political leaders...More often than not, however, Rosenbaum has made up his mind on something before he goes after any advice and his mind can seldom be changed by one person alone." Bulkeley could be almost embarrassingly accurate: "People who think they've swayed him generally find, on rethinking the conversation, that he was asking questions designed to get the response he wanted." (Bulkeley was on target in noting that I do spend time seeking opinions before I make up my own mind, but she may not have known that I listened most carefully to my old mentor, Gordon Howe, an astute and artful politician, and our county manager.)

Whatever the reasons, the win was ours. I knew I'd done a good job using brains and hard work; as I told the press, "We outworked, out-imagined, and out-innovated the Democrats"—and that had meant working twenty-four hour days for twenty-two months. My reward came when party leaders, led by Governor Rockefeller, asked me to come to Albany to talk about my winning strategies and to write a how-to-win mini-textbook that other Republicans could use in their own campaigns. (I did it. The title of the pamphlet is "They Said It Couldn't Be Done," a copy of which is in the Library of Congress.)

We were the "magical team" in New York State politics at that moment. We were so potent that the governor and his wife, Happy, joined us for our victory dinner in late January, three months after the election. Almost twenty-five hundred Republicans gathered at Rochester's War Memorial for the celebration. The rafters rocked when the governor announced that he'd picked Rochester for the site of the next state GOP convention, and that he would use the occasion to be nominated for his fourth term. The dinner and the governor's announcement that his statewide campaign would begin in our hometown was a splendid conclusion to two years of hard, non-stop campaigning.

The post-election weeks, however, had not all been smooth. Between the election and that triumphant victory dinner, we'd hit a nasty patch: Democrats challenged the residential legitimacy of one of our city council winners, Michael Roche. This was a fight we couldn't afford to lose: without Roche, not only would we lose our majority grip on the council, but the next mayor might well continue to be Democrat Frank Lamb. My expectations for a smooth transition of power within the city were blasted, and we found ourselves in a real donnybrook. It was a black day for me personally when the local newspapers featured a photograph of the two contesting mayoral candidates—one Democrat, one Republican—literally fighting over the gavel.

I quickly recruited some of the best legal minds in the community to defend our cause, including retired New York State Court of Appeals judge John Van Voorhis and my future law partner, Jack McCrory. Within a month the quarrel was over. Roche's primary residence was determined to be within the city limits, and we took control of the city council, five to four. As promised in our campaign, we tapped Stephen May to become the city's new mayor. Steve, who led our ticket with more than 49,000 votes, had a special charisma; a bachelor, he lived in a four-room basement apartment and drove an eight-year-old Volkswagen convertible—he was also bright, attractive, hardworking and personable.

In January 1970, hard work of another sort began for me. Although some two thousand city and county jobs would continue to be held by their incumbents, more than a thousand positions would be left vacant by departing Democrats. Suddenly I had no peace! Everyone wanted a job. I couldn't go out to dinner with my wife and have a quiet evening; some guy would come over to our table, tug on my sleeve, and say, "What about that photographer's job?" or, "I hope you'll keep me in mind for that opening at the court house." It became really onerous. Job seekers would show up at my house on Sunday mornings, bringing gifts as though I was some potentate. I discovered that the worst part of my job as county chairman was dispensing patronage. I disliked it intensely.

If the patronage problem was a pain in the neck, I also realized that I seemed to be suffering from a mild case of post-election blues. I'm a fighter: I'd loved every minute of the last two years, doing what everybody said couldn't be done, winning both the city and county. Suddenly, my fights were all small and, in comparison to the past twenty-two months, rather petty. I guess I'm a sprinter, rather than a long-distance runner. I'd won my big fight; both the city and the county seemed to me to be in competent hands, with May as mayor and Gordon Howe as county manager. After two and a half years as county chairman, I needed a new challenge.

★ ★ ★

One day I answered my jangling phone and heard Gordon Howe say, "I want to talk to you about something." He continued: "Cass Henry is resigning from the supreme court, so there's going to be an opening. I think we should go over and talk to Harry Goldman about it." Clarence (Cass) Henry was a lawyer's lawyer, a brilliant guy able to sum up to a jury for two solid days without looking at a note. Harry Goldman was then presiding justice of the Fourth Judicial Department, which includes a total of twenty-two counties and encompasses Syracuse, Rochester, and Buffalo.

I was interested. Shortly after Gordon's phone call, we met with Harry Goldman and I told him that I would be very interested in being appointed to fill Cass Henry's uncompleted term. "You ought to do it," he told me, "Carpe diem." In fact, the idea of becoming a state supreme court justice had been on my mind for some time. One thing motivated me tremendously—my father. I loved my father deeply and I wanted to do something for him. I'd been lazy in college; I hadn't got that Swope Award in history, and I felt I'd let him down. I decided I wasn't going to let him down twice. I knew my being named state supreme court justice would make him tremendously proud. He'd bust his buttons.

After talking with Justice Goldman, I went right home and called Jack Tenney, an old law school classmate and former county chairman, who was then a state supreme court justice in Utica. Jack told me there was a movement afoot to require any county chairman of a political party seeking a seat on the state supreme court to wait two years after

No Room for Democracy

resigning the chairmanship before announcing his candidacy. "If you're going to do it, do it now," Jack advised. "Carpe diem," I thought, recalling Goldman's advice. "I'll do it."

I found my successor as party chairman in young Bill Dwyer, a former radio journalist who had been for years an imaginative and hard-working campaigner for the GOP. Asked by a reporter about his past role with the party, Bill downplayed it all the way. To my amusement, a profile on him in the local press began with this quote: "I was the guy carrying water to the elephants."

Not everyone is familiar with the obstacles that lie between an aspiring candidate and a seat on the Supreme Court of the State of New York, the highest trial court. Here, in brief, is what's involved. Each political party holds a judicial convention to pick its nominees for the available court posts (sub-groups within a party—for example Conservatives, Liberals, or Independents—may meet separately to choose their own candidates). In my upstate New York district, delegates convene from eight counties, but the outcome is essentially controlled by the most populous, Monroe County. However, to reach a fifty-one percent majority, Monroe's delegates must be supported by delegate votes from one of the other seven counties; most often today, the swing votes come from Seneca County, including the town of Seneca Falls, home of the National Women's Hall of Fame.

Candidates for seats on the state supreme court are rated by their peers. The various bar associations poll their members through a questionnaire designed to determine the strengths and weaknesses of the candidate under consideration, and the results of the poll are made public using the generalized terms "qualified" or "unqualified." (In recent years, a third designation, "highly qualified," has been added.) Because I had tried so many cases over the years, I was well known in the legal community—and there was a lot of evidence on which my qualifications could be judged. Gordon Howe later told me that I had the highest score on the bar poll ever recorded in our district—ninety-nine percent. (If I ever find out who the other one percent was...just kidding!) For some years now, a candidate seeking appointment to the bench needs to be found "highly qualified" by the governor's screening committee in order to be appointed.

* * *

On July 22, 1970, Judy and I were at Rochester General Hospital where our son Matthew, 6, was undergoing a tonsillectomy when I was called to the telephone. This was a call I'd been waiting for—it was Governor Rockefeller, appointing me to complete the state supreme court term of Cass Henry. "My son's tonsils and word of my appointment are coming out at the same time," I quipped, when a reporter called to confirm the news. At 39, I was the youngest ever appointed to the high court in the Seventh Judicial District—comprising eight counties including Monroe, home of Eastman Kodak, and Steuben, home of Corning Glass—in the Fourth Judicial Department.

I'll never forget the day I was sworn in. The ceremony had to be moved to the Appellate Division in order to have a room big enough to hold the throng that gathered—some two hundred friends, family, and colleagues. My old friend Justice Goldman, who had encouraged me to seek the post, did the honors. He concluded his remarks on a light note, saying (with a gesture to my bald pate), "You'll be a shining example on the bench," and, with a smile, added an afterthought: "One thing is sure, the lawyers won't be able to get in your hair!" Then he gathered up the robe, slipped it over my shoulders, and said "Ladies and gentlemen, I give you Mr. Justice Richard M. Rosenbaum"...and my father burst into tears.

I took quite a cut in salary when I accepted the appointment. State supreme court justices then made about $39,500 a year. I mentioned to fellow justice Jacob Ark my concern about what this cut might mean for the Rosenbaum family budget. I remember Jake saying, "I don't know why anybody would need more than that to live on." How things change!

The local newspaper made a big deal of my appointment, in part because I was so young. Some of their comments were amusing; I especially liked this one, written on the day I moved my office into Rochester's two-year-old Hall of Justice (then the envy of most cities in the state): "[Rosenbaum] has a hearty laugh, a voice with the delicacy of a

sonic boom, and he has an unbreakable habit of enjoying horrible puns…
but for all his jesting and sometimes booming ways, Rosenbaum grows
quiet and deeply serious when he talks about the law." The reporter was
right. My life rests on four pillars: my family, my faith, my respect for
the law, and the profession of politics.

Suddenly I was in the situation I'd wanted. I loved my chambers—
the big room, the spacious library. I'd call my father to come down for
lunch and as we walked down the street, people would stop and greet
me: "Hello, Your Honor." He loved it, and I was proud, too.

Four months later, of course, in November, I would have to run for
election for the post to which I'd been appointed. I'd just spent two years
knocking myself out winning an election for my GOP team—you'd think
I'd had enough. But this time, I was the candidate. Immediately I was
fully charged once again, off and running, all the juices flowing. I easily
won the nomination from the GOP camp, but I also tapped lawyer colleagues to fill the court's two other empty seats. (This brash move ran-
kled more than a few people, among them Rochester's district attorney
Jack Conway, who'd wanted the job himself. With some justification,
Conway went around grousing, "Rosenbaum appointed himself to the
bench." Which was basically true, but so what? That didn't phase me.)

My picks for the two empty seats on the court were Jim Boomer,
Rochester's former corporation counsel, a great judge with a great
intellect (who tragically drowned in a flash-flood while on a camping
trip), and Steuben County judge Alton J. Wightman, also an intelligent
and well-respected gentleman. It amuses me to recall those days—
these guys were all older. I was the baby, but the baby was running the
ballgame. They were kind of watching in awe from the sidelines as I was
making it happen.

I was pretty confident about my chances in the election, but in typi-
cal Rosenbaum style, I wanted to win with a flourish. I embarked on what
I consider one of the greatest coups of my career. I made a beeline for the
Democrats' convention and asked them to endorse me. What *chutzpah!*
I'd just beaten the Democrats into the ground in the city election—you'd
think they'd run me out on a rail. Charging into their meeting room, I

eyeballed Bob Quigley, the party's county chair. "Bob," I said, "let me talk a little *tachlis* [straight talk] to you. You can spend a lot of money trying to beat me, but you know I'm going to win this election. It's up to you, but let me tell you, I'd love to run on your [ballot] line." Quigley said, "Let me take it up with the convention." Well, as you might imagine, there was a tremendous uproar. But my "you can't beat me, so why not join me?" tactic worked, and the majority voted to endorse me. (Bob Quigley and I were what you might call friendly enemies. I really liked Bob, and when he died soon after—at age 49—I truly regretted the loss.)

Now I had the Democratic endorsement, but I still wasn't satisfied. I decided to go for the Liberals, too. I was fishing pals with one of the key guys in the Liberal Party and one afternoon at a pond in nearby Brockport, I asked him "Would you consider giving me your endorsement?" "Are you kidding?" he shot back. "Having your name on our ballot would be great for our party. You want it? You got it!" Then, in a final burst of *chutzpah*, I went to the Conservatives, who were led then by my friend Leo Kesselring , and they said yes, too. This four-party endorsement had never happened before in our district—and it's never happened since.

Even though there was no way I could lose, I went around campaigning like a madman—and I didn't give away a dime! I was having the time of my life. I tell you, I just ate it up with a shovel! Of course, all three of us—Boomer, Wightman, and I—were elected. As leader of the pack, I made sure I was appointed first—by minutes. That sounds like a pure ego move, but I had my family in mind; with seniority, I would rarely be called to preside over cases in Steuben County, thus avoiding an overnight stay away from home.

I was young, full of piss and vinegar, and ready to take on any case. The older judges loved that. Judge Peter Blauvelt would come to me and say, "I've got a case over in Auburn. Do you want to take it?" and I'd answer, "Sure!" (I enjoyed working in Auburn; the site of a federal prison; criminal cases there were often especially interesting, and it was close enough to Rochester that I could be home for dinner.) After a year I was given a permanent court reporter: Harry Hadley. Harry and

I hit it off great. He went with me everywhere; on road trips, we'd sing songs in the car, with me beating out time on the dashboard. Harry was both smart and helpful; when a case had concluded, I'd ask him, "Harry, what did I do wrong?" He'd been around the court for a while, and I really wanted to learn.

I was always out there looking for cases. I remember Judge Dominick (Mike) Gabrielli saying to me late one afternoon, "Dick, it's five o'clock. Aren't you going to go home? You're killing the union." I didn't care how long it took or how hard I had to work. I may not have been as conscientious in college as I should have (that guilt still lingers), but when I became a lawyer, things changed. I understood that now I was dealing with other people's lives, and I felt that responsibility very strongly.

In my campaign, I was fond of quoting from Sir Francis Bacon's essay "Of Judicature,"

> Judges ought to be more learned than witty, more reverend than plausible, and more advised than confident. Above all things, integrity is their portion and proper virtue…. Patience and gravity of hearing is an essential part of justice and an overspeaking Judge is no well-tuned cymbal.

At the same time, I was constantly challenged to restrain my admittedly unruly sense of humor—acting "sober as a judge" definitely was out of character for me. I suspect I overstepped my limits the day (this was before I went on the bench) I offered advice to my colleague Bill Clay, who was about to argue a case against another Rochester lawyer, Mordecai Greenberg. "Bill, when you go before the jury, pretend to stumble over his name and call him 'Mediocre Greenberg.' He'll go so crazy he won't know what he's doing." (He didn't.)

***

Every once in awhile a case would come along that would strike my funny bone. Topping the list was *Gonsenhauser v. Davis,* the culmination of a four-year property payment dispute involving a cattle sale that came before the bench in 1971. When I learned the identities of the principals, I could hardly wait for the fun to begin.

I knew the plaintiff, Max Gonsenhauser, a cranky, stubborn German Jewish livestock dealer from Brighton. A total contrast to Max was the defendant, Chester C. Davis, a suave New York City lawyer who on paper owned a large farm in Unadilla in Otsego County, New York. I happened to know that Davis actually was the front man in the landholding enterprises of Howard Hughes, the eccentric aeronautical genius and multimillionaire.

For four years, Max had been trying to get paid for a shipment of cattle purchased by Davis's farm manager back in 1967; the sale price then had been $10,275. Country bumpkin vs. city slicker was what the case looked like on the surface, but I knew Max was as simple as a fox. Davis's farm manager, Ernest Scheller, was a sod-buster who might have served as Max's *doppelgänger*, but without Max's brains.

On the witness stand, Scheller claimed that several of the cattle bought from Gonsenhauser had been defective; that's why payment had never been made. "Some of those cows had mastitis," Scheller told the bench. When I asked him to explain that term to the jury, he said, "Well, they were a bunch of three tit-ers." With that, he held up his hand and waggled three fingers suggestively, like teats on an udder. I'll tell you, I had to hide my face behind the charge book and struggle to keep from laughing out loud.

After three long days of bickering, the jury eventually found for Gonsenhauser. The next day, a Rochester newspaper cartoonist perfectly captured the scene, using images of an irate farmer pointing, three fingers extended, at a sheepish-looking defective cow. The headline writer was as amused as I was, since the article was topped with the line: "Gonsenhauser Wins Moo(la)."

***

One of the counties I presided in was Yates, whose county seat is the Finger Lakes town of Penn Yan. I remember well my first day on the bench there. The day began when I had to walk on a plank over a muddy yard to get to the courthouse, an inauspicious start, I thought. As I tried to adjust to this new environment, the phrase "walking the plank" actually came into my superstitious mind. Once in my chambers (to use the word loosely in this circumstance), I was checking things out when the door slowly swung open. Expecting to see another lawyer, I was startled to be greeted instead by a big, droopy-eared Bassett hound; the dog looked up at me as though I was an interloper. Clearly he felt this was his domain, not mine. I later learned the dog belonged to Lyman Smith, the resident justice,

That term, one of the cases involved a bridge over Keuka Lake Inlet, the question being: Who should maintain it? The Village of Penn Yan or the Town of Milo, which encompassed the village? The Milo town counsel submitted as evidence of control a photograph of the parking meters that lined the bridge; each bore a little cloth cover bearing the words, "Merry Christmas! Village of Penn Yan." After examining the photograph, I loudly exclaimed, "This evidence is prejudicial!" "Why?" asked the puzzled counsel. "Because it doesn't say 'Happy Hannukah!'" I quipped—and the courtroom burst into gales of laughter.

* * *

Later, back home and in a more sober frame of mind, I ordered cleanups at two migrant worker camps in Wayne County, whose proximity to Lake Ontario's shoreline has made it a rich agricultural belt. Conditions at both camps were deplorable. I ordered camp owners to comply with the state's sanitary codes or close down, arguing that camp residents were "dangerously deprived of privileges." The following year my popularity skyrocketed in Monroe County when I issued two "law and order" decisions within a week; the first strengthened legal support for victims, the second called for harsher punishment of criminals.

Of the many cases that came before me, I believe the most important was *Gannett Co. v. City of Rochester*—important because my decision had constitutional implications regarding free speech. If I have any judicial immortality, it rests on my decision in this interesting case. Rochester at that time was home to the corporate offices of the Gannett Co., Inc., which has since become the largest newspaper empire in the nation. Back in 1972, Gannett already owned newspapers in many cities, and under the leadership of publisher Paul Miller was flexing its muscles to acquire more.

In December 1971, the city of Rochester passed an ordinance requiring that every newspaper vending machine on the city's sidewalks be licensed, at a cost of ten dollars for each license. (Specifically, to use the language of the ordinance, licenses would be required for "each table, box, stand, newspaper vending machine or other device" used on a sidewalk for the sale, display, or storage of newspapers or magazines.)

Gannett, which daily stocked 209 vending machines in Rochester alone, challenged the constitutionality of the ordinance and the case was brought before Justice Richard M. Rosenbaum early in 1972. Representing the defense was the city's corporation counsel A. Vincent Buzard (later to become president of the New York State Bar Association). Buzard challenged Gannett on the grounds that privately-owned vending machines and similar objects used for newspaper sales and storage were potential hazards obstructing public sidewalks.

Gannett called into the ring Jack McCrory, one of the feistiest lawyers in the stable of the city's top law firm, Nixon, Hargrave, Devans, & Doyle. McCrory rested his case on two Constitutional amendments—the first, which guarantees freedom of speech and the press, and the fourteenth, which guarantees equal protection under the law. He was supported by counsel representing the American Civil Liberties Union. The case would be decided without a jury. (No jury was required, because the case was presented as "a motion in special term," a phrase familiar to lawyers, but of little consequence to others.)

This was a tough case, and I really struggled over the facts, the precedents, and the implications of my decision. At the same time, I worked hard to achieve the required judicial objectivity. Beyond the strictly legal implications lay the usual human factors; after all, it was my hand-picked slate of city councilmen who had passed the ordinance, while McCrory had been part of the legal team that succeeded in resolving the fight over councilman Mike Roche's residence. I had personal ties to both the prosecution and the defense—and no jury to turn to. The decision would be all mine.

Shortly after the case was introduced, a strange thing happened. I was at a dinner meeting at my alma mater, Hobart College, when I suddenly became ill. My discomfort—severe abdominal pains—rapidly worsened, and I realized I would have to leave immediately and drive home to Rochester, an hour away. I hadn't gone far when the pain became so acute that I pulled the car over to the side of the road and vomited repeatedly. Somehow I managed to get back home, parked the car, and staggered into the house. Judy took one look at me, helped me to bed, realized something was terribly wrong, and called the doctor. At midnight, surgeon Morrie Shapiro operated on what turned out to be a strangulated hernia (probably brought on by wild dancing at a Rockefeller party in Manhattan.) My circulatory system had shut down; without surgery, gangrene would have followed. It took six weeks of rest, punctuated by frequent sneak trips to the law library, for me to recover.

The enforced distance from the bench was salutary; in fact, it was a godsend to me. Both lawyers submitted huge memoranda that I worked on in my bedroom, analyzing the fine points of each position. After three months, I submitted my final 18-page decision—in favor of Gannett. While recognizing the right and duty of the city to regulate the use of its public streets and sidewalks, I pointed out that that right "must be set against the preferred place given to the freedoms that constitute the life blood of democracy"—including the freedom of speech and press. The ordinance, I wrote, was "guilty of overkill similar to shooting down a fly with a cannon."

My decision, I wrote, was made "to preserve an untrammeled press as a vital source of public information…A free press stands as one of the great interpreters between the government and the people. To shackle it is to shackle ourselves." The vending machines, I pointed out, made newspapers accessible to non-subscribers who had a right to the daily news. The city appealed the decision unsuccessfully. With that corporate headache solved, Tom Curley, then a Gannett executive, said that a statue of me should go up in the lobby of the Gannett Building on Exchange Street. (It didn't.)

* * *

One less than salutary episode during my term involved James Wilmot, an entrepreneur of some renown, who called me in my chambers and asked me if I would like to be a federal judge. Jim had heavy Democratic credentials and was a personal friend of Hubert Humphrey. He said he could make that happen but he wanted the "right decision" on one of the cases before me in which he had an interest. This was a criminal act which I resented. The case had no validity and I decided against Mr. Wilmot. To my surprise he appealed and the Appellate Division unanimously affirmed my decision.

In my two-and-half years serving on the state supreme court, I took on every case I could; I probably did ten years' work during those thirty months. I was beginning to think about what my next step upward might be—probably an appointment to appellate court, the next highest division. That's what I had in mind one morning, when my secretary told me that Governor Rockefeller was on the line.

"Richard," the governor said, "I want you to come down to Pocantico [the Rockefeller estate in Westchester County]. There's something I want to talk over with you." Here it comes, I thought. He's going to raise me up to the appellate court. Instead, Rocky had something else in mind—and that call would open a new chapter in my life, and bring about a sea change in its direction.

Chapter 10

Rocky and Rosie

I got a rude, but enlightening, shock at the 2004 Republican National Convention in Manhattan. Someone among the powers that be had me in tow, and many greetings and introductions were underway. The moment came when, with a hand on my shoulder, my introducer turned me toward a young delegate from a Midwest state, saying, "This is Dick Rosenbaum. You know, he was Nelson Rockefeller's right arm." I watched in amazement, and then with wry amusement, as the young man's face registered both puzzlement and incomprehension. The name of Rockefeller, once the very symbol of American wealth and power, meant little or nothing to this Gen X youngster. *Sic transit gloria,* apparently.

I was probably not much older than that kid when I first met the man who would become my mentor, confidante, and *hero* for so many years. That our lives would come to be linked so closely never occurred to me back in 1958 when I had served as a young sergeant-at-arms at the state Republican convention in Rochester. The atmosphere in the convention hall was electric the day that Rockefeller, until recently a political unknown, announced that he would challenge Averill Harriman, the incumbent Democrat, for the state's highest office. Both Harriman and Rockefeller were blue-blooded multimillionaires from Westchester County, the silk-stocking exurbia north of the Big Apple. "The Battle of the Titans," as that election campaign came to be called, was about to begin.

As a young lawyer, just three years out of law school, I was both fascinated with the action, and impressed with the way Rockefeller was shedding his upper-class mantle and becoming a populist. Already he had perfected his signature greeting, the genial "Hiya' fella!" accompanied by a big smile and a friendly slap on the back. When the convention crowd shouted deliriously, "Who else but Nels?"—a chant repeated whenever he appeared—my voice joined with theirs. (When greeting women, Rockefeller's approach was much gentler. And, if the woman was attractive, his "Hello there!" usually was accompanied by a grin, probably testosterone-triggered.)

A relative stranger to local politics, Rockefeller was as familiar with the corridors of great power—both political and financial, national and international—as any man alive. Born in Bar Harbor, Maine—that summer playground of New York's "400"—he had graduated Phi Beta Kappa from Dartmouth College in 1930. Rockefeller's distinguished college record was doubly remarkable because he was seriously dyslexic. Little then was known about that learning disability, but a series of private tutors helped him read and interpret the printed words that often danced before his eyes. "If not for that [dyslexia]," he used to say, "I might have amounted to something."

As the third son of John D. Rockefeller, one of America's wealthiest men, Rocky was intimately linked to a vast network of political strength and corporate wealth. But among all his brothers, he had a special gift—the personality and charm that would move him out into a public world, one that extended far beyond the family's very private (in fact, semi-secret) sphere of money and influence.

Nelson's special talents were recognized early on. The fact that he was fluent in Spanish was neither unimportant nor overlooked. During World War II, America was troubled by the presence of a strong fascist strain in Latin America, particularly in Argentina, where Nazism was evident. As a counter measure, President Franklin Roosevelt appointed Rockefeller director of the Office of Inter-American Affairs in 1940, and four years later promoted him to assistant secretary of state for Latin American Affairs. As a result, Rockefeller was instrumental in keeping Argentina within the Allies' fold during World War II. A decade later, President Eisenhower tapped him as undersecretary of the U.S.

Department of Health, Education and Welfare, and later appointed him his special assistant for foreign affairs.

Rockefeller understood the intricacies of politics at the highest levels of government, but he was a babe in arms when it came to grassroots politics. He had always been appointed, never elected; he'd never taken part in the rough-and-tumble of a campaign. When the idea first surfaced that here was the man who could go toe-to-toe with Harriman, it was clear that the newcomer would need a mentor, someone who understood the everyday world of local politics. That mentor was Malcolm Wilson, then a member of the New York State Assembly (and, like Harriman and Rockefeller, also a resident of Westchester).

In a curious facsimile of the now-famous "road-trip" films of the forties and fifties, featuring Bob Hope, Dorothy Lamour, and Bing Crosby, Malcolm bundled Rockefeller into his own car (deliberately choosing a very plebeian model, almost a jalopy) and for months they crisscrossed the highways of New York State. In every city and major town, Malcolm introduced Rockefeller to the power players, especially the Republican county chairmen, promoting him as "Rocky," not only a good guy, but an electable candidate who commanded virtually unlimited private resources. By the opening of the gubernatorial nominating convention in Rochester in 1958, everybody knew Rockefeller. While the taint of John D.'s reputation as a "robber baron" lingered (a taint the family's famous philanthropies could never quite erase), his son won the public relations battle—and eventually the election, by a modest 10,000 votes.

Fast forward fourteen years to his call to my chambers in Rochester's Hall of Justice, and his command: "I want you to come down to Pocantico. There's something I want to talk to you about." Rocky was then beginning his fourth term as governor, and I was in the middle of my third year as state supreme court justice. Our paths had crossed many times over the years; the governor had been particularly impressed with my success in winning the city of Rochester and the county of Monroe back to the Republican camp in 1969.

I had worked hard in all four of Rockefeller's gubernatorial campaigns, and he knew I could be effective; at our frequent lunch meetings in Albany, he usually said, "I want you sitting next to me." (Rocky often operated as though he had a royal fealty. If we extend that metaphor, I might at that time have been perceived as his "lady-in-waiting," an image that amuses me greatly.) He had, of course, also appointed me to the state supreme court, where I filled Justice Cass Henry's unexpired term on the bench (after which I was elected to a full fourteen-year term with the support of all four political parties). Now, I thought, as I put down the phone, he's going to elevate me to the appellate court.

* * *

So in early summer of 1972, Art Richardson, then president of Rochester's Security Trust Bank and a Republican stalwart, and I drove east along the New York State Thruway and south through the beautiful Catskill Mountains to the hamlet of Pocantico Hills near Tarrytown. As anxious as I was to know what was on Rockefeller's mind, I couldn't help but be impressed at what lay spread out before me as we began our long drive up to the mansion, having been waved in by the uniformed guard at the gatehouse.

The estate, some 3,000 acres, much of it surrounded by an iron fence, is comprised of the mansion and its support buildings (over a hundred houses), two pools (plus an inside pool), an eighteen-hole golf course, and extensive gardens; at that time, the estate's groundskeepers and maintenance men alone numbered more than a hundred. Several houses on the grounds were at the disposal of visitors and key staff; for example, Rocky's advance man, Joe Canzeri, lived in one of these, but scarcely had time to take advantage of its splendid swimming pool. Others were used as "holding stations" for defeated candidates, retreats where they could regroup after the battle.

Art Richardson and I were welcomed warmly by the governor, ushered into Rocky's study, and offered refreshments after our five-hour drive. Frankly, I was both astonished and upset when the governor explained why he'd summoned me: he needed a new state chairman for the Republican Party and he wanted me to take the job. "Well, Governor," I stalled, "I don't think I can do it. I already have a job on the bench, and you're the one who got me that job in the first place."

My mind was whirling; I knew that accepting the chairmanship would mean a total commitment, signing a 24/7 contract that might well wreak havoc in my young family. My wife, Judy, has always been my strongest supporter, but her affection for the political rough-and-tumble has never been high enough to register on any known scale. She definitely would not like the idea that I was giving up a state supreme court job to get back into the political trenches. We had four young children (ages four, eight, nine and eleven) and a new house; our life was pleasant and manageable. How could I throw all that away? Every time I demurred, Rocky would counter: "You need a new house in Albany? I'll get you a new house," and the sparring would continue.

After lunch that day, the governor called for his town car and, leaving Art behind, we drove into Manhattan, stopping somewhere on the Upper East Side. Standing at the curb waiting for us was Louis Lefkowitz, then the state's attorney general. Louie hopped in the car and we drove around for hours; Rocky and Louie really worked me over, telling me how much the party needed me, and how important it was for the state that I agree to take on the chairmanship. They explained that Chuck Lanigan, the current chairman, wanted out, and an infusion of new energy was badly needed. I had that energy, they kept insisting; Rocky trusted me, I was the only man for the job.

I was not naïve, and I knew Rockefeller. He knew how to use people, and I saw that he wanted to use me; given my wary temperament, that made me very nervous. I also knew that Rockefeller had an unusual talent for making you want to be used—if he didn't ask you to take on some huge, difficult task, if he chose someone else for the job, you almost felt left out, even offended. That was, in fact, one of his strengths as a leader. I left Pocantico that day without giving him an answer.

* * *

Three months later, months of murderous pressure and intense personal struggle, I still hadn't agreed to take the job, even though George

Hinman, a key player on Rockefeller's team and a Republican national committeeman, was continually beating me on the head to do so. George, an otherwise courtly gentleman and a partner in the venerable Binghamton law firm of Hinman, Howard & Kattell, knew upstate New York politics; his father had run for governor in 1902. Apparently he also was convinced that I could do the job.

While I agonized, the weeks passed. Somehow I had to come to a decision, because I knew that Rockefeller hated to be kept waiting. In delaying my decision, I was on risky ground, as I learned some years later when the governor asked my advice for a senatorial appointment. I told him my first choice would be Kenneth Keating, a popular representative from my own district. "Not on your life," Rockefeller, said with umbrage. "I wouldn't appoint Keating if he was the last man on earth. Back in 1958, I had to beg him to run for the U.S. Senate, and he kept me waiting for three days while he made up his mind."

I could understand Keating's hesitation. He already had seniority in the House; what was the point of his becoming a freshman senator, if that meant losing some of his power? Of course, he did eventually accept, was elected, and did a good job in the upper house, after which the carpetbagger Robert Kennedy beat him. As a result of Keating's delay, however, his relationship with Rockefeller soured. I've often been amazed that the governor put up with my three-month delay in accepting the state chairmanship.

Finally, the Rubicon had to be crossed. At a meeting in Albany, I brought up the most important of my reservations: "You know, Governor, you have the reputation of using the chairman as your errand boy. I can't be that. If I take this job, I'd need to be part of every important political decision you make, every key meeting you schedule. I'd need to know the details of every plan you project, every deal you make. I can only take the job on those terms."

Actually, I sensed that I had the governor in a vulnerable position. If I stayed on the court, I would outlast him, since he was nearing the end of his fourth term. However, I never played that card; I respected Rockefeller too much. I also knew that I would love the rough-and-tumble—and the power—that the job promised. I asked the governor that day why he wanted me for the job. His answer was pure Rockefeller: "I like to get people around me who are brilliant, who are hard-working and who know what they're doing, who I can trust, etc., etc." You know it's pure bullshit, but you love hearing it! You leave thinking, "If he says I'm that good, I really must be something!"

By the end of our meeting Rockefeller had agreed to everything I asked for. Now I truly was caught. After that meeting, I drove home, walked into my house, told Judy that I'd accepted the job—and burst into tears. Just the thought of telling my father the news had brought me back to earth in a hurry. I knew that in his opinion, becoming a state supreme court justice should have been the apex of my career. He was proud of my position, and reassured by the prospect that I had "job security." I knew he was haunted by the memory of that period back in the early 1940s when he had no job at all. He wouldn't understand my giving up a secure job for the uncertainties of life in politics. When I told him the news, he merely shook his head and said, "Dick, nothing you ever do again will surprise me."

In the Ring with the GOP Elephant

On November 20, 1972, at a raucous luncheon at the Roosevelt Hotel in Manhattan, the GOP committee unanimously elected me state chairman, to succeed the previous chairman, Chuck Lanigan. When I say raucous, I do mean over-the-top jubilant—there were close to two thousand exuberant delegates, spectators, public and political officials, and newsmen packing the place. As Judy and I walked down the center aisle of the main ballroom, hand in hand, and up to the podium, the band struck up and the place exploded with cheers. Balloons cascaded down from the ceiling and everybody went wild. To tell you the truth, I was so overcome that I think my acceptance speech was the worst speech I ever gave in my life. (I really can't tell—I couldn't hear what I was saying.)

I was almost embarrassed when I heard Governor Rockefeller's praise; he told the group that this new chairman possessed "youth, energy, brilliance, organizing genius, new ideas and one of the most inventive and original minds I've ever encountered." The whole affair—the praise, the band, the cheers, the balloons, the meeting's venue in the heart of glamorous, powerful Manhattan—left me shaken and somewhat overwhelmed, to tell the truth. At that moment, I finally realized the enormity of the job that would be mine for the next few years.

At the end of that luncheon, I learned a lesson in how fractious the metropolitan area's political organizations could be. Judy and I were just about to leave the dining room when a group came over and asked if they could have a photograph taken with me; they identified themselves as the GOP delegation from Queens. The photographer did his work, and I went back to talking with departing guests. A few minutes later, a second group came up and asked if they could join me for a picture. Like a broken record, the leader of this group also said, "We're the delegation from Queens." I learned later that the party had split into two factions. Each group, I realized, would use the photograph for its own purposes, and each would claim to have an inside track with me.

Frankly, I was annoyed with this petty party turmoil, and likened it to "midget wrestling," a phrase picked up and popularized by others. (Suffolk County on Long Island had the same problem: I labeled their constant wrangling "Dodge City," after the rambunctious town familiar to TV Western watchers.)

* * *

A week or so after my election celebration, in December of 1972, the Rosenbaum family packed up and moved to Albany. We had found a pleasant house in the neighboring town of Bethlehem, a name with a heavy connotation. At one of my first speaking engagements, I told the audience that I had made the move in spite of some misgiving. I recalled that another man of my religious persuasion also had come to a town called Bethlehem—"and he got crucified." When the crowd laughed, I added the punch line: "But look at the organization he built!" Around Albany, that line never failed to bring down the house.

We remodeled that house extensively to fit our growing family's needs; the fact that an executive golf course was nearby was appealing (not that I ever had time to use it). The remodeling process was a head-ache, since it was being monitored long distance from Rochester. After a call in the middle of winter from the carpenter, who told us the heat had gone off and the doors were all warped, I wondered if accepting the state chairman's job wasn't the dumbest thing I'd ever done.

In fact, the final results pleased us very much. Our four children were enrolled in public school, but soon complained that they were bored. Whether they missed their friends in Rochester or the schools really were boring I can't say, but Judy and I listened—and then enrolled them in the local Hebrew day school, where they all thrived.

As for me, I immediately moved into the state chairman's office at 315 State Street, and began to make connections with my staff, which at that time numbered about thirty. I spent the first couple of weeks assessing the political landscape within my own office. At the top was Jack Vandevoort, who had run the office for the previous two state chairmen, Charlie Schoeneck (a prominent lawyer from the Syracuse law firm of Bond, Schoeneck & King) and, more recently, Chuck Lanigan, from Rome, New York. Because of a crisis in the Schoeneck family that kept Charlie almost totally distracted, Vandevoort had developed his own operation and was essentially the office's executive director.

Well, I knew that having two bosses within the same organiza-tion wouldn't work (at least not when I was one of them), so after a few months I let Jack go. When the news broke that Vandervoort had been shoved out the door, Arvis Chalmers, a leading political writer at the Albany *Times Union* and a friend—and key news conduit—of Jack's, wrote a scathing piece about me, predicting I'd have the shortest tenure of any state chairman. I called the staff together the day the article appeared, and told them that I'd be around longer than Chalmers, and they could put that promise in the bank. (Listening to my harangue that morning was our telephone operator, who happened to be Vandevoort's mother-in-law. She was very good at her job, a real pro. I liked her, and kept her on the staff.)

Of course, I needed a chief of staff, but that person had to be my guy, somebody I could count on to cover my back. Every chairman needs someone like that, someone smart and intensely loyal—someone you can reason with, who'll perform, and who knows who's boss. I knew the perfect person for the job: Don Mack, a young fellow from my old town of Penfield. Don had always been grateful for the fact that, years earlier, when I was Republican leader of the Town of Penfield in Monroe County, I'd appointed him—a Catholic— to the town's otherwise solidly Protestant GOP committee. He really wanted to come to Albany with me (and wanted it enough to live for more than three years in an attic across from the office). The fact that he was a numbers guy made him even more valuable. (Eventually, he did buy a house.)

My other senior staffers were both skilled and colorful. In retrospect, I realize that office held a really yeasty brew of personalities. Eunice Whittlesey, the party's classy vice chairman from Oneida County, often tangled with office manager Mary Ann Knauss, a bold, gutsy, aggressive woman (who married congressman Hamilton Fish). Eunice and Mary Ann did not have a smooth relationship; to say the least, their personalities clashed, often noisily.

Stirring the pot would be my press secretary, Nick Cammero, a brilliant, seasoned pro who knew where all the bodies were buried. Nick had a terrible temper, and, when annoyed, spewed language worthy of a drill sergeant. (Some of his worst epithets were saved for the mornings when Eunice would usurp his parking place. He'd burst into my office swearing a blue streak and I'd say, "Nick, I really don't like that kind of talk. Calm down." Finally he'd stop—I guess when his tongue got scorched.) Nick was a real asset, though; he could write a great speech and he drafted excellent press releases.

The fifth member of my senior staff was Tom Spargo, our counsel, a very bright lawyer from Schenectady, who is now known as the state's great expert on election law and a former justice of the supreme court in the Albany area. Tom had studied to be a priest, but gave it up.

Perhaps the most reasonable person in that office was my secretary, Ruth Swan. Ruth never raised her voice, she was totally efficient, and she had a quintessential understanding of the role and of her boss. She'd had lots of on-the-job training—she'd been secretary to at least three of my predecessors.

No Room for Democracy

***

Of course, it was the governor who had the strongest personality of all, and very quickly he became the focus, the magnet that held us all in thrall. I have to confess that I was still very impressionable (and, at forty-one, relatively young). Even though I had been a state supreme court justice, somewhere inside I was still that kid from Oswego. As a result, the Rockefeller aura was very seductive. Sometimes I could scarcely believe that Rocky expected me to have lunch with him almost every day in his office on the second floor of the New York State Capitol, where we'd drink Dubonnet (his favorite preprandial) and talk together about the day's events and strategize our plans for the weeks to come.

Many other meetings took place at the governor's mansion, a great rambling brick edifice on Eagle Street, and one of Albany's historic sites. (I used to amuse myself by thinking, "If I ever become governor, I'll change that name to 'Bald Eagle Street' to match my hair style.") The mansion's second floor is so vast that Arthur Levitt, then state comptroller, could live there, despite being a Democrat surrounded by Republicans; so did Louie Lefkowitz when he was in town, and others, as the need arose. That whole second floor of the mansion was known as "Boy's Town." Behind the mansion was "the playhouse," a not-so-little building adjacent to the pool, with a billiard room, kitchen, etc. On hot summer weekends, I'd sometimes take the family there to spend the afternoon; they loved it.

Often I'd take advantage of the fact that the playhouse had a ping-pong table and challenge the governor's counsel, Howard Shapiro, to a game; we were both pretty good players. Joe Bruno, who would later become the state senate majority leader, would challenge me, too, although those contests usually took place in Don Mack's basement. Many nights I'd stay on at the mansion for dinner, an event always preceded by caviar, shrimp, and fancy cheeses. Life in Oswego was never like this!

At the same time, part of me was uncomfortable with what quickly became a daily routine. I didn't like being away from my family at dinner-time, or getting home at ten or eleven almost every night, well after the children were sound asleep in bed. Judy has never forgotten the day she came home and found a note from me on the refrigerator: "Sorry I missed you. I've gone to Oregon with the governor." And Amy, our oldest daughter, once told a friend, "The only way for me to see my Dad is to watch the six o'clock news on TV." That's what the family put up with for four and a half years. Now, more than thirty years later, I still feel bad about it. Of course, my crazy schedule was my own fault: I'd asked to be totally involved with the governor and my request had been granted—in spades.

What made it all worthwhile was the excitement of the game and the electricity generated by the governor. If I had to use only one word to describe Nelson Rockefeller, that word would be "inspirational." I could go into his office on a day when things weren't going well and walk out two feet off the ground, totally energized. He had enormous enthusiasm, and he was a marvelous teacher. I learned a lot about how to handle people—reporters especially—from him. I also liked his strong sense of loyalty to those who worked for him, a quality that inspired us to go the last mile on his behalf.

At the same time, I was fascinated by Rockefeller's penchant for keeping his private opinions to himself. It was a real eye-opener for me to see Rockefeller, the politician, at work, saying things in public that I knew he didn't believe. I'd seen it years before when he castigated New York's Ken Keating to me privately, while praising him in public.

Perhaps the most vivid example of Rocky's unforgiving memory involved Jake Javits, who at the time of this incident was about to become a candidate for another term as the state's senior senator. A big announcement party for Jake was held at the Waldorf, with Rockefeller acting as master of ceremonies. Rocky made a long, flowery speech in support, ending with "...and Jake, we love you." When Jake got up and said, with real *schmaltz*, "The most important thing in life is to be loved," we all thought the B.S. was about to reach the waistline.

The next day, the governor and I were flying on the "Kosher Kamikazi" (the nickname I used for his small Israeli-built plane) to Boston to meet with Massachusetts Republican governor Francis Sargent. Thinking over the previous days' events, and knowing Jake was famous for

No Room for Democracy

playing his own ballgame, I said to Rocky, "What was this business last night about loving Javits?" To my shock, Rocky spit out his response: "That double-crossing S.O.B. I hope I get a chance to get even with him."

★ ★ ★

As close as I was to Rockefeller, I couldn't get him to share my predilection for ethnic humor, although he learned to put up with it. On one occasion, I barely defused a bad gaffe on my part by doing an about face and aiming for the funny bone. Shortly after my appointment, Rocky told our little group of insiders that he wanted to appoint a man named Salvatore Pirro to the state parole board. The announcement was a rude surprise to me. I lost my composure, and burst out: "Governor, you can't do that! You gave me your word that I would control those appointments!"

Rocky looked at me as though I was out of my mind; nobody talked to him that way. "What have you got against Pirro?" he asked, surprise and puzzlement in his voice. I realized the outburst was inappropriate and quickly switched to a joking mode: "Governor, I don't have anything against him, I don't even know him. If his name was Shapiro, I'd be for him," I quipped. Rocky shook his head, and looked at me as if he thought I was crazy. I could just see him saying to himself, "Where did I get this lunatic?"

★ ★ ★

I learned fast that Rockefeller—who was used to being a law unto himself—could act on occasion without considering the consequences. His public withdrawal from the 1968 presidential race was marred by a very bad political faux pas, although, as fate would have it, his mistake would cause him little long-term harm. Rockefeller had courted support from Spiro Agnew, and Agnew, then governor of Maryland, had agreed to support him. When news broke that Rockefeller was about to hold an important press conference, Agnew assumed that Rocky would tell the nation that he was in the presidential race for the long haul. Agnew gathered his friends around him to watch the telecast, boasting that Rockefeller had assured him he was still in the running. Instead, Rocky pulled the rug out from under him. In announcing his withdrawal from the race, he humiliated Agnew in front of his friends and supporters—an unforgivable slur in politics, particularly to a small-minded man like Agnew.

I could count on being inspired by Rockefeller's vision and power. I also realized that to keep him out of trouble I would have to watch him like a hawk.

Would he appreciate it? I very much doubted it.

Of Early Pitfalls and Sticky Wickets

In 1973, the year I took over the state chairmanship, the Republican Party in New York State was in a strong position. We controlled both the state senate and assembly by a fairly decent margin, and Rockefeller's coattails were strong enough so that he had pulled many people up into positions of power with him. I knew his choosing me was a compliment; usually you bring in a new person when things are going poorly. Over the next four and a half years, I would be often stretched to the limit to meet his, and my own, expectations. Governing New York State is not an easy proposition, and the "state of the state" and the "state of the party" often were closely intermeshed.

Within a few weeks I was confronted with problems—many, if not most, related to the office's modus operandi, that infamous "We've always done it this way" syndrome. Here's a good example: In my first month on the job, January 1973, I took a group down to Washington, D.C., for President Nixon's inauguration. We stayed in the capital for three or four days, and when we returned to Albany, I said to Ruth, my secretary, "Let me know when the bills come in. I want to pay them right away."

Weeks passed and no bills. One day a man came into my office and introduced himself; I immediately recognized the name as that of an Albany real estate mogul. Mr. Big Bucks handed me a heavy envelope; inside was $10,000 in cash. "What's this?" I asked, and he answered, "Well, we have a lot of leases with the government, so every year we give ten grand to the state chairman." Staff, he said, would know what to do with the money. Immediately, I called a staffer in who answered with equanimity, "Oh, we have two other people who each give us ten thousand dollars every year. We keep it in a safe deposit box at the bank and use it when we need it for special expenses. That's how we paid the bills for our trip to Washington."

Well, I was just off the bench; I knew how illegal this was (and is), and I was not about to go to jail for taking kickbacks. To the guy with the envelope I said, "Look, this is your lucky day. I'm going to give you back a third of everything that's in that safe deposit box, and I'm going to do the same for the others. Don't ever come into this office again bringing me money and expecting favors. This is a pay-off, plain and simple. If you want to buy tickets to a party function, fine, buy as many as you want. But I didn't come off the bench to go to jail." The other two "contributors" got their money back, too, and that stopped that practice. I'm a guy who likes to sleep nights.

Hard on the heels of that incident another sticky problem surfaced. Months before my arrival on the scene, the governor had made a deal with Joe Frangella, the party's chairman in Albany County. Rocky had appointed Frangella to a newly created post, secretary of the state GOP; with the job came important perks—about $30,000 a year for one. The money would come from overage on insurance premiums paid by the state to cover bridges and state-owned office buildings. Over the years, I'd had a good relationship with Joe, who in his other life ran a big mushroom sales operation. (Soon after I met him, I couldn't resist saying, "Joe, you're a real fun guy, I mean you're a real fungi!")

When I learned about the arrangement, one that had been made before my arrival, I was furious. I saw this as a train wreck about to happen. Patronage was okay, but this deal was tinged with illegality. I cut off the payments to Frangella, who immediately called me in a rage and then wrote a letter to the governor, accusing him of breaking his promise. In turn, Rockefeller dropped me a note, forwarding Frangella's irate letter, and saying he thought we should honor the agreement; I ignored him.

I soon found, however, that I'd inadvertently triggered a landmine. Frangella had a friend, "Buzz" O'Hara, who was head of the New York

State Office of General Services, which made all those contracts for the state's bridges and buildings and then insured them. Together Frangella and O'Hara caused a grand jury to be convened to investigate the situation. They accused me of setting up the payment deal in the first place. Fortunately, I had Frangella's letter to the governor, complaining that I'd cut off the payments, a letter that totally exonerated me. Believe me, I had kept that letter. I wasn't going to take the rap for something that I had nothing to do with and that could, conceivably, even bring down the governor. (Actually, the charge resurfaced in Monroe County after I'd left the state chairmanship, but that charge too became moot.)

Early on in my chairmanship, I tangled with Jake Javits. One of the first things I did in my new office was run an audit of funds going through the office. The analysis included a listing of $10,000 a year funneled to Javits' staff for "special research." I ordered the funding to be cut off. Javits was furious; he considered himself above the fray. I told him he probably owed the office more than $10,000 for the work we did on his behalf. As a result of this, no doubt, our relationship was never especially friendly. (Jake considered himself a statesman, not a politician.)

Unfortunately, Javits took his good opinion of himself too much to heart and, in doing so, lost the support of the party's rank-and-file. Eventually, of course, his cavalier attitude toward party responsibility (such as not showing up to speak at county rallies, not even keeping his speaking commitments to county chairmen) caused him to lose in the 1980 primary to Alfonse D'Amato, which was a big setback for the Republican organization and its reputation—an example of the triumph of ego over common sense.

I learned from these episodes that I would have difficulty extricating myself from deals that had been made before my arrival in Albany, and that I would have to wend my way through a maze of past promises that could cause big trouble for me, the governor, and the party.

The Underside of Politics

"What fools these mortals be," said Shakespeare's Puck. A half-century in politics has proved to me that Shakespeare knew what he was talking about when he added that immortal line to *A Midsummer Night's Dream*.

Money and power, especially political power, are a dangerous combination, as Spiro Agnew discovered to his shame. Thanks to my father's lessons in rectitude, I was always careful to keep as far away from the GOP coffers as I could. I let someone else handle the money, while I did the work.

Year after year, I would see once-promising politicians indicted for mishandling funds. Some were victims of simple greed and deserved their disgrace. Others were honorable men who had stumbled into the sticky web of tainted money, a web often spun by others. As a man who deeply loves his wife and children, I feel truly uncomfortable when I think of the shame these fools brought down on their families.

The granddaddy of all the downfalls I witnessed was unforgettable. The story begins with a phone call that came to me one day in Albany from the head of the "Italian Desk" at Republican national headquarters. A friend of the caller needed help badly, he said. Would I meet with them in New York City and see if I could help? We agreed to meet at the Hotel Pierre in Manhattan. On my arrival, I was ushered into a small suite and introduced to a handsome man, very well turned out, tweed jacket, salt-and-pepper hair, who was sitting at the end of the room. "This is Michele Sindona," my friend said. "What can I do for you, Mr. Sindona?" I asked. Sindona came right to the point: "I will give you one million dollars if you will speak on my behalf to the federal judge in Brooklyn who has ordered my deportation. I want that order reversed."

At this point in the conversation, if I'd had hair, it would have been standing up. I said, "Mr. Sindona, I can't do this." I couldn't resist asking why he was so upset at being deported. "If I go back to Italy, I will be killed," he said, simply. Classy fellow that he was, Sindona didn't try to convince me. When I told him there was no way I could help him, he offered to pay my expenses for coming to New York, an offer I wasn't about to accept. About six months later, I read in *Time* magazine that Sindona, who had been deported, was found poisoned in his cell in an Italian jail. Three days after he had been imprisoned, he was dead.

I stumbled on Sindona's secret years later, in 1992, when I was campaigning for the GOP nomination for governor. Among my strongest supporters was a group of prominent Italian businessmen who were members of the Knights of Malta, the right arm of the Vatican worldwide. The leader of the group in New York was Michael Morelli, a high-ranking officer at Chase Bank in Westchester. One day I asked Morelli if he ever had heard of Michele Sindona. Not only had he heard of him, he said, but they had lunched together at the Pierre Hotel once a week before Sindona's deportation. Morelli's father, who worked in the top echelons of Interpol, had told him that Sindona had embezzled $500 million from the Franklin Bank, where the Vatican had deep relationships, causing the bank's collapse. Sindona had been murdered, according to Morelli, on direct orders from a very high-ranking Italian government official because he had inside information about Vatican finances and might spill the beans.

No single political party has a monopoly on temptation to corruption. While I was state chairman, Joe Margiotta, the GOP leader in Nassau County, went to jail for taking a kickback on insurance premiums (that old bugaboo); of course, that little episode finished Margiotta's political career.

Another memorable encounter with the spreading waves of pain that result from foolish, misguided behavior occurred in Rochester, back in the sixties. Frank Vicaretti was a small-town local politician who was a friend of Rochester's legendary sheriff Al Skinner. Unfortunately, Frank got involved in some dishonest activity and I had to recommend firing him as superintendent of the highway department in a neighboring town. But it was Frank's son, Frank Junior, who was the really bad actor. He liked to disguise himself as a cop and drive around late at night, following women drivers. He would pull them over on some phony charge and then say he'd let them go—if they'd have sex with him; some of the women who refused were attacked and seriously injured. As a result, Frank Jr. was sent to a maximum security prison downstate for a long time. Every week, for years, Frank Sr. would drive down to the prison to visit his son. Suddenly, when he was in his sixties, the older man died of a heart attack.

I happened to be in Rochester the day of Frank's funeral, and I was asked by the Monroe County GOP chairman to attend; the Italian community would be out in full force and having me there as state chairman would be good for the party. As soon as I walked into the funeral home, Frank's widow and the children became hysterical, crying and yelling out, "The State came to see Daddy! The State came to see Daddy!" I sat quietly in the back for a full hour, waiting for the service to start. Finally, just as I was about to leave, the door to the viewing room flew open and in came Frank Jr., handcuffed and with irons on his ankles, surrounded by state police. I watched in amazement as he threw himself on his father's body, yelling "Daddy, I'm so sorry! Daddy, I'm so sorry!" His mother was crying, "It's OK, Franky!," while his sisters were shouting, "You killed our Daddy! You killed our Daddy!" Pandemonium reigned in that funeral home. It was an awful, awful scene, one I'll never forget.

Incidentally, the day after I fired Frank Sr. from his highway post, I got a call on my answering machine; a man with a very gruff voice told me to call a certain number for an appointment. Curious, I dialed the number. The voice on the answering machine at the other end of the line said, "Parsky Funeral Home." (Parsky's is Rochester's traditional Jewish undertaker.) Fortunately, I haven't yet had to make that appointment.

In my personal hall of ill-fame, Sidney Zipkin, a Rochester bus driver, has a special place. Just before Rochester's mayoral election in 1969 (when we were working our tails off trying to wrest the city from its long Democratic control), Sidney came to the local GOP headquarters and asked if he could drive a sound truck during the last days of the campaign. He had the job for only a day; we discovered that a local ordinance prohibited the use of sound trucks, so we pulled the truck. After the campaign was over, Sidney came back again and applied for a job with the county. Upon checking his records, I learned that he had a police record; he was a "paperhanger," i.e., a forger. "Sidney," I told him, "I can't possibly hire you. Sorry."

Seven or eight years later, after I had served as state supreme court justice and state GOP chairman, Sidney suddenly phoned me at my office in downtown Rochester; he had read in the local newspapers about my return from Albany. Sidney, a man in his forties, said he wanted $500 for the work he had done for the campaign; "My mother says I should have it," he told me. When I refused to give him the money, he said he was going to come out to my house and kill my wife and children. That got my attention. Thinking fast, I jollied him along. "Come to my office at three this afternoon and we'll talk about it," I said. Of course, I had the police waiting when he arrived. Sidney was hauled into city court and with my acquiescence, the judge agreed to let him go if he promised to leave the state; that seemed fine with Sidney, who wanted to go to Las Vegas anyway, he said.

Six months later, Sidney was back in Rochester, and the threats started again. This time he received a two-year prison sentence. When I got his phone call, I had asked, "Why did you wait eight years before asking for this money?" He said, "I had to wait. I was in prison all that time for forgery."

***

Over the years I have learned that the most dangerous political cocktail is a combination of arrogance and greed. The longer a person is in a position of power, the greater grows the arrogance and a sense that he, or she, is above the law. Power *can* corrupt, as Machiavelli pointed out. And when greed enters the picture, a whole family can be ruined. Thus the triumph of ego over common sense.

Puck—and Shakespeare—had it right. What fools we mortals can be.

Chapter 11

Enter "The Iron Chancellor"

Problems within the party, while troublesome and time-consuming, couldn't keep my focus from my main challenge as state chairman—ensuring that the governor's programs were enacted. I had learned that it takes a tough hand to keep a party united, and to make sure everyone on the team is working toward the same goal. Politics is no place for the faint-hearted, and anybody who tried to buck me usually ended up on the wrong side of the ring, clinging to the ropes. When I gave an order, I expected to have that order carried out, and pronto.

One day, at a meeting of the party's state committee, I was barking directions and handing out orders as usual. John Campbell, then a member of the Republican state committee from Long Island and a guy with a very dry sense of humor, turned to George Hinman, one of "Rocky's regulars," and said, "Dick reminds me of Otto von Bismarck, the Iron Chancellor." Well, the name stuck, and before long the political reporters had picked up on it. From that day to this, Campbell calls me "Otto." (I reciprocated, of course. John is one of those Brahmin lawyers who speak with the polished tones of a Bill Buckley. When I learned that he grew up in rural Oneida County I dubbed him "Mud Creek Campbell," a name that stuck, if you'll pardon the pun.)

My "Iron Chancellor" moniker picked up further currency when Hinman was nominated once again to represent New York State on the Republican National Committee. In his acceptance speech, George told the cheering delegation that there was only one reason he was being re-nominated. "Whatever Dick says, I say 'Yes,'" he told them, and again referred to me as "The Iron Chancellor."

The moniker pleased me, I admit. While I'm all for democratic government, there's no room for democracy within a political party. Discipline is the necessary ingredient to getting things accomplished, as any successful leader knows. There's a fine line between respect and fear. Call me Machiavellian, but I believe that a good strong leader needs to inspire both.

"The Cattle Drive"

Immediately after I took office, the spring "cattle drive" began in Albany. This happens annually just before the close of the state's legislative year. As the annual budget deadline approaches, assemblymen and senators (and lobbyists galore) show their muscle, fighting to ensure that legislation important to their constituents and clients is passed. As party chairman, one of my jobs was to ensure that those bills that promoted the governor's agenda had strong support. No legislation comes up for a vote unless it's called up by the leaders; conversely, if a bill is "starred" by one of the leaders (held for further review), it probably ain't goin' anywhere. The next job—the crucial one— is to ensure that the legislation we favor gets passed. A failed bill can be a hard political blow.

In the seventies, cattle drives lasted about two weeks, including weekends. (Today, the battle is waged for months, until either the legislators are exhausted or the public is so fed up that lawmakers are forced to reach an agreement.) As Rocky's major domo, I was obliged to be there by his side every day of the drive, advising him on the political ramifications of the legislation being proposed. Working closely with us (sometimes at cross purposes) were Perry Duryea, then Speaker of the state assembly, and Warren Anderson, majority leader of the senate, and their counsels. We'd meet every Tuesday morning for breakfast at Albany's Fort Orange Club. (Anderson always called Duryea "the Frontiersman" because of the huge breakfast he ordered, usually steak and eggs. A big man—the size of a lumberjack—and with snowy white hair, Duryea was right out of central casting.) Our job: to lobby legislators to vote for those bills that promoted the governor's agenda.

I rarely left the capitol building during those two weeks. Like staffers and aides, I slept on a couch or on the floor of the executive office. Rocky's staff arranged for food and beverages to be delivered throughout the day. If I left to go home for a shower and to pick up clean clothes, it was at my peril; trying to reconnect with my family for an hour or so, my ear was always tuned to the inevitable phone call summoning me back to the fray.

Rocky understood that Judy and the kids weren't seeing much of me. One afternoon he phoned Judy to apologize for once again expecting me to work late. He began by saying, "Hello, Mrs. Rosenbaum, this is Nelson." Certain that the caller was a practical-joking friend, Judy said "Nelson *who?*" Nelson Rockefeller was the response. Judy said, "You're not fooling me, Bill," referring to the former Monroe County Chairman, Bill Dwyer, who had a reputation as a compulsive practical joker. The governor said, "I *am* the governor," and it was he!

Most governors, I believe, worked the cattle drives from the sidelines, relying on cowboys like me to get the work done. Not Rocky! He was in the middle of the action, grabbing the bull by the horns, personally calling at the office of any legislator thought to be wavering in his support of a bill the governor favored, phoning another to thank him for his vote. That was Rocky's M.O.—and it meshed perfectly with my own: Jump right in the ring and make things happen! (When Malcolm Wilson succeeded Rockefeller as governor, the atmosphere surrounding the cattle drives became much more relaxed. I'd be in my office at nightfall, getting ready to spend the next few hours on the phone lobbying, and Malcolm would knock on the door and say, "Dick, you've done enough for the day. Go home, see your family.")

As a young lawyer, I'd had an offer that would have enabled me to watch the cattle drive from a front row seat. Assemblyman Eugene Goddard, a courtly and reserved gentleman from my upstate district, asked me to become his counsel and legislative assistant. It had taken all my resolve to stay with my new law practice and resist that siren call. Now, a couple of decades later, I was running the rodeo.

In retrospect, it seems to me that legislators in those days—that is, the mid-years of the last century—were (with obvious exceptions) more statesmanlike than many who hold office today. I regret the metamorphosis that has occurred over the last forty years, as politics has become a business rather than an honorable calling. Some legislative seats now seem to have become sinecures, occupied for years by the incumbents to enhance their outside interests.

Our Founding Fathers envisioned a different model—a government in which a citizen was elected to serve his community, his colony, his state, or his country for a few years, and then, having made his contribution to his fellow citizens, he retired to his real work—his family, his farm, his office. As years passed, legislative salaries continued to be relatively low, so election to the senate or assembly was seen as a temporary commitment, a public service, rather than a job to be fought for, term after term. Until relatively recently, most legislators were lawyers who considered the practice of law as their primary source of income. (I think every young lawyer has an attack of politics, the way every young child has an attack of the measles.)

Now, many legislators see this office as their gravy boat; to that end, they pack end-of-the-year legislation with bills that will help get them re-elected. As a result, that original ideal concept—of legislators who offer their time, their energy, and their talent for the good of the state (rather than their bank account)—has become tarnished. At its most corrosive—that is, when a legislator's prime motivation is holding on to his job—that erosion of the ideal spawns the canker of corruption that infects many of our institutions.

The "Narco Judges"

Two trends were developing in America during the early seventies. The first was a burgeoning drug culture, born a decade earlier in the wild-and-wooly Age of Aquarius, a culture seen by many as the dangerous spawn of hippies and love-ins, of Woodstock and Timothy Leary. The second was a growing fear of that drug culture—an alarm strengthened by graphic reports of the ruined lives of thousands of young people who were seen as its victims. During the seventies, these trends were moving inexorably on a collision course. As America's children continued in their mad dash to throw off the cultural restraints of two hundred years, many of their parents reacted by growing more conservative.

The pain associated with drug abuse among the young had scorched a branch of Nelson Rockefeller's own extended family. As the seventies progressed, the cry of "Can't you do something about this, Governor?" came to him ever more frequently, ever more intensely, and from all the varied parts of his constituency.

At the same time, more and more New Yorkers seemed to be growing dissatisfied with what they perceived as "Rockefeller's liberalism" and his "free spending." The very improvements that had made the state a national model under the governor's aegis—its billion-dollar state university system, the wave of new building that rapidly was turning staid Albany into one of the country's most architecturally dramatic capital cities, one whose zenith had not yet been reached—these were becoming liabilities as the state's tax burden mounted. As the first weeks of his fourth term ticked by, the Rockefeller magic had definitely lost much of its luster—and no one knew it better than he (except, perhaps, his hand-picked major domo—me).

Rockefeller had to stop the erosion of his political base—and for a very good reason. From the beginning of his political career, his eye had been on the presidency. (As he once said, "What else is there? I've had everything else.") His divorce and remarriage in 1963 had hurt him nationally. He could not let his own New York State slip away from him, not at this crucial moment, as the end of his fourth term loomed. He believed strongly in all the causes he had espoused; his social agenda grew directly out of the family's need to amend its "robber baron" image by using its wealth and influence to help the country—and especially its home state of New York—achieve their fullest potential. He would never abandon those goals.

At the same time, the changing political climate required that he take a tough, conservative stand somewhere—but that stand would have to be on behalf of some issue he really believed in. He found the issue he needed in the war against drugs. Early in 1973, the governor announced that he was establishing some seventy new state supreme court justices (so-called "narco judges") to handle the growing number of cases resulting from the arrests of drug pushers and users.

It became my job to convince the legislators to support the program. I moved into an office on the third floor of the capitol, where the legislature convened, and began to call in the lawmakers one by one to make our pitch. (Duryea, by the way, objected strongly to my lobbying effort and complained to me. I reported to the governor, who in turn, said to me, "Tell him to go f— himself." His response surprised me, because Rocky rarely used that kind of language.) One legislator tried to bargain with me, saying he wouldn't vote for the legislation unless he was promised one of the new judgeships. "If you don't vote for the bill, there won't be any judgeships to award," I reminded him. He caved, and Rocky loved it.

Now, at the beginning of the 21st century, the Rockefeller drug laws are seen by many as draconian: life sentences for many pushers, long jail sentences for those holding even relatively small amounts of narcotics. With the state's prisons already overcrowded, the drug statutes are under review, and some already have been softened. But back in the seventies, not only was the "narco judge" bill popular with the people, it once again proved that Rocky was the ultimate pragmatist: He was creating a $55 million job package, patronage of the first order. Each justice (eventually the number was reduced to sixty) would be paid $41,000 a year; each would need a secretary, a law clerk, and staff; probation officers, correction officers, court officers, stenos and aides must be hired.

Edward Hall, writing in the *New York Daily News*, translated for his readers what the proposed $55 million meant: "The creation of job goodies, enough to bring joy to any county leader—particularly in New York City—willing to go along with Rocky's idea of a fusion mayor takeover from the then mayor, John Lindsay. In 1974, this kind of miracle could also make a man governor—again."

Let's look more closely at what Hall meant when he referred to Rockefeller's suggestion that what New York City needed was "a fusion mayor."

New York City: A State within the State

To paraphrase lyricist Lorenz Hart, "I love Manhattan, the Bronx, and Staten Island, too." But the Big Apple always has been a big problem for Republicans. Unruly, chaotic, ethnic, and above all Democratic, New York City is in some sense a state unto itself, and (until Rudy Giuliani changed the picture in the 1990s) Gracie Mansion has seldom been home to a Republican mayor.

The city—with its five teeming boroughs—also is an ace that can trump the outcome of a gubernatorial campaign. In order to become governor of New York State, a Republican candidate once had to come out of New York City losing by no more than 500,000 votes; if the candidate lost by 600,000, forget it. Even a strong upstate vote couldn't overcome the New York City margin.

The Big Apple always commands an enormous amount of patronage. That golden egg—and especially the power that it signifies—tempted Governor Rockefeller. Buffalo was the other traditional Democratic stronghold, but New York City—well, that was a potential political Fort Knox. In Rocky's words, "We may not be able to control all the patronage in the city, but something is better than nothing."

In 1972, Rockefeller decided to wrest control of the mayor's office from John Lindsay. The Rockefeller-Lindsay fight is an interesting one. The two men might well have been allies: both were bluebloods, both were wealthy, both were liberal in their politics. And both were smart, personable, outgoing, good-looking men; a war hero, Lindsay had been tagged "the Republican John Kennedy" (although he had been elected the mayor of New York City as an Independent).

I really don't know why Rocky came to dislike John Lindsay so intensely, but to mention his name to the governor was to energize a buzz saw. Maybe this was an alpha male doing what alpha males do. Or it may be that Rocky, a loyal Republican, distrusted Lindsay because he had switched parties. He used to say to me, "I wish Lindsay would become an actor and leave governance to me."

To say that feelings ran high among those supporting Rocky and those backing Lindsay is an understatement, as I learned to my astonishment in the Bronx one evening. I'd been sent by Rockefeller to speak at the Bronx County GOP annual dinner, using remarks prepared by Hugh Morrow, then the governor's speechwriter. One of the themes of the speech, of course, was that Rocky was "the man," not Lindsay. Well, all hell broke loose when I began talking about Lindsay. Everybody started shouting, either in support or in protest, and we had a near riot on our hands. Fistfights broke out and chairs were thrown; certainly no one heard another word of my speech. Neither Johnny Calandra, the Bronx GOP chair, nor Malcolm Wilson, the lieutenant governor, who was present, nor I could do a thing about the chaos. We just had to let it steam itself out, which it did eventually. I recall at one point when the din became particularly loud, Wilson, always the soul of propriety, turning to Calandra and asking if he couldn't do something to bring order. Calandra's rejoinder was right in character, "I can't shoot them in public."

It was a series of disastrous strikes in New York City, culminating in the New York City trash collectors' strike in the sixties that did irreparable damage to the already troubled relationship between Lindsay and Rocky. For weeks, garbage piles moldered in the streets and on the sidewalks, the smell was awful, raising a storm of protest from residents and giving the Big Apple a black eye that could be seen across the country. The strikes cost the city billions of dollars; in each situation, Lindsay eventually was forced to negotiate a settlement with the union involved. Rockefeller saw this as a capitulation and anticipated troubles to come with unions throughout the state.

When Lindsay announced in 1973 that he would not run for re-election, it seemed as though Rocky's prayer had been answered. At the same time, based on past history and New York City's record as a Democratic stronghold, it looked as though no Republican could win the mayoralty there. Undeterred, Rockefeller worked out another strategy: he'd outflank the Democrats by putting all his resources behind a fusion ticket consisting of both Republicans and Democrats.

Republicans, he hoped, would support a new Democratic mayoral candidate, someone with a liberal platform similar to Rockefeller's. After a successful election, the new mayor would appoint Republicans

No Room for Democracy

to key city posts, thus giving Rockefeller the consummate politician, a share of the city's governance.

Rocky's candidate was Bob Wagner, the city's three-term former mayor, who had been out of the office for a decade. Selling Wagner, a liberal Democrat, as our candidate, to the city's GOP county leaders—especially the conservative George Clark in Brooklyn—was going to be tough, what I call "heavy political lifting." I got the job—and it was a doozey. *No Room for Democracy* on display.

For three months, I moved to New York City and took over a suite in the Roosevelt Hotel, where in the forties, governor and GOP presidential candidate, Tom Dewey, held forth. That three months was an education in big-city politics—call it what you will: a zoo, a war zone, a dysfunctional crazy family—like none I'd ever seen. It drove me nuts—and at the same time I was totally fascinated. Here was the world of Damon Runyon writ large, and real. Each of the boroughs had both a Republican and a Democratic leader, of course, *capos* who ruled their own "families." Each district had at least one clubhouse, a neighborhood center managed by the party that served as a true social center. Men would gather at the clubhouse throughout the week to drink, play cards, and talk politics; women would fill the club with anniversary parties, weddings, wedding receptions, and wakes.

Party loyalty (Republican, Democrat, or Liberal) was a way of life for many New Yorkers in those years. A friend who grew up in Brooklyn fifty years ago, the son of a doctor, recalls being taken to his neighborhood Democratic club on several occasions. He says they never left the premises without being asked, "Do you have something for the little black box, Doc?"—and his father would slip a few bills into the appointed receptacle.

Because of the city's predominantly Democratic make-up, our GOP leaders then were relatively powerless. But just thinking about the ones I worked with then makes me chuckle. There was the unforgettable Vince Albano, the leader in New York County (Manhattan), a short, fat rogue of monstrous proportions. A buddy of Cuba's notorious dictator, Fulgencio Battista, Albano was famous for taking friends on no-holds-barred trips to Cuba (expeditions that, fortunately, never included me). Whenever I was scheduled to speak in the city, he would call and remind me to be sure to include a reference to "Vince Albano's New York County." Every one of his telephone calls to me ended the same way: His guttural, whiskey voice would intone over and over again, "I love ya,' sweetheart. You're the greatest chairman we've ever had. I love ya,' sweetheart, I love ya,' I love ya'..." His voice would slowly fade away, as the connection would click off and the line go dead.

In the Bronx, the rooster was dapper, irreverent Johnny Calandra, with his beautiful little wife; in Richmond County (Staten Island), Phil Fitzpatrick, a charming Irishman with some character flaws, controlled the county. In Queens, the GOP boss was Sid Hynes. Knowing the governor's connection with South America, Hynes constantly used the one Spanish word he knew when they talked together: "Sure, I'll do it, Governor!—with gusto!"

Finally, there was George Clark, the GOP leader in King's County, home to Brooklyn—"the fourth largest city in America." Clark was a different kettle of fish. Shortly, he would become my personal nemesis and, curiously, my close friend, as well. A conservative among conservatives, Clark steadfastly refused to support the deal I was selling successfully to the other borough leaders—that we back a fusion ticket in New York City's next mayoral election. He hated the liberal Bob Wagner.

Unfortunately, Bob Wagner was hesitant about running again, so we couldn't get the kind of good solid statements from him that we needed to make a strong case in the media. In a way, I understood his position: He needed assurance that the party would back him one hundred percent. With Clark, the conservative, against him, that would never happen. Finally, after months of negotiating, I got Clark to agree to abstain from voting. I thought I had the game won.

Then, twenty-four hours before our fusion ticket was to be announced, John Marchi, the conservative Republican senator from Staten Island, who would reinvent the wheel every time he spoke, came out of the wings (probably urged on by Clark) and announced that he was entering the race. Very quickly, the support for Wagner that I had

No Room for Democracy

won from borough leaders over the last three months—won with my blood, sweat and tears—all evaporated. Marchi became the official candidate—and lost the election big time to Abe Beame, garnering only four per cent of the vote.

Losing the fight for a fusion ticket was a real blow to me. Rockefeller was in Holland at the time. When he heard the bad news, he was furious. The best I could do in the face of this disaster was to coin a quip, one that quickly made its way into the Rosenbaum lore: "Rockefeller went to Holland—and I got in Dutch."

Lindsay was out of the picture at last, but the defeat of our fusion ticket effort was a big disappointment—for me, for Rockefeller, and, in my opinion, for the party. But the problems of governance within New York State and uncertainty about Rockefeller's political future amounted to small change compared with the *tsunami* that struck the country a few months later: Watergate.

Chapter 12

Watergate and Beyond

It seemed, at first, a relatively innocuous incident. After all, dozens of minor break-ins and burglaries occurred on the troubled streets of Washington, D.C., that third week of June 1972. Some will be overlooked, their reports lost in the morass of paperwork that swamps police files, especially if nothing more than a TV or stereo has been taken, to be exchanged in the neighborhood later that night for a little bag of white powder.

But the break-in at the Watergate Hotel and office complex in the area of the district called "Foggy Bottom" is different. At 2:30 a.m., five men are arrested trying to bug the offices of the Democratic National Committee; one of the men admits he is a former CIA agent. The *Washington Post* is on top of the story as fast as a headline can be written. The assumption in the newspaper's editorial room the next morning is, "Here we go again." Only ten months earlier, the "Plumbers Unit"—a group of insiders ordered to plug leaks in President Nixon's administration—had been caught burglarizing the offices of a psychiatrist. One of the doctor's patients was Daniel Ellsburg, the former defense analyst who had leaked to the *New York Times* the Defense Department's secret history of the Vietnam War, a report that came to be known as "the Pentagon Papers."

In October, four months after the Watergate break-in, the *Post* reports that FBI agents have established that the break-in stemmed from a massive campaign of political spying and sabotage conducted on behalf of Nixon's re-election effort.

Anger and disgust seem to sweep the nation. Yet a month later, Nixon is re-elected in one of the largest landslides in American political history, winning sixty percent of the vote and crushing the Democratic nominee Sen. George McGovern., a doctrinaire liberal. Serving beside Nixon as vice president is a former governor of Maryland, the relatively unknown but already controversial Spiro Agnew.

* * *

Six months after Richard Nixon's re-election, the Watergate scandals were accelerating, every day seeming to bring more damaging disclosures. The president was in trouble. Across the nation, politically attuned Americans avidly watched the nationally televised hearings of the Senate committee appointed to investigate what came to be called simply "Watergate." One after another, Nixon loyalists were discredited: G. Gordon Liddy, John Erlichman, H. R. Haldeman, John Dean, Howard Hunt, and others. On October 23, 1973, a desperate Nixon fired Archibald Cox, the Justice Department's special prosecutor for the Watergate hearings, triggering angry resignations, an event that immediately became known as "the Saturday Night Massacre." The call for impeachment within the Congress was growing. In a defensive maneuver, Nixon supporters countered by promoting the rallying cry, "Do you want Spiro Agnew to be president?"

I had known Spiro Agnew for many years, and my opinion of him was low. (It about matched that held by Washington's elderly social doyenne, Alice Roosevelt Longworth, who once said to Nixon, "Dick, promise me that whenever you fly, you'll take Agnew with you.") When I was GOP chairman in Monroe County, I'd invited Agnew to address our convention. The speech went well, and the next day I arranged to have a driver pick up Agnew, his wife, and me for the drive back to the airport. As soon as they got in the car, Agnew began yelling at his wife for forgetting some pills he'd left on the back of the toilet at the hotel. His wife never said anything; she just seemed to droop under his verbal assault. I thought this was pretty strange behavior and very embarrassing, especially with me sitting next to them in the back seat of the car. That little incident gave me an insight into the type of person he was—and I didn't like it. I went public with my views in January 1973, when a headline in the *New York Times* read "Rosenbaum Views Rockefeller as Better than Agnew for '76." The article was based on a conversation I had with reporters over coffee at the National Press Club in Washington.

I had stronger reasons for disliking Agnew than my disgust with the way he'd treated his wife that day in Rochester. For years, it had been well known that he had been taking kickbacks from contractors, a practice he made good use of during his years as governor of Maryland. A common jest among politicos then was that "the governorship of Maryland paid $25,000—plus tips." (In fact, "slush funds" made up of not-so-secret political contributions were common in both parties. Back in the fifties, Illinois governor Adlai Stevenson, then running for president, kept a slush fund of $60,000 made up of "donations" from contractors.)

Agnew's problem was that he kept up the practice when he was in the White House.

The accusation that pay-offs were being made to the vice president, a charge based on firm evidence, was made public in the middle of the Watergate furor by attorney general Elliot Richardson. The likelihood that Nixon's administration might be facing two impeachment proceedings—one against the president, the other against the vice president—was a potential disaster that had to be met head on. In October 1973, Spiro Agnew resigned rather than face criminal charges and possible impeachment.

Immediately after Agnew's resignation, I got a phone call from George H. W. Bush, then the national GOP chairman. At the time I was a senior member of the GOP national committee. George wanted me to submit the names of three men I could back to fill the now-vacant office of vice president—and to do it pronto, within twenty-four hours. I told him I would submit only one name, that of governor Nelson A. Rockefeller, the man I believed most qualified for the job. Chief contenders for the suddenly vacated post were George Bush himself, Rockefeller, and Gerald Ford who was then House minority leader. Dark horse candidates were representative Melvin Laird of Wisconsin (who later served as secretary of defense); Elliot Richardson of Massachusetts (later attorney general); and Don Rumsfeld of Illinois, then ambassador to the North Atlantic Treaty Organization.

Rocky Bows Out

The final months of 1973 were fraught with consequence. Shrill reports on the Watergate scandal filled the nation's newspapers and airwaves and I began canvassing the state, trying to rally our disheartened Republican ranks. In Albany, we walked on eggshells, uncertain as to the governor's next move. I felt particularly vulnerable, because I was Rocky's guy. Bobby Douglass, Rocky's arrogant former secretary, once had said, "You know, if Rocky goes, you're dead." Those words now carried a very real threat.

The fact that Rockefeller, after fourteen years as governor, was looking for new challenges was not a surprise. He sensed that New York State's economy was faltering, that his popularity was on the wane; a defeat at the polls would cast a pall over his future on the national scene. At a luncheon at the mansion in December 1973, he told a few of us privately that he had decided to resign. Gathered around the table that day were the governor, Malcolm Wilson, Perry Duryea, and myself. Conspicuously absent was Lou Lefkowitz. Rocky's bombshell was to be kept under wraps for a short time, and the luncheon meeting had been scheduled at a time when Lou, known to be an incorrigible news leaker, was out of town. (My principal concern was that the governor himself would leak the news, as he often had done before. I sometimes complained that we had "the only ship of state that leaks from the top.")

One question loomed: Who would take over the reigns of state governance? Lieutenant governor Malcolm Wilson, of course, would finish out the remaining year of Rockefeller's term in office, after which there would be a general election. Both Wilson and state assembly Speaker Perry Duryea wanted the party's nomination. The question was raised that afternoon when Rocky told us of his decision: Who did he favor? Malcolm or Perry? "Well," he said, "let's wait for a while

No Room for Democracy

before we decide that." I practically bounced out of my chair at those words: "No, it's going to be Malcolm!" I said emphatically—and Rocky quickly changed the subject. Later that day, a pleased but embarrassed Malcolm telephoned me: "I told my wife what you said at that meeting," he said. "Where do you get such *chutzpah*?" As a matter of fact, I don't know. The words just popped out of my mouth. I knew both men would be good candidates, but I felt Malcolm had more experience and had earned his chance; he would have even more experience after governing for several months. I also knew that he had Rocky's confidence and I believed that would be useful to the state in the long run.

I also knew that, when Malcolm Wilson succeeded Rockefeller as governor, he had the right to choose his own GOP state chairman, so I went to him and said, "Look, I don't want you to think you're stuck with me. If you have someone else in mind for the state chairmanship, just tell me. I'll be very happy to relinquish the post." He urged me in the most vigorous terms to continue to run the party, so I did. As it turned out, Wilson was in office only through the remainder of Rockefeller's unfinished term. Malcolm was a gentleman, but he was a poor campaigner; he tried to develop his own election campaign, but he got hopelessly bogged down in details. (A recurring vision in my mind is that of Malcolm sitting in his office thumbing through papers in his briefcase.) That, combined with the shadow that Watergate cast over the Republican Party, finished him. He was soundly defeated in the next election by Democrat Hugh Carey, losing—in spite of my best efforts on his behalf—by some 800,000 votes. New York's voters, it seemed, had had enough of both Rockefeller and the Republicans.

***

Immediately after Wilson's loss, I moved to assert my leadership within the party. An article in the *New York Times* in November 1974 captured the essence of my rather pugnacious stance: "While most Republicans had taken to cover [after the election defeat], Mr. Rosenbaum in his customary booming voice called a morning-after news conference to declare his leadership of the party. 'I'm the party chairman and the party leader—I make the decisions,' he declared." Pledges of support for my leadership came in from Rocky and Wilson, as well as from Buckley, Javitz, Lefkowitz, senate majority leader Warren Anderson and assembly Speaker Perry Duryea. Asked if I had requested a vote of confidence from party leaders, I said, "When the time comes that you have to ask for a vote of confidence, when your position is that weak, that's the time you ought to think about doing something else."

As a matter of fact, I *was* thinking about something else: a run for the governorship. Apparently that was becoming obvious to others, although I had never voiced my thoughts publicly. After Wilson's resounding defeat, the Gannett News Service obviously caught the drift: "In asserting his independence, Rosenbaum is not only counting on a role for the state chairman as a political power in his own right, but is also serving notice of political ambitions of his own."

As for Rockefeller, he now faced a major problem. He was relinquishing his role as governor of one of the nation's most important states; how could he remain a force on the national level? His solution: the formation of the bipartisan Commission on Critical Choices for America, and a radical shift in his own position, a rapprochement with the conservative wing of the Republican Party. The new think-tank, organized and chaired by Rockefeller, was created to explore possible responses to the military challenges facing the nation in a post-nuclear world. The commission also would become a useful publicity-generator for the now ex-governor. The group met monthly at Rockefeller's two-story penthouse apartment at 812 Fifth Avenue overlooking Central Park. Key among the commissions' members were Henry Kissinger and Gerald Ford, then GOP leader of the House of Representatives. The latter would come to play a crucial role in Rockefeller's future.

The Watergate Tidal Wave Rolls On

By springtime, rumors about the choice of a new vice president to replace the disgraced Agnew had reached a fever pitch. Various rumors implied that Rockefeller wouldn't accept the vice presidency if it was offered, or, if it was offered, that "it would take forever to confirm him" because of resistance from conservatives. (I attributed both of these rumors to the Bush camp.) Sometime during these weeks, Anne Armstrong, a GOP national committee member from Texas, called me and said that George Bush, the national party chair, was playing both liberal and conservative sides to get the vice presidency. My own phone calls suggested that many in the South—including GOP chairmen Clarke Reed of Mississippi and Clarence Warner of Oklahoma—opposed Bush, and might support Rockefeller. (That was a pretty big "might"; Reed and Rockefeller were considered to be at opposite poles of the Republican Party's political spectrum.) Of course, all the rumors became moot when Nixon chose Gerald Ford to complete the unfinished term of the disgraced Spiro Agnew.

The Watergate drama was far from over, however. In May 1974, President Nixon, under great duress, agreed to make public 1,200 pages of edited transcripts of tapes documenting all conversations and telephone calls in his offices. At the same time, he refused to turn over the tapes themselves, and insisted on retaining recordings of sixty-four conversations, claiming executive privilege. That same month, I told a reporter that "[The president] should have made complete disclosure at the beginning. Nothing appeals more than a person admitting he made a mistake." Speaking of the transcripts, I said, "It is hard for me to understand how the president can decide for the judiciary committee what is relevant to them, when he is the subject they are discussing." I also told the press that I believed that Congress should submit the Watergate issue to the Supreme Court, which could compile the information disclosed and use it as grounds for a resolution of impeachment while continuing to hold the information *in camera*, within the Court. In fact, two months later the nation's highest court rejected the claim of executive privilege and ruled unanimously that Nixon must turn over the tapes.

New York senator Jim Buckley called on the president to resign, to strengthen a country torn by the Watergate disclosures. I held the opposite view, and was quoted as saying, "The stabilization of our country is based on the constitutional process of four-year elections." I pointed out that, since World War II, numerous European governments had toppled when the head of state lost the people's confidence. The same thing might happen in America, I feared, should the president resign because of his current extreme unpopularity. "If we are going to run our government based on a person's popularity, then we might as well elect pollsters to office and let them take polls to run the government," I told the press. (Today, that statement might seem to some more than a little prescient.)

As for Governor Rockefeller, he understood that the scandals meant big trouble for the Republican Party, as well as for the nation. I went on the road practically full-time, trying to reassure the ranks. As Rocky said one day to me wryly, "It's time we got crime out of the White House and back on the streets where it belongs."

Thinking back on that period, I often chuckle when I remember a speech I made in Lima, Ohio, four months before Nixon's impeachment. Fifteen hundred citizens of "the Buckeye State" stood in a bone-chilling rain to hear me say that Nixon would not be impeached and that all the bad news would blow over. How wrong I was.

In July 1974, the House judiciary committee passed the first of three articles of impeachment against Nixon, charging obstruction of justice. Twelve days later, on August 8, Richard Nixon became the first president in history to resign from office, and vice president Gerald R. Ford moved into the Oval Office.

The nation's long nightmare was over.

Chapter 13

Rocky and the Vice Presidency: A Tough Fight

The presidency, of course, was Rockefeller's ultimate goal. He'd been heard to say, "What else is there? I've had everything else." At the same time, he made it clear that he wasn't interested in the Number Two role, often quoting John Nance Garner's pithy comment: "The vice presidency is not worth a bucket of warm piss."

Newsweek's Dick Zander succinctly caught the somewhat erratic nature of Rocky's decades-long quest: "[Rockefeller] has been running, at different speeds, for the GOP presidential nomination since 1960," Zander wrote in 1974.

In his first test of the presidential waters in 1960, Rocky discovered that the party preferred Richard Nixon. The second time around, in 1964, Rockefeller had been the clear favorite to be nominated, but his sudden divorce and remarriage in the months before the election and a brutal frontal attack by conservative forces backing Arizona governor Barry Goldwater brought about a decline in his popularity that he was unable to overcome.

When Rocky stepped to the podium to address the 1964 national convention at San Francisco's Cow Palace, he attempted to offer a platform amendment that would broaden the civil rights plank. As he condemned the John Birch Society, his voice was drowned out by a chorus of hoots and boos that lasted throughout his speech. Goldwater became the party's standard-bearer, and then lost in a general election landslide that also brought down many Republican officeholders.

In 1968 Rocky made his third attempt to reach the presidency. That August, with the election coming up fast, I headed for the national GOP convention in Miami as a young delegate from Monroe County. I was pledged to support the governor, but we all knew that Richard Nixon was the odds-on favorite. Even so, it would take more than three countdowns to knock Rocky out of the ring.

The weather in Miami in August 1968 was so hot you could hardly breathe. Unbeknownst to me at the time, that convention would foreshadow the future of the presidency. I remember walking into the amphitheater and being surrounded by people holding little globes with light bulbs in them. By pressing a button, the bulbs would illuminate the message "Reagan: A Better Idea."

In 1973, the lure of the presidency was still strong. In the middle of the Watergate scandals, Rockefeller hosted a glittering weekend conference for all the governors and their wives; he viewed the event as a way to build a beachhead for one more run at the presidency. Rocky pulled out all the stops. Friday night's party (and what a party!) filled the glamorous Rainbow Room atop Rockefeller Center. Adding pizzazz to the guest list were popular celebrities such as actresses Celeste Holm and the dancer Lynn Fontaine, the chanteuse Hildegarde, prizefighters Jack Dempsey and Floyd Patterson, and newsman Harry Reasoner. Saturday night's dinner was a glittering affair around a candlelit pool within the Metropolitan Museum of Art. Judy and I were a long way from Penfield, New York, that weekend.

The weekend continued on Sunday at Pocantico with a select party for about thirty governors and their wives. Attracting a lot of attention (especially among the women) was Ronald Reagan. Rocky told me to stick close to Reagan so that I could give him a run-down on the California governor at the end of the day. Frankly, I thought he was a lightweight. Rocky was far more substantive than Reagan even on the Californian's best day. On the other hand, Reagan had good political instincts and he had good people to do the real work. Clearly, he was going to be strong competition. Eventually, Rocky decided that—once again—the cards were against him, and he rather suddenly withdrew from the race.

Rockefeller would never reach his ultimate goal, but his power and influence continued to make him attractive to liberals of both parties.

He once told me that the Democrat Hubert Humphrey had asked him to consider becoming his running mate when he ran against the Nixon-Agnew ticket in 1968. Rocky told Humphrey he could never switch parties because of his family's long history of Republicanism, although at times the temptation may have lurked beneath the surface. Obviously his nephew, Senator Jay Rockefeller, harbors no such reservations.

* * *

By 1974 the picture in Washington had changed dramatically. Suddenly, with Nixon's resignation, America had a new president, Gerald Ford (Rocky's old friend from the Critical Choices for America commission). Ford's elevation to the highest office in the land meant, of course, that the vice presidency was open. The contest as to who would be appointed to fill that vacancy eventually came down to two strong candidates: George H. W. Bush, the GOP national chairman, and Nelson Rockefeller. Barry Goldwater remained the favorite of the party's right-wing.

The truth of the matter is that I had been pushing for Rocky as vice president from my very first days as state chairman. On occasion, I may have pushed a little too hard. Early in my chairmanship, my PR guy Nick Cammero arranged for me to hold a press conference at the National Press Club in Washington. Everything went smoothly, until the reception after the conference. Still green as grass, I thought that our cocktail party conversation would be "off the record," a pretty stupid assumption on my part. Amid the general banter, one of the reporters asked me whether I thought Rocky or Spiro Agnew would make a better vice president. Without thinking, I shot back "I don't think Spiro Agnew could carry Nelson Rockefeller's jock strap." The next day all hell broke loose; Ron Maiorana, the governor's press secretary, was furious with me for starting a firestorm. Rocky loved it; he knew I'd been carving out a colorful presence. His response to my critics was perfect: "What would you expect my state chairman to say?"

Promoting Rocky as a VP candidate was not an easy call, but tough problems are my bread-and-butter. Adding to the challenge was the fact that over the years Rocky had said he wasn't interested in playing second fiddle, and he refused to campaign openly for the post. But as his term as governor lengthened, the prospect of moving into the national limelight had become more attractive. (After all, with the assassination of John Kennedy, the nation had just seen that the vice president is only one step away from the presidency.) At a deeper level, Rockefeller carried within him the family's sense of civic responsibility, a kind of *noblesse oblige* that led him to believe that he could be of real service to a country that faced months of uncertainty caused by Watergate and its aftermath.

By August 1974, the contest between Bush and Rockefeller to win the Republican endorsement for the second-in-command was intensifying. Ballots from Republican elected officials and party leaders showed that Bush was mounting a full-scale campaign, led by Richard Herman of Nebraska, and he had the clear endorsement of several national committeemen. I, of course, was working furiously for Rockefeller, while Ford's counselor Melvin Laird was calling the shots from the White House. (Mel had publicly promoted Rocky as VP even before Ford succeeded to the presidency.)

I traveled around the country to meet with as many state chairmen as I could. My job: to test the waters and deflect criticism from conservatives, especially in the South and West. I worked my tail off, trying to counter the belief that Rocky was "too liberal" and that he could never be satisfied being merely "standby equipment" for Gerald Ford. As I told *Newsweek*'s Dick Zander, "This is a new administration, with special problems—the economy in particular—and I think he'll be a full-working partner with the president."

Finally, the day before President Ford was to announce his VP choice, Rocky phoned and asked if I could come to Washington. Of course I could. "Go to the national committee headquarters and let me know what the attitude there is," he said. "You're going to be vice president, aren't you?," I asked. His answer: "You didn't hear it from me." The next day I was at national headquarters in Washington, surrounded by Bush loyalists. Bush, of course, had been running the place, so they were all hoping, even expecting, that he would be Ford's choice.

When the hour came for the announcement, we all gathered around the big television set, I stretched out on the floor in front of the tube, literally lying low. We watched as the cameras caught the scene at the White House. The door to the Oval Office opened and out walked the President. Right behind him was Nelson Aldrich Rockefeller. I let out a great guffaw and then a cheer—but around me you could have cut the icy silence with a knife.

My role in Rockefeller's selection by Ford was headlined by the Rochester *Times-Union*: "Rosenbaum Carried the Ball for Rocky." In a long article, political reporter Phil Currie described how I had helped to "bring out [Rockefeller's] pluses" and "nullify [his] minuses" in the days before Ford's decision. Currie pointed out that the Southern wing of the Republican Party, headed by Clarke Reed of Mississippi, favored the choice of a conservative VP, but couldn't decide on a favorite; clearly, Rockefeller would not be among their top choices. However, as I told Currie, "If they weren't for us, I wanted to make sure they weren't against us."

On a more positive note, I had made sure that GOP leaders in the Northeast would support Rockefeller. I was helped in this by a coincidence of timing. A meeting of governors had been scheduled in Bangor, Maine—well before Nixon's resignation—at which I would be named GOP regional chairman. Instead of flying to Maine that weekend, I flew instead with Rocky in his private plane to Chicago for a meeting of Midwest GOP leaders. I spent hours in Chicago enthusiastically lobbying the Northeast governors by phone on Rocky's behalf—apparently effectively—since the governors issued a statement unanimously endorsing him over George H. W. Bush (he of the summer home in Kennebunkport, Maine) as their first choice for VP. I couldn't talk to all the Republican governors, of course, but I made sure that I rallied every one who was a close friend of Gerald Ford. (Actually, right after Agnew's resignation I had talked with every GOP chair across the nation, so I had built some strong ties in Washington and had a pretty good sense of who was who and where they stood vis-à-vis Rockefeller.) The hard work and the hours of lobbying had paid off.

During his confirmation hearings, Rocky was questioned at length about his legendary gift giving. He called me one day and asked how I thought he should handle the questions. "What if I remind them that the Bible says it's better to give than to receive?" asked Rocky, the life-long Baptist. I told him it wouldn't help him win, but he might as well give it a try.

* * *

I was proud of the fact that I had helped boost Rocky into the vice presidency. But the contrast between Rocky's usual deluxe accommodations and those in this new environment became strikingly clear later in the day of his appointment, when we boarded Air Force Two, the vice-presidential airplane—a genuine relic—and took off to attend a meeting that night in Rhode Island. Both of Rocky's private planes were top of the line, of course, Cadillacs of the air. Impeccable service and tasty mid-air treats were what I'd become accustomed to. When I saw that Air Force Two offered only plastic drinking cups and little containers of Chiclets, I said, "Mr. Vice President, this bucket of bolts is quite a comedown, isn't it? Are you sure you really want this job?" Rocky, of course, couldn't have cared less; he'd had luxury enough to last a lifetime.

Vice President Rockefeller's new business address was the Executive Office Building, adjacent to the White House, and his official residence was the Admiral's House. (At this writing, Vice President Cheney lives in the Admiral's House, and his office is next to the president's in the West Wing of the White House.) In fact, Rockefeller rarely stayed at the Admiral's House, because his own beautiful rambling farmhouse on Foxhall Road, set on thirty-five rolling acres, was much nicer—and it was home, the place where he was most comfortable. (The Secret Service, of course, kept guard in a little gatehouse near the front door, where among other things, they monitored all phone calls coming in and out of the residence.) I was there so often that I had my own bedroom at the top of the stairs.

During Rocky's tenure as VP, a news story broke that he'd had a bed designed for him by artist Max Ernst at a personal cost of $35,000. On one occasion when he had a reception at the Admiral's House, all the guests wanted to do was go upstairs and see that mink-lined bed.

Often, when an event or press conference was scheduled for the White House Rose Garden, Rocky would invite me to join the president's immediate party. He was very thoughtful that way, and tried to include me in everything. He knew I hoped to become governor, and he was really grooming me for the job, introducing me to people and cutting me in on as much action as, in all propriety, he could. Of course, my gratitude was boundless. (See personal letter from Rockefeller to Rosenbaum indicating his support, Appendix C.)

Unfortunately, perhaps, Rocky was never born to be second-in-command. He was too smart (and perhaps too arrogant) to stand in the shadow of a president like Gerald Ford, a good but rather ordinary man who had been sucked into the White House by a scandal-created vacuum. As early as November 1975, I had a phone call from Rocky, complaining that he was bored. "I'm 67 years old," he said. "Why should I stay down here [in Washington] picking do-do with the chickens?" After fifteen years of being the Number One guy in New York State, he sometimes found working with Ford's cabinet difficult. He also had stony words about Elliott Richardson: "He's so stuffy, it's difficult to breathe when he's in the room."

Rocky's attitude troubled me. Almost immediately a major fight loomed, when president-by-appointment Gerald Ford would have to mount a national election campaign. Would the Republican Party stand behind him? Or would they be swayed by the magnetic charm of his rival, the Hollywood celebrity-turned-governor Ronald Reagan?

A Scrimmage with Buckley

Just about that time, I had my own troubles back in New York State. I've always been known as a fighter. I'll try to mop the floor with any opponent, but I know how dangerous it is to make enemies. Once a fight is over, I usually go out of my way to seek a lasting rapprochement.

With New York State senator Jim Buckley, it was a different story. Buckley made no bones about the fact that he found Rockefeller's so-called liberal policies anathema, and, since I was the governor's guy, he did everything he could to thwart my leadership. Buckley had been elected U.S. senator in 1970 as a member of the Conservative Party. Throughout his tenure he would hold that line with the determination of a bull terrier. His unbending attitude made my job of holding the Repubican Party together difficult in the extreme because more conservative members of the Republican Party were followers of Senator Buckley. Adding to my problem was the fact that our war chest was temporarily out of money, the result of our unsuccessful campaign to keep Malcolm Wilson in the governor's office.

Real trouble with Buckley and his fellow Conservatives began in December 1974, when New York's senior senator Jake Javits made a bid to become chair of the Senate Republican Conference, an influential post that would automatically make him a member of President Ford's leadership team. "The Iron Chancellor" told Buckley he had better support Javits or else; the "or else" was that he might lose the support of the Republican Party in his own bid for re-election in 1976, two years down the road. To my disbelief (and anger), Buckley issued his own ultimatum: not only would he not support Javits, he would back Javits' rival for the Senate leadership role, the conservative senator from Nebraska, Carl Curtis.

The Javits-Buckley enmity had begun years earlier when Jake and Rocky had tried to block Buckley, then a relative newcomer, from upgrading his political designation on the ballot from "Conservative" to "Conservative-Republican." (Buckley won that one.) I knew, and so did Rocky, that Buckley was out to cut Rockefeller off at the knees; if he couldn't achieve that, he wanted at least to reduce Rocky's influence on Ford's policies, an influence that would be strengthened if Javits became the leader of the Senate Republicans.

Immediately after Buckley announced his refusal to support Javits, I fired off a salvo that ricocheted through the press: "Senator Buckley was elected by the voters of New York, not the voters of Nebraska. His refusal to support Senator Javits is an act of disunity." Buckley had the support of a couple of influential downstate chairmen, especially Ed

No Room for Democracy

Schwenk of Suffolk County, a protégé of Perry Duryea, minority leader in New York's assembly. Ergo, I had Duryea to deal with, as well as Buckley. I knew that the Duryea/Rosenbaum match would have to be fought at some point, exclusive of the conservative issue. I was thinking seriously about a run for the governorship, and I knew Perry had the same idea. Sooner or later, we would have to duke it out.

A strange triumvirate developed as a result of Buckley's need to raise his own war chest. The recently introduced campaign finance reform bill would have hurt his fund-raising efforts; in lobbying against that bill he allied himself with both the liberal American Civil Liberties Union and with senator Eugene McCarthy, a liberal favorite. In addition, Buckley was making a move on the international scene; he embarked on a well-publicized trip to Russia and returned with widely reported condemnations of the "police state" he had witnessed on his tour. Buckley and McCarthy were beginning to talk about developing a third party, one that could mount its own presidential campaign. I doubted their idea would succeed, but I saw only trouble ahead from Buckley, and stepped up the barrage against him.

"People who try to divide the party will meet with strong resistance from me and the county chairmen," I told a Gannett reporter. We would buck any effort by conservatives if they tried to drop Rockefeller from the ticket, I said, adding "We're not going to sell the party out. Nobody's going to blackmail this party. If the Republican Party expects to elect a president and vice president in 1976, the ticket will be Ford-Rockefeller."

To my dismay, Rocky adamantly refused to let me, or anyone, promote him as a vice-presidential candidate. However, I immediately went to work to ensure that Ford's name would be on the Republican ticket, in spite of opposition from the conservatives. In June 1975, a year-and-a-half before the next presidential election, the Associated Press reported my success in New York State:

> Rosenbaum engineered a unanimous vote of the state Republican Committee endorsing President Ford for the 1976 Republican presidential nomination—a step clearly

aimed at rebuffing Buckley's suggestion that conservatives should consider trying to dump both Ford and Rockefeller....
Part of the purpose of this elaborate ritual of endorsement and non-endorsement...was to signal to Ford that Rockefeller knows his political fate is in the President's hands.

At the same time, we had tendered a severe rebuke to Buckley by threatening to deny him party backing.

The game is called "hard ball," and we knew how to play it. Now we had to move the game from our ballpark out into a national arena—the 1976 Republican Convention in Kansas City.

* * *

In October, 1975, I was appointed to head the GOP state chairmen's association by Mary Louise Smith of Iowa, the party's national chairwoman. If Mary Louise was the party's pope, I had just become her chief cardinal. My appointment was interpreted around the country as a sign that President Ford was leaning toward Rocky for his running mate in 1976. Politicos sensed that President Ford had given me his seal of approval, and that I was chosen deliberately to broaden Rocky's base of support among party dissidents.

As the GOP's "chairman of the chairmen," I wanted to keep Gerald Ford in the White House. As a New Yorker, I wanted to persuade Rocky to stay at Ford's side, a breath away from the presidency. I knew how much sweat, savvy and skill it would take to make that Ford-Rockefeller ticket happen, and Rockefeller's half-hearted attitude troubled me. Nonetheless, I strapped on my gloves and got ready for the political fight of my life.

A Fight of a Different Order: Rosie v. Floyd Patterson

Early in March 1975, I got a call in Albany from Frank Guelli, an old friend and husband of one of my former clients, Jennie Roncone. Jennie's family once owned a popular restaurant in Rochester where the city work crews often ate lunch; that included me, when I worked for the city during college summer vacations.

Frank was a good athlete and he had always been a nut about boxing. Now, he told me, he was promoting a boxing exhibition in Rochester and he had booked the War Memorial, a big downtown arena, for April 8—a day that just happened to be my birthday. Frank had already signed some of the great names in boxing, including Willie Pep, Carmen Basilio, Billie Graham, and Kid Gavilan. I nearly dropped the phone when I heard what he wanted: For the main match, he wanted me to enter the ring against former world heavyweight champ Floyd Patterson!

As a junior at Hobart I had won the heavyweight boxing title and Frank, who kept track of such things, knew all about it. I agreed: I thought it would be a hoot. I was in good shape for a guy in his mid-forties and Floyd was no spring chicken either. I should have started training right away, but I kept putting it off—training is boring, and, after all, this wasn't a serious fight, just an exhibition. (I hoped Floyd knew that, too.) About ten days before the event I started to do a little shaping up.

I began jumping rope and doing push-ups every day, and I sparred with my good friend Joe Bruno, then a staffer and later majority leader in the New York State Senate. Joe knew boxing; he'd been a light heavyweight champion when he was in the Army in Korea in 1954. We'd had many ping-pong matches in Albany over the years and we were both high-spirited and highly competitive.

Two days before the match I pulled a muscle in my left calf while jumping rope. I was worried. It was bad enough that I was going to be in the ring with Patterson. Was I going to have to limp away from him? That's hardly my style.

On the day of the exhibition, I drove to Rochester from Albany and visited my friend the late Ozzie Sussman, a legendary trainer of fighters. Ozzie gave me a good rubdown and managed to loosen the tight muscle in my leg. I booked a room at the Holiday Inn (then on Main Street) and took a nap. Two hours later, when I awakened, I couldn't believe my eyes. Once again, Rochester was being hit by a major snowstorm, and it was growing stronger by the minute. Soon the roads were treacherous, some impassable. How many people would come out on a night like this?

My fears were unwarranted. The fight crowd, always interested in mayhem and drawn to the arena by the famous boxers on the card, came out in droves. Several matches began and ended and, as the evening wore on, Floyd had not made an appearance. (I was hoping he was afraid to show up!) No such luck. Floyd turned up, accompanied by an entourage of family and seconds, the guys who come to advise and encourage a fighter. My seconds were my dear friends, the late Don Mack, later to become Penfield Town Supervisor, and Don Jeffries, a local travel agent impresario.

Finally, Floyd and I climbed in the ring, were introduced and touched gloves, the customary boxing ritual. I never have been quite sure whether Floyd thought this was just an exhibition or something more substantial. Whatever he thought, Floyd came out of his corner like a shot and landed some body punches that sent me almost immediately to the canvas. This wasn't the kind of plodding old heavyweight I'd hoped to meet. He was just plain fast. I managed to pull myself together and make it through the round by covering up and landing a few harmless left jabs. I was having great difficulty catching Floyd, not only because he was so quick but also because my pulled calf muscle showed up again and with it the limp.

In the second round Floyd pummeled me into the ropes, but I managed to get in a few shots under the ribs. At that point, with about twenty seconds to go, Floyd decided he wasn't going to take any more guff from this rank amateur. He uncorked a left hook that caught me flush in my right eye. The crowd let out a groan, I held on to Floyd, and the round ended. By now I was seeing double and bleeding into my mouth. The referee, Arnold Cream, better known in the fight game as "Jersey Joe" Walcott, came over to my corner and held up two fingers,

No Room for Democracy

and said "How many?" When I answered, "Four" the show was over.

Floyd, always a gentleman, came down to the dressing room and apologized, which was completely unnecessary. Still, it took nearly a week before the bleeding completely stopped and I could see normally again. The *New York Times* carried a story about the whole affair and I received numerous calls from friends questioning my sanity. Perry Duryea, the state assembly Speaker and a rough-and-ready guy in his own right, called and told me he wouldn't even go into the same building with Floyd.

A few months later, governor Hugh Carey, a Democrat, appointed Floyd chairman of the New York State Athletic Commission. When I read the news, I wrote to congratulate Floyd and opined that this was his reward for beating up the Republican state chairman. Almost twenty years later, Floyd came to Manhattan to endorse me for governor and we posed for campaign pictures together on the steps of City Hall.

Chapter 14

Rockefeller: The Sunset Years

As for the years following that heady Kansas City convention, I'm tempted to say that I went into a hole and disappeared for four years. Of course, that's not the real story. But suddenly Rocky was disappearing from my everyday life and, although we were still in close touch, much of the spark and excitement that had energized our partnership had faded. I missed it—and I missed the close camaraderie. No doubt I also suffered from a mild case of burnout. I'd been charging full-tilt for four years now, and my batteries may have been getting low.

Certainly there was nothing now in my political life to match the magic that was Rocky at his best. When I first went to Albany as state chairman, Nelson Rockefeller had seemed to me all-powerful. As a kid from upstate, his aura—his sophistication, his self-confidence—fascinated me. I'd never met anyone with such charisma, such an ability to make things happen. An example of that ability is contained in Chapter One, "Let There Be Light."

Now it was politics as usual, and I had to get on with it. Soon after the 1976 convention, Jim Baker, then undersecretary of the U.S. Department of Commerce, was picked by President Ford to chair the President Ford Committee, the group that had been convened to support the Ford cause in Kansas City. I was one of eleven regional chairmen chosen post-convention to keep the effort going in the face of Jimmy Carter's strong surge nationally. The job was interesting, but it didn't have much zing—and I missed "zing."

After the convention, there was much speculation in the press that I would be named the Republican Party's national chairman, but

Gerald Ford decided otherwise. I was seen as too close to Rockefeller to unite the party. In addition, the Ford-Dole ticket had suffered some damage among women voters when it failed to support the proposed Equal Rights Amendment as part of the party's convention plank. Having Mary Louise Smith (referred to by some as "the Iowa grandmother") continue as national chair would help minimize those losses; Mary Louise was in fact a very effective national leader. During the final hours at Kansas City, I enthusiastically nominated her myself, beginning my speech of support by shouting "Good morning, Mary Louise!" into the famous white telephone that had been the focus of the convention's most publicized fracas. Eventually, Mary Louise relinquished her position to Bill Brock, a centrist from Tennessee whose job would be to continue the effort to reunite the party.

Immediately after the Kansas City convention, we began preparing for the upcoming election that pitted Ford against Jimmy Carter. I set up a tour of key cities where Jerry could "meet the people" of New York State. I won't forget the dark, rainy afternoon in my hometown of Rochester when the president addressed a crowd gathered at the airport. I'd arranged to have my mother and father near the podium, and the rally had barely started when I heard my mother calling out, loud and clear, "Dickie, put on your raincoat!" (Once a mother, always a mother, I guess. Certainly everyone within earshot got a kick out of that remark.)

As the campaign was coming to a close, I committed a nearly fatal slip of the tongue, a colossal blunder that still causes me to shudder when I think of it. After two years of non-stop campaigning I was exhausted. One night toward the end of Ford's tour of New York State, we found ourselves in an airfield hangar in Islip, Long Island. In front of a huge crowd, I stepped up to the podium to make the introduction. After my usual flowery three-minute speech, I concluded with: "Ladies and gentlemen, I give you the president of the United States—and the next president of the United States: Gerald R. FRAUD!" The place went crazy—and I was marginally suicidal. Ford was very forgiving. He understood that I was almost at the end of my tether. So did former heavyweight boxing champion Joe Frazier who was in the crowd that night; Joe came up to me afterwards and said, with a sympathetic shake of his head, "That's just tired."

I *was* tired. When I'm on a mission I'm totally involved, 24/7. Sometimes the fatigue shows. As state chairman, I used to stay at the Doral Park Hotel at 38th and Park Avenue in midtown Manhattan. Often I'd get up early and get copies of half a dozen newspapers from the newsstand near the hotel lobby and take them back to my room to peruse, so I could keep informed about what was happening around the state. One morning, the stand had run out of copies of the *New York Times*, so I put a coat on over my pajamas and headed down Park Avenue toward Grand Central Station. I hadn't realized that about a foot of pajama leg was sticking out from under my coat until I met Charlie Urstadt, then head of Battery Park City. "Mr. Chairman," said Urstadt, "what's the matter with you? Are you sick?" "Nothing's the matter," I replied. "I just didn't feel like getting dressed." Charlie has never let me forget it.

* * *

To tell the truth, during those months I was still steaming privately at the way the national party leaders had dumped Rocky. I couldn't be one hundred per cent sure in my heart that Ford deserved to be president. Even Rocky had his doubts about Ford's ability to lead the nation. When I once questioned him about the specifics of one of Ford's policies, he shrugged and said, "Don't ask;" in other words, "There's not much there." In fact, Rocky held Ford "in deep contempt" (his exact words), even though Jerry had said he hoped Rocky "held no hard feelings." Fat chance.

In hindsight, I see Jerry Ford as a kind, decent, honest man who grew into the demanding role that was handed him. His pardon of Nixon, seen by some as an exchange of favors, was an absolute necessity to start the nation's healing process. Unfortunately for Jerry, he made some serious mistakes during the ensuing campaign. His claim that the nations of Eastern Europe were free, when in fact they were still under Soviet domination, stopped his momentum in its tracks at a time when he was coming on strong. That helped Jimmy Carter and the Democrats take the presidency.

It was the Southern conservatives, of course, who eventually pressured Ford into dumping Rockefeller from the ticket, saying they couldn't hold out against Reagan unless he got rid of Rocky. In my opinion, Ford should have called in those Southern leaders and said, "Look, I'm president. I want Nelson Rockefeller in my White House. You go back home and build up some support for him. If you don't, you won't get the support from me that you need to stay in power—not to mention those pork barrel projects you hope to get." Instead, Ford called Rocky in and said, "Nelson, I'm getting a lot of pressure to drop you from the ticket. What do you think?" Of course, Rocky got the message right away, and he said, in effect, "Listen, I don't want to do anything to hurt you. I'll announce that I'm not going to run again on the ticket, or you can announce it." That's the kind of person Nelson Rockefeller was.

In fact, it was Don Rumsfeld, then White House chief of staff, who was instrumental in getting rid of Rocky, and he made sure the decision was made quietly long before the party gathered in Kansas City. The *New York Times* made the situation clear as early as November 1975: "For six months, White House chief of staff Donald Rumsfeld has left no particle of doubt he was using his recognized talent for political infighting to remove Nelson Rockefeller as the vice-presidential candidate next year. In Washington, Rocky was viewed as having joined the walking dead." Rumsfeld knew that Rocky would outshine President Ford in a four-year term and convinced Ford he was better off with Rockefeller off the ticket. And when President Ford hard-lined out of the park a request for a federal bail-out of New York City it was seen by the *Times* as "an insulting demand for [Rockefeller's] political scalp." The *New York Daily News* headline summed up the city's attitude: "Ford to City: Drop Dead." (Ironically, the *Daily News* supported Ford in the general election.)

Here's the real irony of ironies. When it was clear that Ford would be in trouble at the convention, Ford, Rumsfeld and Rogers Morton had to turn to Rockefeller (and New York State) to win the delegates Ford

No Room for Democracy

needed. I wanted to make a big deal of this whole thing as it was happening, and Rockefeller wouldn't let me. I told him I wanted to use my speech to the convention delegates to tell them what a great job Rocky had done in New York State and as vice president. He said, "I'm begging you not to do that. It may touch off a demonstration against Ford and I don't want to do anything to hurt him." That was the way Rocky was. (I wouldn't have been so gracious.)

The Ford people had hinted that if Rocky withdrew, he would have a strong voice in the vice-presidential selection and would play an influential role in formulating policy planks in the platform at the convention. My response: "Baloney!" Policy planks don't mean a damn thing (as Ford admitted privately), only that you can wave a flag and appeal to this or that special interest group. But Rocky continued in his support for the Ford/Dole ticket. During a gathering of the Southern states chairmen's organization shortly after the convention, three of us were breakfasting together, Rocky, Clarke Reed (chair of the party in Mississippi) and myself. Reed began by complimenting Rocky, telling him how grateful the South was for the hard work he'd done for the party. Rocky immediately laid his cards on the table: "You guys wanted me off the ticket. You got me off the ticket. Now get off your ass and get this ticket elected." It was an order he repeated virtually verbatim that same day at the general meeting of all the Southern chairmen.

Unfortunately, Gerald Ford failed politically to be an effective president. His problem, in my opinion, was this: he'd been in Congress for too many years. Because Congressmen are distracted by the short-term nature of their jobs, they find it hard to make decisions, so they compromise on everything. They have to run for re-election every two years, so at least half their terms in office are spent building up their bases of support by agreeing with everybody, and raising money. In Ford's case, when he got to the White House he didn't know how to use the presidency to get what he wanted. He just didn't understand how to use politics at the presidential level.

I believe that dumping Rocky cost Ford the election. With Nelson on the ticket we could have carried New York State, and other states as well, because Rocky was such a superb campaigner. Ford went into the election with at least two strikes against him: he hadn't been elected to the presidency, and he represented a party still under the shadow of Watergate. During the campaign, with the help of my politically savvy friend, Bob Baker, the campaign Executive Director, we managed to help close a thirty-point gap in the polls, and then—disaster. In a debate with Carter, Ford referred to the states of Eastern Europe as "free," when in fact they were still under Communist control. This infuriated any number of ethnic groups, descendents of people who had fled those states. Despite that, we almost pulled off the election. At the risk of sounding like a broken record, I believe that if Rocky had been on the ticket, we would have won, since New York State went for Carter by only a small margin.

* * *

The night of the election in 1976, Judy and I were at Rocky's penthouse at 812 Fifth Avenue, part of a small dinner party that included the Kissingers and four or five others. Kissinger kept standing in front of the television set, asking me to interpret the trends and results as they flashed on the screen. (Later Henry gave me a copy of his book *The White House Years*, inscribed "To my political mentor, Dick Rosenbaum.") That night, one of the few amusing moments was the announcement that Jay Rockefeller, Nelson's nephew and a Democrat, had been elected governor of West Virginia. As the returns were flashed on the television screen, Rocky said, wryly, "Well, it's a small state—but it's ours."

After Ford lost the election, Rocky went back to his office on the fifth floor of the Rockefeller Center, resigned at last to the fact that he would never be president. He must have been bitter. He'd given many years of his life to the Republican Party and much of his fortune, only to have the party turn against him.

Rocky's marriage was not in good shape, either. I was in his office one day when the bill came in from his accountant for Happy's recent trip to Europe. He looked at the figure, shook his head, and said to me: "How could she spend $50,000 in one week? That must have been one hell of a vacation." Happy, of course, could tell her own sad story about the disintegration of a marriage that had started with high hopes—and that had been consummated at great political cost to the bridegroom.

* * *

If Rockefeller had personal problems, I had my own—and they were all focused on my professional future. How could I continue to play a power role in the party now that the public—both state and national— viewed Rocky with disfavor; our names certainly were closely linked in the public mind. Painfully, regretfully, I realized that—with Rockefeller withdrawn into private life—New York State needed a new Republican Party chairman. My term as chairman would end in 1978—I needed a new job. Advances were made to me by various law firms in New York City, including the silk-stocking firms Webster & Sheffield, Proskauer Rose, Rosenman & Colin, and others. I danced around their offers like a kid at a prom who wants to be friendly, but who didn't want to be stuck with the wrong girl. Politics, I realized, was in my blood, and I didn't want to get out of the game.

For at least a year, I'd been considering going for the Big Prize— the governorship in 1978. Rocky, who knew that Perry Duryea probably was going to make a move in the same direction, was willing to throw his support to my effort, since he and Perry had never been simpatico. In 1977, Rocky called me to Pocantico Hills and said, "Let's get this ball rolling. I'm giving the eulogy today in Manhattan for Gus Levy [a Goldman Sachs mogul]. After the service, you and I and George Hinman will take the helicopter up to Pocantico and we'll make our plans." Later that afternoon we met in the new little temple-style building on the estate grounds; it had just been built in anticipation of a visit from the emperor of Japan. In this fantasy pagoda, we talked over all aspects of my putative campaign.

"You'll probably have to resign as state chairman," Rocky said, "otherwise it will look too political." This I knew. He also pointed out that I would need some powerful allies in the business community. To that end, he volunteered to get me involved with The Group of 400, a national club of influential CEOs who could be useful in fund-raising. Then Rocky said he would call a meeting of all the GOP county chairmen and push to have Joe Margiotta, the powerful leader of the party in Nassau County, take over for me as state chairman. There would be one big "if," he told me: in order to get Rocky's support, Joe would have to pledge to support me in my run for the governorship. This, I realized, was a big "if"—Joe was a downstate colleague and close friend of Perry Duryea, my chief rival.

Rocky scheduled the meeting and, because I had family commitments on the day picked for the meeting, he promised to act as my surrogate. That night when I got home, rather late and dead tired, I found a phone message asking me to call Dick Zander, chief political writer for *Newsday*. When I reached him, Zander said, "Dick, I hear Rocky is backing you for governor. The word is out here that you're going to leave as state chairman to run for governor and Joe Margiotta is going to replace you. Is it true? If you tell me it's not true, I won't write it."

His question floored me; this was all supposed to be a big secret, at least for the moment. "Dick," I said, "I don't want to talk about it."

"Do you deny it?" Zander asked. "If you deny it, I won't write about it."

"I can't deny it, I answered truthfully. The next day, the news was all over the front page of *Newsday*, and soon on newscasts across the state.

Unfortunately, this was very bad for my gubernatorial prospects; in some ways, it was the kiss of death. I had hoped to sneak up on Perry Duryea, the state assembly leader who thought he had a lock on the Republican nomination. Like any good politician, Perry had been tilling the political soil for years. Every summer he'd invite all the county chairmen to a big lobster roast at his place in Montauk (his family was in the lobster fishing business); that was a great way to draw them in, since the chairmen control the vote. His position as head of the state assembly, a political hothouse, also gave him a big leg up. Perry also looked like a governor. He was a big guy with a shock of silver hair, and he was built like a piece of steel. In spite of our rivalry, I liked Perry.

I knew the odds of my getting the nomination were against me. Without any day-to-day contact with the legislators I was something of a toothless saber-tooth tiger. But I had Rocky on my side. I think he was a little put off by Duryea's power; he didn't like that challenge to his own position. But I was willing to take on Duryea and give the fight my best shot.

Unfortunately for me, the timing was really bad. Many of the county leaders were ticked off by what they saw as Rockefeller's continued attempt to control the party now that he was emeritus. Political correspondent Frank Lynn got the story about right, as usual. In a special report to the *New York Times*, he referred to "the strong reaction of metropolitan and some upstate county chairmen over Mr. Rockefeller's attempt...to make Nassau Republican chairman Joseph M. Margiotta the GOP state chairman so that Mr. Rosenbaum would be free to pursue his gubernatorial ambitions. The move was widely interpreted as part of a Rockefeller-inspired effort to prevent Assembly minority leader Perry B. Duryea from winning the GOP gubernatorial nomination next year."

A lot of vitriol was spilled over this issue, and I had to gather the county leaders together and assure them their voices would be heard in the nomination process, that my running was not by Rockefeller fiat. Apparently my assurances did not convince them.

***

With the prospects of my winning the governorship waning (I realized that Perry had a real political machine, while I had only the state GOP committee and a weakened Rocky), I needed to ensure my political future by holding on to my role on the Republican National Committee. As state chair, I had automatically been a member of the committee; once out of office, I would have to compete with as many as a dozen others to become one of two committeemen (traditionally a man and a woman) elected to represent the New York State GOP at the national level. The state chairman usually appoints the two committeemen, but I was careful to announce that I would not nominate myself.

Politics, as the old saw goes, does indeed make strange bedfellows. In my effort to win the national committee post I found an unusual ally in George Clark, the Brooklyn party leader. In the days leading up to the

Kansas City convention and throughout that wild week, I had battled hard with George who was rallying delegate votes for Reagan. Now, nine months after the convention, Clark sent a letter to all New York State's county chairs urging them to support my bid for the national committee post vacated by my old friend George Hinman. This, he said, "would be a good way to keep our fearless leader on the scene." (He added, "I know he can do a tough job. I saw that last summer in Kansas City. Every night I called home to make sure I still had my citizenship.")

In April 1977 I was elected by the state GOP committee—along with Eunice Whittlesey of Schenectady—to represent New York State on the Republican National Committee. Rather conspicuously absent at the voting was Joe Margiotta. I knew Joe had wanted the national committee post, and even though his Nassau County group voted for me, his absence was noted.

My appointment to the national committee was generally viewed, correctly, as a prelude to my resigning as state chairman. A succession fight loomed. With both Rockefeller and Rosenbaum out of the action, who would run the party? It was generally agreed by onlookers that two men would vie for control: Duryea and Warren Anderson. Anderson had close ties to Rockefeller and Rosenbaum; Duryea, the perceived party favorite, was supported by the conservative Margiotta and by those who wanted to slide out from under the Rockefeller apron.

During my tenure as a member I should mention that I tried on various occasions during meetings of the Republican National Rules Committee to change the structure of the Republican National Committee by passing a resolution which would have broadened the number of members eligible for election to the committee. The Republican National Committee is organized similarly to the organization of the U.S. Senate, so that all states are equally represented. Each state has three seats, one occupied by the state chairman, who serves while in office, and one man and one woman serving as Republican National Committeeman and Republican National Committeewoman.

I proposed that the rules change would allow for a one man, one vote formula. If that change had been instituted, a state with a large population like New York would have had a much greater representation than a small state like Rhode Island. This to me seemed only fair. My argument was that, under current rules, a sparsely populated state, a small state if you will, had as much to say in setting party policy and in running the national convention, etc., as a heavily populated state. An acceptance of my proposal would almost certainly have resulted in an increase of participation and membership by African American Republicans. My resolution garnered very little support and as a result, the image of the Republican Party as exclusionary was enhanced.

I firmly believe that the individual members didn't care one way or the other about broadening the committee membership to hopefully include more African American Republicans, but they also did not want to dilute what they viewed as their prestige as members of a highly exclusive fraternity. Ultimately, there was just *No Room for Democracy*.

Although I had been picked as state chairman by Rockefeller fiat, I knew the days of single-handed power were over, and I set up a special search committee to review candidates for the chairman's job. Although Duryea and Margiotta at first grumbled about the committee's final choice, Utica dentist Dr. Bernard R. Kilbourn became New York's GOP leader on June 8, 1977. Kilbourn, a moderate, was viewed as someone who could effectively serve as a buffer between Duryea and Anderson. In a nice show of unity, his name was placed in nomination by Duryea's ally and my old rival, Joe Margiotta.

Two weeks later, the Rockefeller-Rosenbaum "farewell party" drew 2,200 cheering Republicans to the grand ballroom of the Waldorf-Astoria Hotel in Manhattan. It was, for me, an unforgettable party— bringing together President Ford, former secretary of state Henry Kissinger, former governor Malcolm Wilson, Senate leader Howard Baker, national GOP chairman William Brock, senator Jacob Javits, and dozens of other prominent Republicans.

That dinner marked a momentous changing of the guard. For Nelson Rockefeller, whose voice choked several times during his responses that evening, the star-studded event signaled a final conclusion to an eventful life in politics. For Dick Rosenbaum, it closed a whirlwind of a chapter. Now it was time for me to turn the next page. (See Appendix D, Rockefeller to Rosenbaum Letter, December 23, 1976.)

Chapter 15

Farewell to Rocky

By 1979 I had been serving on the Rockefeller Center board of directors about two years. The board consisted of only seven men, including Nelson's brothers David and Laurence Rockefeller, and it was headed at that time by J. Richardson "Dick" Dilworth, a blue blood from Philadelphia, a true aristocrat and a fine man. The directors met once a month in the boardroom at the center, one of New York City's best-known buildings, on the Avenue of the Americas. Meetings began at 3 p.m. sharp; if you weren't there by 2:45, you could expect Dick Dilworth to phone as to your whereabouts. For me, the meetings were enormously boring, since our main function was to review financial statements of the more than a hundred companies under Rockefeller Center control. By 5 or 5:30, when the meeting ended, I was glad to get out of there.

The board president at that time was Alton Marshall, who had also served as secretary to Governor Rockefeller in Albany for some years. Al had his drinking and domestic problems, but he was a regular guy and Rocky was fond of him. Unfortunately, Al had got caught up living the high life when he was hanging around with the governor, and somehow he couldn't adjust to real life when the party ended. Ultimately, that attitude cost Al his job as board president.

After a few years in the post, Al asked for a sizeable raise in salary, one that he saw as commensurate with that paid to CEOs of other major real estate companies. Mind you, at that time, Al was earning $600,000 a year as board president. He had a luxurious apartment paid for by the company, a car, a chauffeur and an unlimited expense account. On receiving Al's proposal, David Rockefeller, then board chairman, made a counter offer; Al said he wanted to think about it overnight. The next day Al met with the Rockefellers and said he would accept their offer. Too late. You disagreed with the Rockefellers at your peril—and Al was out of a job.

David Rockefeller is a very interesting person. The youngest of the Rockefeller sons served for years as chairman of Chase Manhattan Bank. It seemed to me that he longed to be a regular guy, but couldn't bring himself to act like one. One day at Pocantico we were looking out the window where a big political reception was going on. Nelson was in the midst of it, greeting everyone, slapping backs, and smiling his famous big grin. David shook his head as he observed his brother and said to me, "I don't see how he does it." On another occasion David threw a party at the Rainbow Room at the top of Rockefeller Center. The next morning, he was quoted as having told a reporter who'd asked about the guest list, "Everybody who is anybody was there." His comment, of course, infuriated a lot of people who hadn't been invited, especially as his comment—and the guest list—was printed in the New York papers.

Rocky had cultivated an effective man-of-the-people attitude that stood in sharp contrast to David. One time we went over to Cherry Hills, New Jersey, to honor the local congressman, a fellow with the improbable last name of Sandman. The governor insisted we wear black tie, even though I told him that wasn't mentioned on the invitation. When we arrived at the party we realized, of course, that we were the only "penguins" there. When the governor rose to deliver his speech, he began by saying he hoped the audience wouldn't think we were "a couple of odd balls."

It took a few years of working with the governor for me to understand how my relationship with him was perceived by others. Our deep personal bond created an aura of respect that opened the most exclusive doors, from private houses right up to the White House. Happy, Nelson's wife, was an integral part of the scene. She had agreed with Nelson that I should run for governor in 1978. At the dinner in '76 following Ford's defeat at the polls, Happy turned to me as we were sitting together on the dais, fingered her ears that sparkled with diamonds, and said, "These earrings are going to help pay for your campaign."

To tell the truth, I sometimes was as amazed as others by my close relationship to Rocky and his family. In the early days of my chairmanship, I stayed either in the tower at the Waldorf or the penthouse at the Hilton when I was in New York City. You had to see the opulence to believe it. On occasion I would have my family stay over for a sumptuous breakfast—anything you wanted. A coterie of five waiters hovering over the children while they devoured mountains of fresh strawberries and blueberries on waffles smothered with whipped cream. As the children grew up, their sophistication widened as they met senators, congressmen, mayors, presidents and vice presidents, giving them an air of self-assurance that has stayed with them.

* * *

The governor was such a great friend and mentor to me that his sudden death came as a terrible shock. After all, he had nurtured me and included me in an unbelievably exciting adventure. I'll never recover from the fall-out, nor would I want to. I was awakened at our home in Rochester shortly after midnight on January 26, 1979, with a call from a reporter, who asked me for a statement concerning the governor's death. I could not believe my ears. After all, I had just been with him the week before. He had told me he had been to see a doctor about his heart, but—always the optimist—he showed no concern.

Whenever he complained about what he saw as Happy's extravagances, I thought about his antique car collection (some forty choice vintage models) lined up along the oval driveway in front of the mansion at Pocantico when the family was entertaining. I considered the prestigious art collection stored in the mansion's basement, including "Car Man," a modern sculptural extravaganza by Ernest Trova, a golden figure shaped like a car. I thought of the helicopter summoned to make sure I made the trip from Pocantico to Albany to the little executive golf course near my home (or vice versa) quickly and safely. I recalled Pocantico's golf course and the indoor and outdoor swimming pools, the opulent New York penthouse, the elegant furnishings (both antique and contemporary) in all the Rockefeller residences. I couldn't help but think of the informal art lessons the governor gave me at the mansion in Albany. I could only conclude that the governor had come to resent Happy for her bitterness and her drinking, just as she resented him for his amorous escapades.

* * *

In the years of his political ascendancy, Rockefeller's enemies had feared his liberal influence should he be elected to high national office, a concern that eventually focused on his role as a potential vice presidential candidate. That concern ultimately led to his downfall, in large measure because of a rising tide of conservatism in America.

A letter written to me by Rockefeller on January 18, 1979, shortly before his death, suggests that that concern was unwarranted. I had once asked him to consider the possibility of restructuring the vice presidential role and in his long letter he was explicit about his views—that such a restructuring would be both impossible and undesirable. He wrote: "I have known well all the Vice Presidents since Henry Wallace, and I think it is fair to say that all of them were frustrated. But a Vice President need not be frustrated if he simply accepts, prior to taking the oath of office, that he is assuming a standby position, and that whatever useful purpose he may have will be as a loyal assistant to the President—without any executive power or responsibility in his own name."

He continued: "During the period I was chairman of President Eisenhower's Advisory Committee on Government Organization, between 1952 and 1956, we examined ways in which the role of the then Vice President, Richard Nixon, could be expanded and made more important and useful. After an extensive study, we recommended to President Eisenhower that, both Constitutionally and functionally, this was impossible." Over the next three pages, he explains his reasoning, and concludes: "I therefore recommend not making any major change in the traditional role of the Vice President and the original constitutional concept of the office."

Rockefeller also believed strongly that any candidate for the role must always be selected by the party *after* the presidential nominee had been chosen, so that the nominee would have the final say in determining who his running mate would be. "The President has enough problems to worry about in this really impossible job without having to cope with a recalcitrant or conniving Vice President at his side—which might be the case if the Vice President were chosen separately by the delegates of the party at the Convention, on the basis of political expediency. This could end up in a disaster," he wrote. (See Appendix E, Rockefeller to Rosenbaum Letter, January 18, 1979 for a complete copy of this historically interesting letter.)

★ ★ ★

As many people know, the governor was with his mistress in her Manhattan apartment. During the fatal heart attack she panicked and froze. Perhaps if an ambulance could have been summoned sooner, Nelson Rockefeller might have survived the attack and lived many more years. At the time of his death he was only 70.

Nelson was, of course, the most unforgettable person I've ever met. To this day, I cannot pass Rockefeller Center without getting a lump in my throat.

Chapter 16

"Next Year in Jerusalem"
My First Trip to Israel

In the spring of 1978, during the Passover holiday, I made my first of three trips to Israel. Over the years my friend George Klein, a Republican Jewish leader in Manhattan, had introduced me to various dignitaries from the Israeli government, including Menachem Begin, the prime minister, and my interest in visiting Israel had been growing steadily.

The spark that ignited this trip was the fact that Amy, our oldest daughter, had won a scholarship to Tel Aviv University. I gave Amy permission to go, over her mother's objection, but I was the one who would cry whenever she telephoned home. This was the first time any of our children had been away from home for any length of time, and I was really uncomfortable. Amy, I realized, was in an environment where I had no control. There was good reason to worry. On hearing the news that an Arab suicide bomber had blown up a bus in Amy's neighborhood, killing eleven people, we tried desperately to phone her, but all communication had been cut off. Eventually Amy called, telling us not to worry, that there were soldiers on all the rooftops in the neighborhood. Somehow that wasn't very reassuring.

Judy and I decided to assess the situation ourselves, and to take along the rest of the family. I asked George Klein to notify the Israeli government that we would be on our way shortly. We purchased tickets on El Al, the government-operated airline that had never had a mishap and which was thoroughly guarded whenever it was on the ground at JFK. A last minute strike by El Al personnel resulted in our flying Swiss Air instead, a flight that went as smoothly as a Swiss watch. Our first stop was in Zurich where we were given very comfortable rooms for a few hours' nap. When it was time to board the plane for Israel, we all had to march out on the tarmac where Israeli soldiers armed with Uzis insisted on opening every suitcase and inspecting everything inside. It was a frightening experience for children, and our youngest daughter, Julie, then eight, shed copious tears.

Fourteen hours after take-off from New York City we landed at LOD airport in Tel Aviv at about four in the afternoon, and hired a car to take us to Jerusalem where we had booked rooms at the Jerusalem Hilton. Tel Aviv was hot and sultry, and we were all suffering from deep jet lag, but the temperature in Jerusalem, thanks to the higher altitude, was very pleasant. After a little meal, we went to bed. I had just fallen asleep when the phone rang next to my ear. The deep, resonant voice that greeted me was that of General Moshe Peled, commander of the Israeli Tank Corps and a hero in every war since the founding of the nation in 1948. The general told us he had arranged to have an army captain pick us up the next morning at ten; he would be our escort for a tour of the area.

In Hebrew we use the phrase *Jerusalem shel zahav*, or City of Gold, to describe this gorgeous capital, where the extensive use of white marble gives the city a clean and inviting appearance. The next day, after greeting Amy with hugs and kisses, we visited the Knesset, where we met Shimon Peres, perennial head of the Israeli Labor Party and now Israel's president. I was surprised at the austerity of the government facilities; Peres's office was four plain walls with a desk and a couple of chairs. The Knesset itself is an attractive, relatively small building and the prime minister's office within is extremely spartan by American standards. In glorious contrast, however, are the great Chagall murals that flank the entrance to the auditorium.

Our driver took us to the Dead Sea, where the water is so salty almost nothing sinks; when you swim in those waters you experience amazing buoyancy. While there we gazed up at the ancient hill town of Masada, where in ancient times many Jews in the surrounding coun-tryside were massacred by advancing Roman hordes. When it became clear that those remaining couldn't hold out against the invaders, the

No Room for Democracy

settlers drew lots and killed each other; so history tells us. We also visited Hebron, sacred burial site of our beloved patriarchs, an area that is the scene of so many nasty confrontations between Jews and Arabs. As I walked around some young teenage boys confronted me and asked if I was a Jew or Muslim; I ignored them, but I could feel their hostility.

On this visit, we celebrated a Passover seder at a tank base at Ashkelon. It saddened us to see so many widows, many of them young wives of tank personnel killed in the various wars between Israel, Egypt, Syria and Jordan. Miraculously, Israel had won each of those wars: the War of Independence in 1948; the 1967 war when Israel took control of Jerusalem and made it the nation's capital; the 1974 Yom Kippur War, when General Ariel Sharon outsmarted an Egyptian army that would have been completely obliterated if not for the intervention of the U.S. and Russia.

As we toured the country on an ultramodern highway, we marveled at the sight of Arab tents and goat herders, primitive settlements just off the highway where people were living just as they had centuries ago. Our driver could only speak Hebrew and Amy interpreted for us. We were amazed to discover that the Jordan River, Israel's border with Jordan, is little wider than a good-sized creek. Exploring near Jericho we walked a rough hillside path, our son Matt scuffling along in the manner of most kids his age. Suddenly Matt bent down and picked up a dirt-encrusted object that looked like a flattened piece of gum. On closer inspection it turned out to be a coin, later identified by experts at the Rochester Museum & Science Center as dating from the second temple of King Solomon.

Many Jews devote two full days to celebrate Passover with feasting and prayers. The holiday, of course, celebrates the Exodus, when Moses led the Jews from bondage in the land of the pharaohs and when the Red Sea parted, according to the Old Testament, allowing the Jews to escape, and then suddenly closed, drowning the pursuing Egyptian army. Amy joined us that first day as we visited the Western Wall, where the outer wall of King Solomon's temple stood, the site of perpetual prayer and worship. Tradition dictates that the faithful put notes of supplication in the cracks of the wall, beseeching God to answer their prayers.

We also visited an Arab *souk*, or marketplace, in Jerusalem. Each vendor has his or her own stall from which to sell goods. (Amy had to intercede when I got into an argument with a vendor about the cost of his goods.) The Christian Stations of the Cross were on our itinerary as well, and, of course, we had our photos taken riding camels.

The second day of Passover, the captain assigned by General Peled again came to pick us up in a staff car to take us to another tank base, this one near Jerusalem. On our drive we passed dozens of burnt-out tanks along the roadway. We were taken up to the Golan Heights which form the border between Israel and Syria and which were won by the Israelis in the 1967 war. An armored Syrian division controlling the heights could swoop down on Israel into the essential port city of Haifa, cutting Israel in two, which is why Israel insists on controlling this sensitive area.

We spent the night at Kfar Blum, one of the *kibbutzim* established near the Lebanese border to create a buffer zone between the two countries. Kfar Blum is surrounded by a number of large industrial farms where avocados, clementines, flowers and dates are grown for export. The community is self-sufficient in most respects, and is run in a style that seemed almost communistic to me. Our sense that danger was ever-present here was heightened by the fact that an Uzi-bearing guard was stationed outside our bedroom door—and by the presence of an underground shelter in the center of the kibbutz, a refuge for the community in case of attack.

As we boarded our El Al plane for the return to the States, we were puzzled by a delay in take-off. Finally, we watched in amazement as a red carpet was unfurled and the prime minister, Menachem Begin, and his entourage entered our plane. They soon were ensconced in the bubble of our 747 and we became airborne. During the flight, I had a note delivered to the prime minister saying that I was a friend of George Klein; he responded by inviting me to come up and visit with him. We had an interesting conversation about the security of Israel.

For the vast majority of Jews, a trip to Israel is a deeply emotional experience. On arrival, as we approached LOD Airport near Tel Aviv, the

Israeli national anthem was played on board the plane and everyone sang the song in Hebrew. If I had hair, it would have stood straight up. Even before we left the States, I had already experienced a sense of great pride in what my people had accomplished, not just in war against an overwhelming foe, but also in the progress that this tiny country has achieved in the arts, sciences, and other endeavors important to mankind in general.

As our plane left the ground on our return flight, I was totally overwhelmed by my feelings—my people had made the desert bloom. Years before, when my friend John Shakespeare, a Christian, met me in Manhattan after his first visit to Israel, he had greeted me with these words: "Rah, rah, Jews!" I couldn't agree with him more.

* * *

My Jewishness is so deeply imbedded in my soul that it can't be contained, nor would I ever want it to be. I'm proud of the fact that all my children are deeply observant, thanks to Judy who makes sure we never forget to honor the holy days. Our grandson Michael Steklof may become a rabbi, and another grandson, Jacob Rosenbaum, seems headed in the same direction.

I love the sound of Yiddish, that flow of language that surrounded me in my childhood. It's warm, colorful, exotic, and frank. I regret that I'm not fluent, but a fair amount has stayed with me, and bursts forth sometimes when I least expect it.

One of those times occurred as I was being interviewed by network reporter Chris Wallace during the 1984 Republican National Convention in Houston, a moment in history when the conservative wing of the party was in the ascendancy. Mollee Kruger, columnist for the *Jewish Week*, made the most of my outburst in a column headlined "Unholy Writ." She told her readers about how "moderate New York delegate Richard Rosenbaum used words like *farshtoonken* (smelly) and *farblonjet* (lost) to express his feelings toward the ultra-conservative party platform." She concluded her column with this bit of amusing doggerel:

When, in the passage of human events,
A Jew is surrounded by masses
Who cause him to feel he's an alien breed,
A déjà vu over him passes.
He hastens to Yiddish to try to express
Frustration and sheer disbelief,
Especially when there's a question at stake
Of "where is the flanken?" *(or beef).*
And poor Mister Rosenbaum, back to the wall,
Engulfed in the blandness of Texas,
A platform with Moral Majority tahm,
Reverted to ancient reflexes,
Resorted to Yiddish, a breath of fresh air,
Prime time and of network dimension.
(Who'd ever expect mameloshen *to grace*
this Helms-Falwell-Schlafly convention?)

Tahm = plainness
Mameloshen = "down-home" storytelling

I love using Yiddish words. Sometimes this gets me into trouble, as it did on the occasion of one presidential reception during the Ford administration. President Ford was entertaining Yitzhak Rabin, then prime minister of Israel, and Judy and I were invited to join the dinner guests at the White House and I had memorized a welcoming phrase in Hebrew.

As we stood patiently waiting in the receiving line for our turn to shake hands with the prime minister, I practiced over and over again my Hebrew welcome. Everything went fine, until—having greeted Rabin in flawless Hebrew—I took two steps to the left where the president was waiting, his hand outstretched. "Good evening, Mr. Rosenbaum," I said to President Ford, and then flushed to where the roots of my hair once had been. What a *mashugina* I can be!

No Room for Democracy

Chapter 17

"Mr. Clean" Comes Home

In the summer of 1977, I pulled up stakes and came home to Rochester. My return was heralded in the local papers with a big headline and photo: "Mr. Clean is back in town!" I'd finally had my fill of politics; after 15 years, I was ready for a new chapter. Some of my friends thought I would be depressed about leaving the fray, but I really wasn't. My attitude has always been, "Go for the new adventure."

Since my calendar at the moment was empty and because I needed some thinking time, I took the family out West for a few weeks, making the circuit of the great tourist sites—the Grand Canyon, Las Vegas, Hoover Dam—and eventually we found ourselves back home in Penfield in our old house on Denonville Ridge. I had asked our builder Ted Jablonski to renovate the whole house and property, and I told him, "Ted, when I come back, I want to see the American flag flying from the flagpole in our front yard." As we drove in to the driveway, we were greeted by the Stars and Stripes.

As for my next career move, returning to the law seemed to be my most likely option. I did not have to quit my seat on the Republican National Committee. I'd interviewed with several big New York City law firms and I'd had offers, but I had declined them because I knew Judy didn't want to live in Manhattan. She was ready to return to Rochester, and that was fine with me. The problem was: what was I going to do next? I'd just finished five years with the governor, had won a modicum of fame in my own right, and here I was walking the streets looking for a job, just like a kid out of law school.

One Saturday I wandered up Main Street in Rochester and went into the offices of Goldstein, Goldman, Underberg & Kessler, and found my old friend Alan Underberg (later the firm's senior partner) sitting at his desk. We had a high old time reminiscing, and I walked out with a deal. They offered me $75,000 a year and my name in the firm's title, always a good ego-booster. I told Alan I'd get back to him in a month. A week or so later, Alan called and invited me to a party the firm was having for some members of the bar. I went to the party, circulated around, and noticed there was a fair size contingent from Rochester's biggest law firm, Nixon, Hargrave, Devans & Doyle (now Nixon Peabody). Nixon, Hargrave at that time was relatively small, a blue-blood firm, conservative, quietly wealthy from its business ties to Eastman Kodak, Bausch & Lomb, the city's powerful newcomer Xerox (sprung from the old Haloid Corporation), and estate work for the millionaire families who had made their fortunes in Rochester.

A few days later, I had a call from Bill Morris, a senior partner at Nixon. "Some of us were having lunch the other day," he said, "and we were talking about you, wondering what you were going to do. So, what *are* you going to do?" I said, "Bill, I don't know, but whatever it is, I have to do it pretty fast!" Bill set up a *sub rosa* meeting with the two of us and a Nixon associate at the Drake Hotel in New York City. When one of the Nixon lawyers said, "We're prepared to pay you $100,000 for openers," I knew I would take the offer, not only for the money but for the association with this highly respected firm.

However, I felt really guilty about backing out of my tentative deal with Underberg. The fact that we'd had a sort of a gentleman's agreement and that I was breaking it really troubled me. I finally called Alan to tell him I was going with Nixon. Almost immediately his old partner Harry Goldman, then the presiding justice at the appellate division, called me. "Dick, are you sure you want to do this?" he said. "If you don't get $100,000, you're a fool," he added. "Judge, I respect your opinion," I said, "but I'm no fool. I've decided to go with Nixon."

The meeting at the Drake Hotel led to another meeting at the Rochester home of Julian (Joe) Atwater with a large number of the other Nixon partners. I recall saying facetiously to some of the fellows in attendance,

"Don't you guys have a real office?" At that meeting, someone asked if I had ever done anything that might embarrass the firm. I countered by asking whether the firm had ever done anything to embarrass me. Mike Tomaino, another partner, later told me he was impressed with the self-confidence that verbal exchange demonstrated.

I've already mentioned the fact that I have a real talent for embarrassing myself, and I did it again on my very first day at Nixon. I'd visited the firm several days earlier and had been introduced around by Joe Atwater. This morning, my first on the job, I pulled into my designated parking spot, and locked the car—with the keys inside. Good news: On looking around, I was relieved to see that one of the car's back windows was partially open. Imagine the sight that caught Bill Morris's eye that morning when he came to work: Rosenbaum, all six feet two of him, his rear end and legs protruding from the back window of his Buick trying to retrieve his car keys. Morris probably thought, "Where did I ever find this guy?"

I was the first partner to come in laterally, without having worked my way up the food chain. At that time, new hires at Nixon were on probation for one year. In that sedate atmosphere, I must have seemed like the proverbial bull in a china shop; I'm a big guy with a loud laugh, I like to talk and joke, and I like to whistle. (The only rebuke I ever had at the firm was from Jerry Kennedy, a swell guy, who met me barreling cheerfully down the hall one day. He muttered, "No whistling in the halls," as he passed, and walked on, smiling.) Somehow, we all managed to survive. About four months after my arrival, there was a knock on my office door and in walked Bill Morris and Dave Hoffberg (a young partner whose sister I used to date at Cornell). They came to tell me my probation was over and I was a full member of the firm.

My first work with the firm was arguing cases before the court of appeals in Albany and I enjoyed that greatly. However, my forte became bringing in bond business, an area in which Nixon, Hargrave at that time had a problem. In order to get bond work, a law firm had to be listed in a "Red Book"; in order to be listed in that book, you had to have handled bond work—a real "Catch 22" situation. I was able to get some small Industrial Development Agency bond work that got us a Red

Book listing, and that was the start of what would become a thriving bond business for Nixon.

As a result of my political connections, I was also bringing in other lucrative work. About this time, a scandal broke concerning certain savings and loan institutions whose names still resonate among those unlucky enough to have entrusted them with their money. When some of these banks went belly-up, the Federal Deposit Insurance Corporation (FDIC) stepped in and demanded reform and oversight. Here was a perfect role for me. My old friend Bill Seidman, a buddy from the Jerry Ford days, was heading the FDIC operation in Washington. Surely he would see the wisdom of appointing Nixon, Hargrave as lead counsel to one of the banks working their way out from under. At the urging of my partner Harry Trueheart, I took a team of the firm's lawyers down to meet with Bill, and before long we got the job of overseeing the reforms at the Bank of New England. (In truth, it was the Nixon lawyers who secured the job that day, while Bill and I spent a couple of hours at a nearby watering hole, swapping stories and having a few laughs. As a catalyst, I'm not bad.)

Any hardworking lawyer who reads this may resent the deal I had at Nixon: no time sheet! I have a different way of working, that's all there is to it. Look, if I can make a fifteen-minute phone call that saves a client fifteen million dollars, what am I going to do? Charge them for the time it took to make the phone call? Forget it! That's why I love the firm so. To paraphrase Frank Sinatra, they let me "do it my way."

***

In 1980 I told the partners that I was interested in running for governor. A skeptic may think the partners would have balked at my proposal, that in running for such a high office I would take too much time away from the firm. That's not the way it works. The partners knew, as I did, that in order to get business, you have to be a player. By supporting me in my run for the gubernatorial nomination, they helped place me at the center of the action. I was expanding my contacts, getting my name out there—and all of this helped the firm. The business poured in.

Here's an example. I'd made a friend of Mike Blake, the Republican chairman of Suffolk County on Long Island. "Mike," I said to him one day, "you've got a lot of development going on out there. I'd like to talk to you about getting some bond work." He said, "Let me bring in the head of the IDA (the Suffolk County Industrial Development Agency) from Deer Park" (one of the smaller towns on the Island). We talked, and he sent us a pretty good piece of business. This was the beginning of Nixon's work on Long Island, which grew to include better bond work, general obligation bonds used to float various projects. During my first year soliciting bond work, I brought in fees totaling seven million dollars, the details of which were then completed by other lawyers in the firm.

I was amused to learn that my colleagues were calling me "the Rainmaker." The firm never gave me assignments; I just had a free rein. I had a nice corner office and my secretary even had an office. I conducted seminars on government with the young lawyers, and I never complained about the income ceiling that was in effect in those days. I just wanted to be left alone to do my thing, and the results won the firm's respect.

In January 1981 the firm merged with Green, Sharpless & Greenstein, a small law firm from New York City, while keeping the Nixon name. I was a big supporter of that move, because I knew the importance of expanding our market. New York had the potential to be a big profit center—and it was. December was always the time of a big work push; bond deals have to be completed by the end of the year because of tax implications. If you have fifty bond deals to complete in a hurry, you have to hump. At that time, the Rochester office would send lawyers, clerks and secretaries to New York City to help get the work done. I'd walk into the office after a concert or party like some potentate, and say "How ya doin'?" I didn't know what the heck they were doing. My job was to get the business, not work out the details, and to put out fires. More than once I felt not like a potentate, but like the guy with the scoop who follows the elephant.

After the merger, the home firm in Rochester realized it had a tiger by the tail. The New York lawyers didn't have the same point of view as the Rochesterians—they wanted to be paid for what they did; no salary limits for them. This caused some hard feelings, and eventually forced Nixon to initiate a bonus system based on work units. As I've said, that ceiling didn't bother me. I knew I could make more money in Manhattan, but I didn't want to live that way, I didn't want my kids to grow up there, and I wanted to keep my wife happy.

The great thing about Nixon, to this day, is that it has great people who can handle almost anything. That's why it's now one of the top fifty law firms in America, with offices in nineteen cities. The work product coming out of Nixon is as great as you'll find anywhere in America—and that's not hyperbole. Those guys are *good* lawyers, and I've always had a real love affair with the firm.

Chapter 18

Rosenbaum for Governor

The year was 1980, and the political bug that had gotten under my skin when I was just a college kid apparently had insinuated itself right into my DNA. While I thoroughly enjoyed my work at Nixon, Hargrave, that old itch for the rough-and-tumble came back and I just couldn't scratch it away. My work with Rocky had given me an insider's view of the state's highest office, and that's where my sights increasingly were turned. I'd watched Rocky perform his duties, and said to myself, "Hell, I can do that job."

As an example of my eagerness to run for governor, at the 1980 Republican National Convention I had a severe attack of foot-in-mouth disease. I shrugged off a young reporter who kept asking for an interview. She looked so young I really didn't take her seriously. When she persisted, I invited her to sit in on a press breakfast, thinking I was doing her a big favor. Over bagels and sweet rolls the next morning, I was embarrassed to learn she'd been assigned by the Associated Press out of Albany to cover me. (Bad move on the part of RMR.) In a fit of guilt, I thanked her for being patient and said, hoping to mollify her, that she wasn't at all like that persistent, obnoxious political reporter from Albany, Dave Shaffer. A minute later I discovered that she, Mary Fiess, was in fact Mrs. Dave Shaffer. An hour later, Mary came to tell me she had just talked with her husband. "He said he feels the same way about you!" We both laughed (although my laugh may have been a bit weak). Both Mary and Dave were fine reporters and we remain friends to this day.

I knew very well that working to get the Republican nomination would put me over the high hurdles and put enormous pressure on my family, as well. Judy and the kids were getting used to seeing me at the supper table again and I knew they weren't going to be happy about still another disruption in our family life. The years with Rocky had been tough on them. After months of deliberating privately, it was Rockefeller who helped me make the decision to go for it. As far back as 1976, at the conclusion of the Republican convention, Rocky had slapped me on the back and said, "Dick, you've done one helluva job for the President [Ford] from one end of the country to the other. I'm for you for governor in 1978."

I'd cleared the way with my partners at Nixon, Hargrave, who realized the connections I would forge across the state and the frequent mention of the firm's name on TV and in the newspapers might well be advantageous. Raising the money I'd need was another matter. I figured I'd have to raise several million dollars to mount and run a campaign. With one kid in college and three more approaching college age, I was really worried about that; I couldn't afford to spend the bulk of my own hard-earned dough with all those tuition bills looming.

I had money on my mind when I arrived at the Rochester airport one morning and ran into an old friend, Fedele Scutti, a local car dealer and a big investor. I told Del I was seriously thinking about going for the party's nomination for governor and asked if I could count on his help. Without blinking an eye, he said, "How much can I give?" When I told him I thought the limit was $45,000, he brought out his checkbook and handed me a check for the full amount right then and there. (When I returned to the office I researched and found that legally Del could have given me $52,000. I have a pretty good supply of *chutzpah*, but I didn't have enough of it to call him and ask for the last $7,000.) Del is a diamond in the rough if there ever was one—his cursing is legendary—but he has a heart as big as the world. His generous gesture made me think raising money for my campaign would be easy. I soon learned the cold reality that it would, in fact, be very hard.

Of course, I wasn't the only one looking to be the party's choice to beat Hugh Carey, then said to be seeking a third term as governor. The competition from upstate was tough, beginning with my old Hobart classmate Edward (Ned) Regan, then state comptroller and a Buffalo resident. Other upstaters in the early running were congressman Jack Kemp, a former Buffalo Bills football star who later ran for vice president, and state assembly minority leader Jim Emery from Geneseo. The big-money guy who worried us all was suave Lew Lehrman of Manhattan, an owner of the Rite Aid drugstore chain and a political newcomer with strong ties to the Conservative Party. (Lehrman, who had courted the downstate Jewish community assiduously throughout the campaign, shocked everyone after the 1984 election when he converted to Catholicism, influenced by Bill Buckley.)

Once I'd made the decision to run, I quickly developed a top-notch team of advisors. Heading the list was Barber Conable, the influential congressman (and later World Bank chief) from the upstate town of Alexander. When Barber agreed to be my finance chairman, I couldn't have been more honored and delighted; his reputation for wisdom strengthened by old-time honesty was legendary. Also working on my behalf was a committee of high-powered executives—Amory Houghton of Corning Glass; John Whitehead, co-chair and senior partner at Goldman Sachs; Dan Roblin, CEO of Roblin Industries in Buffalo; and Tom Gosnell, CEO of Lawyers Cooperative Publishing Co. in Rochester, to name just a few.

For help with nuts-and-bolts strategizing, I hired John Sears, the Washington lawyer and political consultant who had been Reagan's guru (and my old adversary back in '76 when I supported Ford over Reagan). Sears would come up from Washington and stay at our house, which quickly turned into "control central." John was then, maybe still is, a tough character. I'd pick him up at the airport and drive him to my home; after some small talk, he'd head for the basement where we'd set up an office. At that time, John was chain-smoking three packs of cigarettes a day, sending up a poisonous cloud that soon overwhelmed the exhaust system. Finally Judy objected, and John moved downtown to the Strathallan Hotel.

To tell the truth, I never really understood John. He never spoke about his family. Our daughter Jill, who since became a veterinarian, graduated from Cornell that year, and John's son was in her class. I don't, however, remember seeing John at the graduation. As the campaign developed, so did my problems with John. He'd miss important strategy sessions, and sometimes he'd simply disappear for days at a time. Still, what a guy! He could stay up all night, drink close to a fifth of Scotch, and the next morning you'd think he'd gone to bed at eight o'clock with only a cup of warm milk inside him. I was so worried about his health that I privately gave him about three months to live, and thought, "I'd better get him while he's still alive." In fact, John's still going strong, though how he does it, I'll never know.

After working behind the scenes for several months, testing the waters, the time finally came to make my public announcement at a campaign kick-off in Rochester: February 2, 1982, a really unfortunate piece of timing. Early in December, shortly after I'd picked the date, my mother called from Florida to tell me my beloved father had had a massive heart attack and had died. I should have known then that that shadow would darken my life for months and years to come.

Nevertheless, we had planned a grand event at Rochester's Genesee Plaza/Holiday Inn, and friends from all over the state had called in advance to say, "We want to be there with you." The Dixieland band was polishing up its brass, the banners emblazoned with "Rosie's the One" were unfurled, the press was at the ready. A chartered plane was on stand-by to whisk us off to similar events in Manhattan, Albany, Buffalo and Syracuse as soon as the hometown celebration was over. We went to bed, confident that everything was under control.

And then—disaster. A sudden storm barreled down on us from Canada the likes of which I have not seen since. The wind howled like a banshee, keeping me awake throughout the dark night; by morning, all area airports were closed. At 6 a.m., a group of sheriff's deputies arrived to escort me from our suburban home to downtown Rochester; the 20-minute drive took an hour and a half. Barber Conable, who was to introduce me, never made it in from Washington and our perennial

No Room for Democracy

county congressman, my friend Frank Horton, did the job instead. The press, the band and the balloons were there, but the crowd was a fraction of what it would have been. Still, considering the weather, I was surprised to see several hundred supporters, cheering and clapping when I entered the room.

Among my supporters that morning was Andy Wolfe, editor of a group of suburban newspapers and a man with considerable political clout in upstate New York. Andy watched as still another friend commiserated with me on the storm's bad timing, and he heard me reply with a grin, "No big tuna!" (I have no idea where that expression came from that morning, and I've never used it since). He wrote a dynamite editorial supporting my candidacy, noting that the coolness with which I'd handled this crisis suggested that the state would be in good hands under Governor Rosenbaum. He headlined his editorial: "No Big Tuna!"

Forget the idea of a whirlwind statewide tour; the winds assured that the plane I'd chartered wasn't going anywhere. We finally made our New York City announcement a week later, but by then the news was stale. The press showed up and gave me some good coverage, but it was four or five reporters, not forty. The next week, when the weather had settled, we finally made the rounds of the state's major cities.

Throughout my campaign I emphasized the need to create a federal economic development plan for New York State. The first wave of Sun Belt migration was well underway, and Rochester, along with cities all over the state, was hurting. I made my case in a white paper that I called "Social Security for our Aging Cities." In it I outlined a radical new urban public policy that would include a federal municipal bond agency that could offer guaranteed no- or low-interest loans to qualifying cities, as well as preferential treatment for aging cities in obtaining government contracts. I campaigned for gun controls, emphasizing the need for better crime prevention methods and stricter laws regarding punishment; at that time, all four candidates advocated the death penalty as the ultimate deterrent. I broke with my opponents in rejecting a movement to reduce state taxes (I believed such a move was unrealistic in the current economic climate) and in being strongly pro-choice on the abortion issue.

For almost two years I stumped the state, making many friends (maybe causing a few headaches in certain quarters) and operating as I always do—full steam ahead. I had an impeccable upstate team and a great organization downstate, including strong support within Jewish, Italian, Black and Hispanic communities who traditionally voted Democratic. My own county, of course, was strongly behind me, as was downstate Bronx County and several other small counties, all of which encouraged me from the start.

I also hoped to win the backing of the delegates from Onondaga County (Syracuse) and its leader, Norm Rothschild. As state chair, I had helped Norm win his appointment as head of the New York State Fair. This was no mean feat, since then-lieutenant governor Malcolm Wilson had had his own candidate for the job, an upstate farmer by the name of Johnson who perhaps was a more logical choice. This was payback time, in my opinion, and I lobbied the Onondaga delegation at least half a dozen times. As the months rolled on, I knew I had my work cut out for me, even though I could count on the support of about a dozen county chairmen.

Among my many endorsements was one from former president Gerald Ford. Some weeks later Ford was questioned by a reporter about my standing in the polls. He assured his questioner that I hadn't yet hit full steam on the campaign trail. "Rosenbaum's in second gear in a three-gear car," he quipped.

As the GOP convention date approached, another candidate surfaced: Paul Curran, a popular Manhattan lawyer and a former federal prosecutor, who had strong backing in Manhattan and Long Island. Curran also had staunch backing from Malcolm Wilson, the state's former lieutenant governor. (Frankly, since I had been a strong supporter of Malcolm in his fight for the gubernatorial nomination in 1974, I was deeply disappointed in his defection from my cause, a defection he made up for in 1994.) Curran's entry into the race siphoned off delegates from all the other candidates and stopped my momentum in its tracks. Now it became a struggle not only to gain more support, but to hold on to the support I'd worked so hard to win.

No Room for Democracy

* * *

A week before the convention, I waited all night for a phone call from Rothschild in Syracuse to let me know the results of the Onondaga delegation's caucus vote; he'd promised to let me know the results as soon as the balloting was over. The next morning, as I was checking into the Hilton, the bad news came. The caucus had thrown its gubernatorial support to Lehrman and had supported me unanimously for state attorney general, a post in which I'd never had any interest. The support of the Onondaga delegation made the difference in having enough support to automatically enter the primary struggle.

As I have often said, "In politics there are no true friends, only shifting alliances." I guess that statement depends on your definition of the word "friend." It turned out that I'd been undone by the work of state senator Tarky Lombardi, Jr., the highly respected member of a Syracuse family, who had led the Lehrman raid on the Onondaga delegation. To say I was keenly disappointed is to put it mildly. I had tried everything I could think of to court primary support, including hosting a weekend in the Catskills at Grossinger's for all the county chairmen.

By the second week in June, 1982, when 450 GOP state committee members met at the Sheraton Centre in Manhattan to pick the party's gubernatorial candidate, they were met by a noisy claque shouting at the top of their lungs, "We want Rosie!" The Democrats already had narrowed their gubernatorial choice to two men: lieutenant governor Mario Cuomo and New York City mayor Ed Koch. Four of us were still in the running for the GOP nomination: Lehrman, Emery, Rosenbaum and Curran, the newcomer. Convention rules were clear: to win the party's endorsement, a candidate must garner 50.1% of the delegate vote. It was obvious to all that trouble lay ahead. I needed 25% of the vote just to qualify for the primary, and the going got tough.

Simmering just under the surface of this fermenting political stew was an effort to convince me to drop out of the gubernatorial race and run instead for a seat in the U.S. Senate. I continually had to fend off well-meaning people who urged me to change course, but I knew that if a candidate gives even a glimmer of interest in some other office, he can kiss bye-bye to the office he *really* wants.

Traditionally, candidates do not appear at the voting place, but remain sequestered in their hotel suites with their campaign manager and a few supporters, where they receive frequent reports by phone. After the first round of voting, I was about five percent short of the twenty-five percent I needed and I began lobbying fiercely to make up the deficit. Suddenly came a ray of hope. The Suffolk County delegation from Long Island, led by my old friend Mike Blake, decided to switch its votes to me. I was now within one percent of the votes I needed.

Now the horse-trading began in earnest. A call came in from Dan Mahoney, at that time the Conservative Party's chairman from Manhattan, offering me the party's endorsement if I would run for the U.S. Senate. With the support of both the GOP and the conservatives, I knew I would be nominated—but only for a Senate seat. By this time, I knew I was the underdog in the gubernatorial race. Worse than that, I was out of money (I'd only raised $800,000) and I was out of votes. I told Mahoney I'd sleep on it and give him my decision the next morning when the delegates reconvened. Believe me when I tell you that after an effort like the one I'd put out, my ego urged me to grasp at an offer like a senatorial nomination.

I didn't sleep much that night. Instead I met with my long-suffering wife, my daughter Jill, my advisors (including Sears and Joel Barken, a staff member I affectionately referred to as "Barken-up-the-wrong tree"), and two of my law partners, Bob Witmer and Tom Clement. Somehow, I couldn't get enthusiastic about the senatorial idea, and when my son Matt phoned from college and said, "Dad, if you do this we'll never see you anymore," my decision became clear.

The next morning, at a hastily convened news conference, I announced my decision: no go. I'd served as a leader in our county legislature and hadn't really enjoyed it. Like Rudy Giuliani, my personality doesn't lend itself to participating in long deliberations and compromises. In the final hours of the convention, I addressed the gathering and vowed absolute support for the ticket; I heard the place erupt with cheers; Ham Fish, the congressman from the era of FDR, called out "I'll

No Room for Democracy

do everything to see you make it to the Senate." At the final tally, Lou Lehrman emerged the winner, having spent a record-breaking $5.7 million to achieve his goal.

Sure, I was disappointed. For two years, I'd worked my tail off promoting a plan to strengthen the state, a plan I believed in wholeheartedly. I'd marched the long road, and had a good time doing it. But I've always believed that our party is bigger and more important than any single individual, so I lost, I hope, gracefully. I was proud of the effort I had made. I'd been "the man in the arena," to borrow one of Teddy Roosevelt's favorite phrases, and I went down swinging and with a lot of respect from my colleagues. As Ron Starkweather, then Monroe County's GOP leader, said at the time: "Dick is a fighter, but he's a unifier, too."

As I left the party's gala wind-up dinner (not so gala for me), I realized that once again it was time to regroup. Before leaving for the plane the next morning, I made a phone call that would change my life in ways I couldn't then imagine. As it turned out, the next chapter in the Rosenbaum story was about to begin.

Chapter 19

Getting Integrated

The phone call I made the morning after the state GOP convention in Manhattan—when I lost my bid for the party's gubernatorial nomination—would have ramifications for me and my family far beyond my expectations. This was the first in a number of similar calls I would make to those who had supported my gubernatorial campaign with both money and time. In failing to win the GOP nomination I felt I had let these people down and I wanted to thank them personally for their help.

That very first call went to Jay Zises, executive vice chairman of the board of directors of the Manhattan financial services firm Integrated Resources, Inc., who, with his brother Sig (Selig) had contributed generously to my campaign fund. I'd been introduced to the Zises brothers by my friend George Klein, a prominent Manhattan real estate developer, a Republican power broker and a devout Jew who seems to spend more time in temple than in his office. One day during the campaign, George said, "Dick, there are some people I want you to meet. Their name is Zises, they have a huge business, and they're very successful. I think they'll like you."

We hopped in George's limo and drove down to 666 Third Avenue, just off 42nd Street, and took the elevator up. As George and I walked past the receptionist into their office, here's what we saw: Jay Zises, lying on a couch with his chin on his hand, wearing a beat-up, moth-eaten old sweater and an old pair of corduroys. Sitting next to him was Siggy, who I knew had the reputation for being an absolutely unmitigated financial genius, dressed the same way. This was just the style of a couple of brilliant fellows who I came to greatly respect. It was as far from the Brooks Brothers world as Gus's Pickles in lower Manhattan is to Zabar's, the uptown, upscale gourmet market. I thought to myself in wonderment, "And these guys are running a huge, successful corporation?!"

After some small talk, the brothers got right to the point. "As a candidate for governor, what is your economic program?" Siggy asked. I stuttered along for a while, spouting some platitudes, until Jay broke in: "You don't know what the hell you're talking about, do you?" And I replied, "As a matter of fact, I don't." We all laughed uproariously, and from that day on it was a love affair. The Zises finally had found a politician who admitted he didn't know what he was talking about. From then on, they went to most of my fund-raising events in Manhattan, and on many occasions they passed along another $5,000.

Siggy had founded Integrated Resources in 1972 when he was about thirty. The company sold financial products—shallow shelters—that took advantage of the then-current tax code. Their products included insurance, business partnerships, land, oil, gas, real estate and shopping centers, which the company would buy, package and sell to investors. At that time, Integrated Resources was a real money-machine. The brothers had pulled together a coterie of very smart young lawyers (I'd say ninety percent of them Jewish) from top New York law firms who knew how to put the products together, and a group of about 4,500 smart salesmen to market them.

The morning after the campaign ended, it was a chastened Rosenbaum who phoned their office. "Jay," I said, referring to my campaign for governor, "I'm sorry, but this is one investment that's not going to pay off. I tried hard, but I just couldn't make it happen." Graciously, Jay told me he'd had a good time following my progress and he had no regrets; this was the first time he'd ever been thanked for any of his numerous political contributions, he said. Now that the campaign was over, how would I like to take a chunk of Integrated's business back to my law firm? Those were the sweetest words I'd heard in the last two years. I scheduled a time when I could bring a couple of Nixon, Hargrave tax lawyers from our New York office to meet with the brothers. We walked out of the office that day with a retainer agreement for $60,000, small change now, but a rather substantial amount at the time—and a foot in the door.

About three months later, Jay called and said, "How would you like to join our board of directors? We need a person with some political savvy on board." I said, "Jay, I'd love to, but I don't really have a clue about what you guys do." "Don't worry, we'll teach you," he said. At their office a few days later, I picked up a huge stack of executive summaries describing their work and started reading them on the plane back to Rochester. I continued to peruse them carefully, with Nixon partners Joe Atwater and Tom Clement helping me decipher the small print.

Soon I was fascinated. The financial atmosphere in New York City was electric in the eighties. So much money was floating around it was like confetti. Integrated had business everywhere, and a large sales force. The composition of its seven-member board also intrigued me. Sig held the top spot, Jay chaired the executive committee, and then there were three guys who were as Waspy as you could get, including lawyer Henry Clay, a descendent of *the* Henry Clay; Struve Hensel, former undersecretary of the Navy; and John Ellis, from the silk-stocking investment firm Blythe Eastman Dillon. I would become the seventh member of a board shrewdly developed to emphasize integrity and credibility (and to soften its richly Jewish nature).

The contrast in the board members' styles at times made board meetings very entertaining to me. If trouble was brewing, Jay often would use Yiddish to reply to a question asked by a Waspy board member. I remember him saying once, "If this doesn't work out, we'll be *chub in drerd* (in deep do-do)." How I'd laugh! It was so incongruous, I just couldn't keep a straight face, especially when I realized that at least three of the board members, including the one who'd asked the question, had no idea what Jay was saying.

I dove into the work like a shark. It was really interesting to me, and I was learning and learning. One day Siggy said to me, "You know, you're the only board member who works hard for his pay. Good job!" I said, "Well, I like to know what I'm doing, especially where big money's concerned." Siggy then said, "I'm going to go to Israel next week with our oil man from Denver, Jack Rule, to look at some oil leases. I'd like you to go with me." I asked Judy what she thought about it and she said, "You love those guys. Go."

What a trip—first-class all the way! We flew El Al, and sat up in the 747's luxurious little 12-seat "bubble" with Prime Minister Rabin's wife, where we enjoyed delicious food and beverages from the mahogany bar. In Tel Aviv, a limo was waiting at the airport to take us to our suite at the opulent King David Hotel in Jerusalem. My room overlooked the old city and every night when Arabs were called to prayer, chills ran up my spine at the haunting sound. I was sobered by the sight of the bullet holes on the outside wall just below my window, a chilling reminder of the 1967 war between Israel and a number of Arab nations.

Sig had scheduled meetings almost every day—and parties almost every night. It was a crazy circus, all the time. He did reserve some time for sightseeing. One day in the market, we came across a young Arab offering camel rides. I was the one who had to ride the camel. As I climbed awkwardly off the beast's back, the driver kissed my bald head, a sight that sent Siggy into gales of laughter. "That means you're engaged, you know!" he chortled. What could I do? As we drove away, I called back to the Arab, "Don't forget to write!"—and once again Siggy broke into hysterics. As for the oil leases that had been the reason for the trip, we passed on them all, although we spent a couple of days in meetings in Tel Aviv and in Lebanon. We returned on El Al in the bubble again. At our stopover in London, we tried for seats on the Concorde when our own flight was delayed. "You're too late buying tickets," said the airline representative. No wonder the Concorde went out of business. The airline lost more than $10,000 that day by refusing to let the three of us buy tickets.

The day after our return, Sig called me into his office and said, "We'd like to have you come to work for the company full time. It looks as though the tax laws may be forced to change, and I need somebody I trust who can counsel me." I said, "Siggy, there are a dozen reasons why I can't do that. To begin with, my wife would never stand for it. She

No Room for Democracy

doesn't want to live in New York." Siggy said: "I'm going to give you an offer in writing. Show it to your wife; if she still feels that way, no problem, you're still part of the family." I showed his letter to Judy who took one look at it and said, "You have to take this offer." I did, and became executive vice president of Integrated Resources, Inc., director of the firm's public relations and special counsel to the chairman.

I had a great salary, a huge office right next to the chairman's, and, during my first year, a studio apartment in the U.N. tower, where I met any number of dignitaries, both foreign and domestic. On my floor in the tower there was an indoor swimming pool and a workout room. The first day on the job, I heard music from the street; opening the window, I saw a band playing on the corner. I remember thinking to myself, "Here I am, in my own apartment in Manhattan. I've finally made it to the major leagues."

Siggy knew I'd miss my family, so we arranged that I'd leave Manhattan on Thursday afternoon and be home in time for dinner. I'd spend all day Friday at Nixon rainmaking (I was still of counsel to the firm), and be back in the office at Integrated by 10 on Monday morning. As Judy said, "This will take care of our kids," who in those days—with Jill in veterinary school, Matt in law school, and Julie about to enter law school—required a sizeable chunk of my income. (Our oldest child, Amy, a teacher, was already out of college, and I missed my visits with her at Hartford University; she was, and still is, a wonderful daughter.) A special perk of life at Integrated was the business seminars the company scheduled for up to a thousand attendees (spouses invited) in attractive places like the Napa Valley and Hawaii, with lots of time off for sightseeing, golf, and fine dining.

Just before Christmas in 1985, Phil Cohen, Integrated's comptroller, stopped by my office to tell me that Sig and Jay wanted me to move into Sterling Plaza, a residential complex at the corner of 42nd Street and Second Avenue where the company owned an apartment. At first, I resisted; I was used to my comfortable, convenient life at the U.N. tower, where every day an afternoon tea was served with all the trimmings. (Actually, I rarely attended, but the idea that I could attend had its appeal.) Phil handed me a set of keys and convinced me to check it out. I walked over to check out the apartment and loved it. (Sterling Plaza, by the way, was owned by Fred Wilpon, owner of the New York Mets. To this day, Fred remains a friend, and still gets me World Series tickets. At the time, the Mets' first baseman Keith Hernandez also lived at Sterling Plaza; whenever I saw him, he was usually accompanied by a beautiful woman, not always the same one.)

While I was enthusiastic about the move, the apartment was unfurnished—and I was just about to leave for a two-week vacation. No problem: the company hired a decorator who asked me what style of furnishings I liked. "Country French," I told her (although I knew very little about it), and left town. When I returned, the transformation was complete. The nice kitchen with picture windows overlooking Second Avenue was lost on me, since I never ate lunch at home and rarely dinner; I did eat breakfast in the little breakfast nook. The living room was double the normal size, the two large bedrooms had balconies and there were two bathrooms and a powder room. A very nice added benefit was the fact that the company paid for the services of both a laundress and a cleaning woman. Not long after moving in I initiated a short-lived Monday night poker game. The tradition ended the night that a table, overloaded with the food I'd ordered in, collapsed. What a mess! The next day I had the company carpenter come in and reinforce the table, which to this day serves me quite well in my Florida house.

A while later, Integrated sold that apartment for more than a million dollars, and I moved ten blocks north to La Triomphe, a building at the corner of 59th Street and Second Avenue. While not quite as opulent, this apartment had windows overlooking the Hudson River and the tramline which links Roosevelt Island to Manhattan. Every morning I would spend thirty minutes on the NordicTrack trainer while watching the tram riders on their way to the city. My walk to work was a little longer now, but I often caught up with Paul Voelker, an old friend who was then head of the Federal Reserve and who was walking my way, and we had interesting talks about the economy.

At work, I was in my element. Some of the brightest, most interesting people I had ever met also had offices on the coveted sixth floor where the Zises held forth. In many ways, life at Integrated reminded me of a college fraternity, and I was having a ball. A big part of my job was to travel around the country and lecture to the firm's sales force, more than four thousand attorneys and accountants located in major cities. I was their coach and cheerleader, keeping them up to date on the company's products and their tax implications. In between seminars, I was in Washington, picking up clues as to what legislation was coming down the pike.

* * *

I may have chalked up a lot of successes over the years, but sometimes I made a real boner. Here's another one to add to the record—and it's a dandy.

At the 1984 GOP convention in Dallas, which I attended as a member of the Republican National Committee, I worked hard for Integrated, buttonholing senators and administration officials and urging them to support our position. On the night when Ronald Reagan was to be nominated for a second term, I decided not to stay on the convention floor to hear the speeches (after all these years of conventioneering, I knew what to expect from them) but instead to schmooze with reporters, an art I'd learned from Nelson Rockefeller. When I saw the actor Charlton Heston, then chair of the National Rifle Association, ascend the podium, I knew I'd made the right decision. I've never been a gun-lover, and I just didn't want to hear Heston's harangue.

As it turned out, he wasn't haranguing. As a result of my leaving the convention floor that night, I stumbled into an embarrassing (but hilarious) gaffe the very next day. The president was hosting a luncheon for some of his biggest supporters and I brought along my son Matthew, now a state supreme court justice but then a young convention page. Just as we were sitting down, I spotted Don Regan, former White House chief of staff and at that time secretary of the Treasury. I made a beeline over to Regan, hoping to convince him to buttress Integrated's position on the tax legislation. As we were chatting, who should come over to join

Regan's table but Charlton Heston. Shaking his hand, I told the actor how much I'd enjoyed his remarks the night before—remarks, of course, that had never met my ears, since I'd been off the floor at the time.

When I returned to our table, Matt asked me what I'd said to Heston. "I told him I'd enjoyed his remarks last night." Matt gave me a look of disbelief: "Dad, he gave the Pledge of Allegiance."

* * *

My dream job clouded over in 1986 when the issue of tax reform moved closer to center stage. We were doing all we could to convince various members of the U.S. Senate not to pass legislation that would change the laws pertaining to tax shelters or at least to help "grandfather" existing laws so that our financial products would be protected. Often I would have to testify before the Senate in defense of Integrated's investments.

Part of our strategy was to hold fund-raisers for key senators and congressmen who might support our cause. Wherever we could and in whatever way we could, we were trying to make friends in preparation for the showdown we knew was coming. We lobbied practically every Republican member of the Senate, including Chuck Grassley of Iowa (later chairman of the Senate Finance Committee), Alan Simpson of Wyoming, Bob Dole of Kansas, Howard Baker of Tennessee, John Heinz of Pennsylvania, John Chafee of Rhode Island, and others.

One of the senators we lobbied hard was Bob Packwood of Oregon, who was then chair of the powerful Senate Finance Committee. One night in Manhattan we raised close to $500,000 for Packwood, who gave us his support, saying in his address at our fundraiser, "I like the tax laws the way they are and see no reason to change them." A short time later, he proceeded to stab us in the back when he sponsored legislation that would revoke the very laws we were depending on to protect our products. (Later, I could feel little sympathy for him when he was forced out of the Senate for disgraceful conduct with women.)

Other senators who benefited from our fundraisers were Bob Dole, then majority leader of the Senate, Chuck Grassley, and Barry Goldwater. One day after voting for the legislation Bob Packwood had sponsored, John Heinz visited us at Integrated looking for Senate campaign money. I told him right to his face I thought he had a lot of nerve coming to us after he voted for legislation he knew would hurt us. We gave no money. Later on John was killed in a collision between a helicopter and the plane he was in. Personally I liked John but I couldn't okay money for him.

* * *

Alas for Integrated Resources, in 1986 the tax reform bill passed. That hurt the company badly, since it made shelters of any size illegal. That wasn't my only worry, though. I had been with Integrated Resources for three and a half years, and I'd been taking notes through all the meetings. When controlling stock interests in Integrated were acquired by the Kentucky insurance company ICH, a corporate raider known for whittling down the sale price of a company as a deal was about to reach closure, I saw trouble ahead. I warned the Zises about ICH's methods, but Siggy and Jay had sold their stock to ICH and to Bob Shaw, ICH's CEO.

As the picture darkened, I got antsy, worrying about the firm's future and my own $250,000 investment. Ultimately I lost it all.

And still the brothers didn't want me to leave the company, Siggy saying to me, in effect, "After all we've done for you, you've got to stay and help us with the board. If you don't, they'll throw us out." (Of course, with the sale of their stock, so went their power.) I told them, "Sorry, I'm not staying, even though I really love you guys. There are a couple of things that mean a lot to me, and one of those is my reputation. If this firm folds, there might be trouble. I'm not going to be here for that."

Ultimately that's exactly what happened. Some large investors thought the selling price agreed to by the brothers was below what the stock was worth. But the brothers weathered the storm, and we are pals to this day.

Inevitably, Integrated Resources was sued by its derivative stockholders. And who was the court's chief witness? Me. As a result of my careful note taking during meetings, I had to sit in hearings day after day for a month being cross-examined. Four suits were filed in Delaware

Chancery Court against Integrated and its top officers, in an attempt to block the stock sale to ICH. Representing the company were Skadden Arps, a major New York firm; Proskauer Rose; and Rosenman & Colin (Sam Rosenman had been a key advisor to F.D.R.). One suit was filed by Stephen P. Hoffman, an attorney representing stockholder Arnold Bloom; another was filed by Samuel P. Spoon, attorney for shareholder David Ackerman; two other suits soon followed. Individually, we were represented by the old Main Line Philadelphia law firm of Wolf, Block, Schorr and Solis-Cohen. Though it cost us plenty, we prevailed. Ultimately, the investigation revealed no wrongdoing.

When I first hooked up with Integrated, Benjamin Netanyahu, former prime minister of Israel and at that time ambassador to the U.N., was staying at Sig's opulent apartment at 80th Street and Fifth Avenue; since I spent a lot of time there, too, Bibi and I became friends. Over the years, my friendship with the brothers has remained strong. When my son Matt took his bar exam in New York, he stayed at Sig's, as I often do when I'm in the "Big Apple." In fact, during the Republican Convention in 2004 Siggy cleared out for his home in the Hamptons and Matt and I and a friend from Washington, Karl Ottosen, moved in.

My time with Integrated Resources was golden for me: fun, exciting, and profitable. Even though I left after I'd been with them three years and nine months, the brothers, for whom I have great fondness and respect, paid me for the full five years of my contract. At the same time, I was getting paid for working one day a week at Nixon, Hargrave in Rochester, a very unusual break. As a result, while I am not in the same class financially with the Zises of this world, I can walk to shore with enough *gelt* to see me through.

All in all, the wild ride with Integrated Resources was a great experience. Most of the fellows I met and worked with there are still close friends. Each one had his own niche and developed products which the company could sell at big profits. Some of the lawyers whom I knew in New York City referred to the company as a "money machine," which was essentially true until late 1986.

After the company deteriorated, almost every one landed on his feet.

No Room for Democracy

Marv Goldklang became a baseball executive; Steve Goldsmith became a prominent banker; Art Goldberg, Dick Ader, Dan Davis, Dave Silvers, Steve Simms, and Jay Chazanoff became wealthy investors; Ben Fein is a successful lawyer; and Gary Krat made so much money he retired years ago in Florida.

I think all of them would agree: Our time at Integrated was one exciting roller coaster ride, a thrill a minute!

Elise and me in 1938, ages 9 and 7.

The Rosenbaum family: father and mother, Jack and Shirley, with sister Elise, and me, April 1932.

Wager the dog and I are in front of my grandparents' store on West Seneca Street in Owsego, New York, 1941.

As a Star Scout in Oswego, age 13, August 1944.

Hobart College lacrosse team; I am number 64 in the back row; spring 1949.

"The crowd thrilled as underdog 'Rosie' Rosenbaum counterpunched muscular Ken Witherow to a unanimous decision for the heavyweight diadem."
Echo of the Seneca, Hobart College yearbook, 1951.

Richard and Judith Rosenbaum, married in Rochester, New York on June 1, 1958.

Congressman Barber Conable, National Republican Chairman Rogers Morton, and me at a Monroe County GOP fundraiser in Rochester, April 1968.

Raising money for the Lend a Hand Fund which helped needy people in the Rochester community, September 1968.

At a Nixon Republican campaign rally in Rochester, October 23, 1968.

Judge Richard M. Rosenbaum, New York Supreme Court, circa 1972.

Joking with Betty Ford, Margaretta "Happy" Rockefeller, and the boss, Nelson Rockefeller, circa 1975.

Floyd Patterson, former heavyweight world champion vs. Richard Rosenbaum, Rochester War Memorial, April 23, 1975. Above: One of my seconds at left, Donald Mack, and referee "Jersey Joe" Walcott, former world heavyweight champion.

Speech for Gerald Ford's presidential campaign in New York City's
Chinatown, 1976.

Political cartoon for the 1976 GOP Convention, Kansas City, Missouri.
Hy Rosen, cartoonist, courtesy of *Albany Times Union*.

In the Oval Office with President Ford and Dick Cheney, White House Chief of Staff, plotting campaign strategy, summer 1976.

Rocky and Rosie at the GOP nominating convention in 1976.

Before the start
of the 1976
Republican
Convention.

Floor of the
Convention.

Speech at the 1976 GOP Convention;
waving to the New York Delegation.

After President Ford's nomination in Kansas City, Missouri, August 1976.

President Ford and the Rosenbaum family bidding farewell in the Oval Office, January 15, 1977.

Secretary of State Henry Kissinger and me at the Rochester Museum and Science Center dedication, September 1978.

"Richard M. Rosenbaum, former New York State Republican Chairman, reacts to a statement by former President Gerald Ford ... Ford is in Rochester for GOP fund raising." January 23, 1980.

Announcing my candidacy for New York State governor, Rochester,
February 1982.

Campaign poster,
1982.

To Dick Rosenbaum
With best wishes,
Ronald Reagan

With President Reagan, August 1984.

With President Bush at a White House reception, 1989.

Secretary of Defense Dick Cheney addressed the crowd at a fundraiser on the aircraft carrier *Intrepid* for my second gubernatorial campaign, November 1992.

Elizabeth Dole and I are cutting a rug at a Washington, D.C. fundraiser, winter 1998.

With Senator Al D'Amato and former senator Bob Dole at a New York City GOP dinner, 1998.

Judy and me in March 2000. We celebrated our 50th wedding anniversary in 2008.

To Richard
Best Wishes

With President Bush and New York Governor George Pataki at the Rochester Convention Center, May 2003.

Rudolph W. Giuliani
SG Horton Distinguished Speaker
October 8, 2005

R·I·T

With Rudy Giuliani at Rochester Institute of Technology, Rochester, New York, October 8, 2005.

The Rosenbaum family, including our four children, their spouses, and our twelve grandchildren, January 2004.

I swore in my son, Matthew Rosenbaum, as a New York Supreme Court Justice, Monroe Country Courthouse, March 29, 2005. Judy is looking on at right.

Chapter 20

"New York, New York... It's a Wonderful Town!"

In New York City, anything can happen—and usually does. Certainly I've been caught up in some rare episodes there. I've often wondered whether I have some special magnet that draws me into bizarre happenings. Some of these adventures turn out to be fortuitous (or just funny). Others...well, let's just say I've been known to find some bad worms in the Big Apple.

* * *

I left my apartment in the U.N. tower about 5:30 one afternoon in December 1985 and was walking up Third Avenue on my way to a black-tie fundraiser for Ned Regan, then the state's comptroller. As I approached 46th Street I heard a great pandemonium, people yelling and shouting, sirens wailing. Naturally, I ran up to see what was happening. When I saw two bloody bodies sprawled out in front of Sparks Steak House, I thought I'd stumbled into a movie filming. Minutes later, I realized that the cops cordoning off the area with yellow tape certainly weren't actors. Blood was everywhere—and it was *real*.

The stiff in the street was Paul Castellano, *capo* of the Gambino crime family; his driver lay dead on the sidewalk. I learned the next day that I'd been among the first on the scene of a mob hit choreographed by Gambino's rival, John Gotti.

New Yorkers at that time were pretty cynical about mob violence; they saw a lot of it. The murders made big headlines the next day and one of the articles (I think it was in the *Post*) included quotes heard on the street shortly after the shooting. From a neighboring restaurateur:

"What great publicity. I'd like to pull the bodies over in front of my restaurant." And from a driver who obviously had had it with Manhattan traffic: "How come it takes me two hours to get from 42nd Street to 56th at this time of night, and the guys who pulled this rubout were out of here in ten seconds?"

My favorite was two guys standing outside Sparks who were reported to have said, "If we hurry, maybe we can get their table." Typical New York City reactions.

* * *

I have always found the pulse of New York City to be irresistible. Even the fading light over the city gave me goose bumps, and still does. It truly is a city synonymous with adventure. One night, I was at P. J. Clarke's great jazz joint with the late circuit court judge Dan Mahoney and his wife Pat, listening to music and enjoying a few drinks. Like many married couples, Dan and his wife occasionally would get into an argument while they were out on the town. When that happened, Dan simply would put his head down on the table and fall asleep.

On this particular evening, I was watching the time because I had to argue an important case the next morning in front of the New York City Council. I was arguing against allowing women to join private clubs that were, at that time, exclusively male bastions. The women plaintiffs were arguing that they were being deprived of equal business opportunities by being excluded from the social activities and business discussions that take place within the confines of these clubs. The defense's essential argument was that club members had the constitutional right to control the makeup of the club's membership and to associate with whomever they pleased.

I left the Mahoneys around midnight to return to the Doral Hotel at 38th Street and Park Avenue where I was staying at the time. Truth be told, I was feeling no pain, and since the hotel was only a few blocks away, I decided to walk. As I approached the Doral's front door, I heard the screech of brakes. Turning, I saw a cab door open about twenty feet away and out jumped a couple of hookers, one tall and one short. The short one came up and threw her arms around me and said, "C'mon, honey! Let's party!" I fended her off somehow, and got safely (I thought) into the hotel. As the elevator rose, I felt for my wallet. Gone. The day before I'd attended a Rockefeller Center board meeting, so there was an extra $300 in that wallet. Twenty-five years ago that was a very tidy sum, and I didn't want to lose it.

I quickly pushed the elevator's "down" button and ran into the street. Across Park Avenue I saw a guy leaning against the lamppost. Yes, he'd seen a couple of women run into an alley that led to the back of the hotel. I charged down the alley, and reached them in time to see them emptying my wallet. As soon as they saw me, running at them with a full head of steam, they split. The tall one ran across 38th Street; the little one ran up toward Fifth Avenue, with me in hot pursuit. I was about to catch her when she jumped in a waiting cab. I called to the driver that if he left I'd have him arrested.

By this time, I'd sobered up enough so that I had at least enough of my wits about me to get his cab number and company. The driver, who'd started to pull away, stopped dead in his tracks when I threatened him. The little hooker jumped out and threw herself on the trunk of another cab moving down Fifth Avenue. By this time, the police had arrived. They stopped the second cab, and caught the girl. I checked my wallet and found my VISA card missing as well as the money that was soon returned when the girl reached down the front of her dress and pulled out the dough. The cops walked the little hooker back down to the alleyway. Sure enough, there in a planter behind the Doral we found the missing card, and, in a planter next to the nearby Lord & Taylor store on Fifth Avenue, we found my Hertz rental card. When I ran into that alley I must have made a lot of noise. I recall windows going up and shouts of "Pipe down, we're trying to sleep."

I told the cops I wanted to file a complaint, so we all went down to the local precinct office where I filled out the necessary forms. The cops insisted on keeping my Hertz card, which they claimed was necessary to show the judge as evidence, and advised me they would be calling me in about six months. By this time, it was about three a.m. and I was all fired up. In the excitement, I'd almost forgotten that I had to be up at seven for my big presentation.

The next morning my head was *very* painful. I still recall vividly how difficult it was to argue my case with so little sleep, especially with people like Ruth Messinger, the liberal conscience of the New York City Council, opposing me vigorously. We finally won, but the decision held for only a short time. (By the way, I never heard back from the New York City police.)

* * *

There is, of course, the other New York, a friendlier one. In 1992, while I was once again seeking the Republican nod for governor, I arranged a meeting with Sandy Weil, then chairman of Travelers Insurance Co. and later chairman of Citibank, hoping to raise some much-needed campaign money. The day of our meeting turned out to be both snowy and icy, and as I rushed up 52nd Street toward Fifth Avenue I slipped on the ice and hit the ground like the proverbial ton of bricks. I lay there, stunned and helpless, as several men just walked on by. Finally a nice lady stopped, helped me up (I must have been three times her size) and asked if I was OK. Who says all New Yorkers are unfriendly and unfeeling?

You know by now that I'm an avid sports fan, but my enthusiasm pales next to my son Matt's passion for baseball. Back in 1976, when Matt was ten, I took him to Shea Stadium, the temporary home of the Yankees. I let the Yankees' general manager, Gabe Paul, know that we were coming and he couldn't have been nicer. When we arrived, Matt and I were ushered onto the field where we watched batting practice up close and personal. Matt was invited into the dugout before the game where he garnered a whole slew of players' autographs, before we headed for the owner's box and our VIP seats. The box projected slightly beyond the dugout so the owner, his friends, and (for just this one time) Matt and I could look right down into the dugout. Matt went home with baseballs, baseball caps and shirts. But one of the best thrills of the day occurred during the seventh inning stretch, when the electronic score-board lit up with a sign that read "Welcome Matt Rosenbaum." Matt pasted that day in his memory book for sure.

Speaking of Yankee baseball, I was fortunate to attend a number of World Series games over the years. One time I was at Yankee Stadium for the seventh game in the series, when the Yankees prevailed. I had hired a limo, and we sat in the parking lot after the game for an hour and a half waiting to exit. As we were driving back to Manhattan through the Bronx, we stopped for a red light. In almost no time, a crowd converged on us from both sides and began rocking the car. All of the Bronx was celebrating the Yankee victory, but this crowd was out of control. The driver began screaming at the throng at the top of his lungs and it seemed as though the car was going over for sure. Bob Green, my Manhattan law partner whom I'd invited as my guest, was sitting in the back seat, white as a sheet. Just then, as if by magic, a phalanx of police arrived in the form of a flying wedge and forced the crowd back to the curb. We all breathed a sigh of relief.

Over the years, I've found Yankee fans to be the most unruly I have ever seen, and that's putting it mildly. On another occasion, I took a couple of friends from the state's Unemployment Insurance Appeal Board to watch the Yankees play the Toronto Blue Jays. For some reason, I felt that day like rooting for Toronto. As soon as I opened my mouth, I encountered a vicious backlash from the neighboring crowd and was subjected to both threats and some of the foulest language you can imagine. I actually thought at one point that I was going to have to fight my way out of the stadium. (Surprisingly, the nastiness was being led— and fed—by two middle-age women.) My guests that day—the board's chief judge, Bob Lorenzo, and executive director Joe Kearney—kept begging me to stop cheering for Toronto for fear of mob violence.

For years, the fun at the Yankee Stadium continued. For one game, I ordered steak, lobster, and all the trimmings "to go" from the Palm Restaurant on Second Avenue in Manhattan. When we arrived at the stadium, my friend Mike Blake, former GOP leader of Suffolk County, our driver and my other guests spread a tablecloth over the limo's open tailgate and we fell to. Halfway through our feast, a police officer spied us and told us that tailgating was prohibited. I seduced him by offering him one of our delicious steaks (we had plenty); he joined the party, and we had a lot of laughs.

* * *

One of my favorite New York pastimes, when opportunity knocked, was to attend the big prizefights at Madison Square Garden. Toots Shore's restaurant across from the Garden was a fun meeting place; the fight crowd there included a host of celebrities, fighters, actors, actresses, politicians, and sycophants of assorted sizes and shapes. One evening at a big heavyweight fight, Princess Lee Bouvier Radziwill (sister of Jackie Kennedy Onassis) walked in and took a seat ringside. I always had ringside seats, too, compliments of the New York Athletic Commission, thanks to my friend Manny Gonzalez, one of the commissioners. Since the princess was only a few feet away, I introduced myself and we had quite a chat. She was stunning and stylish, quite petite, and surrounded by bodyguards. (She appeared to have a body worth guarding.).

* * *

One day as I was hailing a cab across from the entrance to Central Park, near the New York Athletic Club, I noticed a woman nearby who kept checking her watch nervously. She seemed to be distraught, obviously upset because someone was late in picking her up for an appointment. My cab came first, but when I moved to the door Mrs. Eager-to-Go stepped in front of me and told me to get out of the way. In spite of her, I managed to climb in (I was late for an appointment) as she hurled epithets at me, the nicest of which was "You old goat!" As the cab sped away the lady gave the door a good kick and me a very nasty look.

Later that same day I took a subway to my New York office, then on Hudson Street near King Street in lower Manhattan. The subway station closest to my office was on Varick Street, about a block and a half from my destination. I wasn't used to riding the subway (town car, cab, or limo was more my style) and when I came up from underground I was lost. On a nearby corner I asked a woman in a jumpsuit if she knew how to get to 345 Hudson. "I just came from there," she said. "They turned me down. I hope you do better." Since I was at that moment chairman of the New York Unemployment Appeal Board, I didn't dare disabuse her of the thought that, unlike her, I was not going to Hudson Street

No Room for Democracy

to seek unemployment benefits.

One time in the dead of winter on a particularly cold day in Manhattan when I had only recently taken over the reigns of State Unemployment, I took a subway to my office only to find I had gotten off a stop too late. I practically froze walking that mile and a half to work. Why didn't I hail a cab? Well, on that particular day there were none available.

For many years I stayed in a suite at the Doral Hotel and developed a first name relationship with the folks behind the registration desk, the bartenders, even the cleaning personnel. Eventually the owners let me occupy the largest suite in the place with a balcony overlooking the city. The staff had a small trophy made for me inscribed in Spanish which translated read, "To Mr. Rosenbaum, the Best Guest in the World."

Chapter 21

Rosenbaum v. George and John Bush

In 1988, just as I was about a week away from leaving Integrated Resources to return to Rochester and Nixon, Hargrave, a story appeared in *New York* magazine that really caught my attention. Based on reliable information, a reporter for the magazine wrote, I was to be the first scalp (hairless or not) on George Bush the elder's belt. In short, I was to be dumped off the Republican National Committee. My sin? I'd supported Bob Dole for president against Bush in the recent Republican primary. (Dole had been my close friend for at least fifteen years and at the time was Senate majority leader, a position that ain't exactly chopped liver.) The "reliable information" included a quote from John Bush, George H. W.'s younger brother.

By coincidence the very next day I was attending a Republican fundraiser in Manhattan, an event I was sure John Bush would attend. When I arrived, John made a beeline for me, and reassured me. I was not to be concerned, he said, because the story was inaccurate.

The "back story" was this: for fourteen and a half years, from January 1973 to June 1988, I had held a seat on the Republican National Committee, first in my capacity as state party chairman and then as the male member of our state's two-person, gender-equal representation. The national committee meets several times a year to set party policy and to organize, set rules for and run the quadrennial presidential and vice-presidential nominating convention. Committee members are elected to four-year terms at a committee meeting immediately following the nominating convention.

Committee members then consisted of two general types. First were the older, wealthy party supporters who seemed to consider membership a great social "perk," an impressive advantage in the games of one-upmanship that go on constantly in those circles. The second group consists of party regulars, and that group included me. Members can enhance their influence by actively working to accomplish rules changes and, at a more personal level, secure advantageous housing accommodations, seating privileges, and parking spaces at meetings and conventions, and invitations for their delegation members to receptions at the White House from the president and First Lady.

About a week after my reassuring talk with John, he phoned and asked if we could meet that very day. I was back with my law firm in Rochester at the time, so I told him that would be a bit difficult since we were four hundred miles apart, but I asked him what was on his mind. "You have to give up your national committee spot," he said. "Who says so?" I asked. "The people in Washington," he said, meaning Lee Atwater, then the Republican national chairman. The *New York* magazine article had been right; supporting Dole in the primary had gotten me in hot water. I said, "John, this is an elected position and there is no way I'm leaving." John said he had to fly to Florida to visit his mother over Memorial Day and we'd discuss the subject further on his return. Before he hung up, he offered me a deal. If I would resign my seat, he could fix it so I could be on the Board of Visitors at West Point, which he considered highly prestigious.

As soon as I put down the phone, I began calling all sixty-two of New York's county chairmen and told them John had tried to force me off the committee. I asked them to support me at the next state GOP committee meeting when endorsements for various offices, including the seat on the national committee, would be made. Promises of support were practically unanimous. John's effort had boomeranged, as most chairmen resented his intervention in a matter that was well within their jurisdiction.

When John returned from Florida after Memorial Day, he called, told me he'd heard I'd been making phone calls, and said that we had to meet in New York City to talk this over. I told him I'd try to accommodate him. At that point the pressure began to build.

Tony Colavita, then the state's GOP chairman, called and told me I should quit the post. I politely but firmly reminded Tony that when he was party chair in Westchester County and wanted to become state chairman, he'd pledged to support me as a national committee member for another four years. I reminded him of what I'd said during that earlier conversation: "Don't ask me to help put you in the driver's seat so you can run me off the road." But Tony insisted I had to leave the committee, and that he was going to put Joe Mondello, the Nassau County chairman, in my place. At that time, the Nassau Republican Committee was one of the strongest and best-financed Republican organizations in the country. Tony said that in order to run the party effectively, he needed Mondello's strong unwavering support. Getting him on the national committee would ensure that.

My problems mounted. My own Monroe County chairman, Barbara Zartman (who once had expressed her undying loyalty to me), now called and said I should quit. Next, Warren Anderson, the state senate majority leader, called and asked me to resign. The rats, it seemed, were deserting what they thought was a sinking ship. The *New York Times* ran a front page article by its ace political reporter Frank Lynn, accompanied by a picture of me with John Bush, concluding that my days were numbered.

Little did they know. I told each caller that one of the advantages I had was that I wasn't afraid to lose (I'd been there before), but that if I did lose I'd give them all a very bloody nose. I reminded them that I was the bald Jewish kid from Oswego who was used to fighting, and that efforts to push me around almost always ended in disaster for the pusher.

As the date of the state committee meeting in Albany drew closer, I called Tony Colavita and proposed that he, Mondello, and I meet in Albany before the convention and thrash things out. I had an arrow in my quiver that I hadn't shot; as soon as I drew my bow I knew they would be in for a nasty surprise. When we met, Colavita immediately asked me whom I would rather see as national committeeman, Mondello or John Bush. I said, "I'd rather see me." With that, the meeting broke up.

A half hour later, the state committee members—450 strong—sat down to meet and eat. Despite the fact that as a national committee member I had a prominent seat on the dais, I did not take it. Instead, I made the rounds of all the tables where members were seated by county, shaking hands and participating in good fellowship. I particularly enjoyed visiting Mondello's Nassau County table. I knew there was seething resentment within that delegation because of Mondello's power grab; he was not only the county chairman, but also the presiding officer of the county legislature. Now he wanted to be national committeeman, too.

As I strolled around seeking support (and creating disorder wherever I could), I couldn't help noticing the smoke coming out of John Bush's ears and hearing the snorts of resentment emanating from State Chairman Colavita, who was having trouble running an orderly meeting. As soon as I sat down, a gaggle of reporters surrounded me and began to ask what I thought was going to happen. I told them I was going to win, and if the effort against me didn't come to an abrupt halt, I was going to let it be known publicly that I had been offered an appointment if I would acquiesce (although I didn't mention the West Point deal directly). When the reporters wanted specifics, I just smiled coyly.

During the final week before the GOP's nominating committee meeting, I called John Bush and told him in no uncertain terms that unless the opposition folded, I was going to call a news conference and reveal the West Point offer, a *quid pro quo* which amounted to a serious political offense.

When the meeting finally convened, there was no opposition to my candidacy. I had stared them all down. John Bush, a gentleman at heart apparently, called me offering his congratulations and said he thought my effort to defeat my opposition was remarkable. I had faced down the party's presidential nominee, the vice-presidential nominee, the GOP national and state chairmen, the New York senate majority leader, and other prominent Republicans.

The *New York Times* made a big thing of my re-election; when Frank Lynn called, he said, "You gave them a real kick in the ass." Bob

Dole called, too, offering congratulations. (He was on his way to a 100th birthday celebration for Irving Berlin where he was going to sing "Happy Birthday" to the guest of honor.)

I took sweet satisfaction in that win. I'd taken a lot of guff along the way; as when early on the *New York Times* had quoted state senator Roy Goodman as having said I was on the outs "for supporting the wrong horse." Imagine how good I felt when, weeks later, after I had prevailed, Goodman called and asked me to intercede with Dole to help him get an important presidential appointment should Bush win. Dole had a say in the matter.

About a month later, I came up behind Lee Atwater, the GOP national committee chair, at a meeting and tapped him on the shoulder. When he turned around and saw me, he gasped and said, "Wow! It's 'Survivor, Incorporated!'"

I was told later that President Bush, riding in a plane from Washington with congressman Guy Molinari from Staten Island, asked, "What is this Rosenbaum thing all about?" Molinari is reported to have told him, "Rosenbaum won, and is now more dangerous than ever. If you go after the king, you must kill him, not wound him."

All through this affair, I couldn't understand why I was being attacked. True, I had supported Dole over Bush in the presidential primary, but they were both Republicans and I had said I would vigorously support whoever was the winner. Months later, someone told me that if Bush were to lose the election, the Washington boys wanted to be sure he got another crack at the prize four years hence. To strengthen their position they wanted my seat on the national committee to be filled by someone whose support they could count on.

It was a hard, hard struggle. But all in all, my victory and the strategy I employed to accomplish it seems to me in retrospect one of my finest political hours.

Chapter 22

In the Running...Again

About a year before the 1992 Republican national convention, I began to think seriously about running again for governor of New York State. I'd learned a lot from my experience in 1982 when I'd tried for the party's nomination, and prominent Republicans all across the state were encouraging me to try again.

In addition to my old friend congressman Barber Conable, former head of the World Bank and my 1982 campaign treasurer, my supporters for this second campaign included John Whitehead, former deputy secretary of state and co-chair of the investment banking house Goldman Sachs; Rudy Giuliani, then mayor of New York City; Senator Bob Dole; Carla Hills, head of HUD in President Ford's cabinet; Arnie Burns, prominent Manhattan lawyer; Bill Weld, governor of Massachusetts; and Bruce and Dick Gelb, who headed Bristol Myers, the big pharmaceutical firm. Both Weld and Burns had been deputy U.S. attorneys under Ed Meese, attorney general in the Reagan administration.

Early in 1991 I'd begun to marshal my forces, and in 1993 I hired Lisa Linden and Steve Alschuler, a talented pair of public relations specialists who had been with the legendary Rubenstein PR firm in Manhattan. Howard Rubenstein and I had been friends for years, and I was concerned that taking away two of his best people would offend him. However, Steve and Lisa were already thinking about starting their own firm and were eager to take me on as their first client. (Lisa's husband, Lloyd Kaplan, one of the top people at Rubenstein, had done PR work for me when I first started at Integrated Resources. Lloyd is one of the best people in the business, so talented that even after Lisa left

Rubenstein, Howard was happy to keep him on for several years. Eventually, Lloyd left Rubenstein and joined his wife at what is now Linden Alschuler & Kaplan in Manhattan.) At the 1992 convention, Lisa, who still worked at Rubenstein at the time, took a short leave of absence to join me, and she effectively worked the floor, getting exposure both for me as candidate and for the issues about which I felt passionately.

One of those issues was the pro-choice/pro-life debate, which was perhaps even more controversial then than it is now. I had made my position clear early on at the state Republican convention. Bill Powers, then New York's GOP chair, expected me to make a speech announcing that I would not run again for a seat on the national committee. (Powers knew that by that time I had decided to leave the committee to prepare for my gubernatorial campaign.) Instead, I used my time at the podium to speak strongly about the need for Republicans to protect a woman's right to choose. The speech received a standing ovation from about half those attending, but I suddenly had become anathema to many of the party stalwarts, including Jack Kemp and Senator Alfonse D'Amato. The media loved it, of course, and I garnered lots of good ink for the cause.

The following year, at the national GOP convention in Houston, it was a foregone conclusion that the Republican platform would contain a pro-life plank. Lisa hit on a brilliant idea to promote the pro-choice stand. We arranged a news conference in Manhattan in front of a Fed Ex office, an event that attracted the media and several prominent pro-choice women, including my daughter Jill, who was then practicing veterinary medicine in New York City. At the appointed hour, I arrived with a large two-by-four wooden plank lettered with the words PRO CHOICE. After addressing the crowd, we took the plank into the Fed Ex office and mailed it to the platform committee at the convention, making the point quite clear that we wanted a pro-choice plank to be included in the GOP platform.

When I arrived in Houston, I was amazed at the amount of interest in the abortion debate. I attended the platform committee meeting the next day and made quite a fuss, insisting that our platform position include a pro-choice statement—at the very least as a minority provision. Pat Buchanan and his campaign manager (his sister, Bay) were carrying on loudly and at great length in support of the pro-life plank. Not only did I refuse to back down, but the more they ranted and raved, the more aggressive I became. A few staff people from the platform committee became upset and asked me to leave, but they backed away pretty quickly when I faced them down. (Actually, I wanted them to physically usher me out so I could make a big PR thing out of it. I would have decked them if they'd laid a finger on me.) With me on the convention floor, I had my son Matt, who at six foot five inches and 240 pounds simply acted as a shield and fended the zealots off.

Partly as a result of the pro-choice brouhaha, I left the convention a day early for the first time in my twenty-four years of convention-going. Republican Party rules call for members of the national committee to be elected following the presidential and vice-presidential nomination. This year, since I was not in the running to succeed myself on the national committee, I decided enough was enough, and my offspring and I went home. I had my own campaign business to attend to.

In the weeks that followed, Arnie Burns arranged an informal meeting for me with Bill Weld, then governor of Massachusetts, at the Massachusetts State House, who I hoped would support my bid for the gubernatorial nomination. I took the opportunity of being in Boston to spend a few hours with our daughter Julie, then teaching at Boston College. After lunch, Julie and I walked over to the governor's office where we met with Bill, his special assistant, and Arnie, who had traveled up from New York City on my behalf. The governor was very encouraging and said he thought we could win. He advised me to hire as my campaign manager and consultant Dick Morris, he of the prostitution scandal and theory of triangulation, which he had developed in Bill Clinton's campaign in Arkansas. (Triangulation is when you work to solve the problem that motivates the opposing party's voters, so as to defang that party politically.) Dick had helped elect at least two governors—Clinton in Arkansas and Weld himself. I approached Dick about taking on the job and his first comment was, "You've been around so long I thought you'd be at least eighty." I was sixty-one at the time. I got a belly laugh at that one.

Dick provided me with an impressive list of references; in addition to Bill Clinton, they included the governor of Colorado and several senators. All said the same thing, in effect: "He's brilliant, but watch your back." Their comments proved to be prescient. Still, as I got to know and work with Dick, I was deeply impressed. He assigned me three books to read, one on education by Daniel Schorr's wife, one on government and one on conservative theory by Judge Robert Bork. Dick said, "By the time we get into the heart of this campaign and people start questioning you on the issues, you'll be like a jukebox, able to respond thoroughly and automatically." John Sears, my former campaign manager, never had given me this kind of preparation and I learned a lot under Morris's tutelage.

Shortly before the gubernatorial race began, Morris advised me to pay a visit to Al D'Amato in Washington, seeking the senator's support. Al told me he hadn't yet made up his mind, but I left his office feeling I had a chance with him. A few hours later at Washington National Airport, waiting for my flight back to Rochester, I phoned my office and my assistant broke the news that D'Amato had just announced his support for George Pataki, the state senator from Dutchess County. So much for D'Amato's candor.

Al's decision didn't discourage me in the least. I announced my candidacy on July 7, 1992, and began to build a campaign team. My efforts began to produce money almost instantly. My finance team, in addition to World Bank president Barber Conable and real estate developer George Klein, included John Whitehead, former chairman of Goldman Sachs and undersecretary of state under George Bush, Sr.; Bruce Gelb, vice chairman of the board of Bristol Myers; and Carla Hills, former HUD secretary. The team was headed by Sheila Levin, a professional fundraiser who'd had a successful record in New York City, especially within the investment banking community. (Unfortunately for us, a previous scandal had resulted in new rules that limited firms involved in bond work from contributing to political campaigns.) Under Morris's guidance, we began advertising on radio. While that effort proved to be less than vote-producing, Al D'Amato later told me it had the Pataki team

No Room for Democracy

so worried, "They shit their pants." We had caught the Pataki people flatfooted and as a result we had two weeks of unanswered advertising, a candidate's dream.

As the campaign took shape, it became obvious that I had to win the Republican primary. If I did, the party would consider me more electable than Pataki, particularly since I was sure to garner a sizeable number of Democratic votes in the general election. We expected those votes would come from Democrats disenchanted with then-governor Mario Cuomo and from those who would support a moderate Republican. Meanwhile I had won the endorsement of the Independence Party, which gave me a line on the ballot. Optimism was beginning to build. We decided that I would not officially attend the state Republican nominating convention. Instead, I would set up camp in an adjacent conference room and stage a puppet show describing D'Amato as the puppeteer and Pataki as the puppet. This caught the imagination of a number of reporters and gave us a fair amount of publicity.

Shortly after the state convention, Al D'Amato called and asked me to withdraw my name. I flatly refused and told him I was in the race to the finish. My team decided the best way to get my name on the Republican ballot was by petition, which would, if we could do it, be a first for the GOP in New York State. The election law required that we gather 15,000 signatures with at least 100, or five percent, of enrolled voters from each of one-half of the congressional districts in New York State. However, we knew that we would need at least 45,000 signatures in order to survive the challenge that was sure to come. The problem was that we had little time before the filing deadline. To solve the problem, I hired an old friend, Karl Ottosen, to come up from Washington where he ran a political consulting business. Karl recruited a team of young people to scour the counties for signatures, mostly in the densely populated areas.

The Independence Party, which was supposed to put together its own petitions on my behalf, let us down badly and forced us to expend money and effort to accomplish the goal ourselves. Rochester pollster Gordon Black and Paychex CEO Tom Golisano had spearheaded the effort to get me on the Independence Party ballot, but when it came time to pay the cost of circulating our petitions they were nowhere to be found. With help from my son Matthew, we beat the deadline for filing. Immediately the Pataki forces challenged us, claiming signatures were phony and addresses wrong. When the *New York Times* wrote a scathing editorial criticizing the challenge, the Pataki forces dropped their effort to knock me out of the race.

Now the battle was joined. Early polls had Pataki/Rosenbaum in almost a dead heat and that news spurred us on. Morris assigned Sue Barber, an associate of Black and Golisano, the task of organizing a series of receptions for me across the state. I sensed trouble brewing when only a few people showed up at her first event in Binghamton, and I told Morris to take her off the payroll. He disagreed, and thought we should give her more time. After several failures, we had a reception in Syracuse where only one person showed up. The papers wrote a humiliating story and I insisted Sue Barber be fired; it was obvious she was getting paid for doing nothing. Political campaigns never run perfectly, although most handicaps can be surmounted. But in a campaign where you are running outside the party organization there is very little room for mistakes of this magnitude. We had been dealt a devastating body blow because we had lost a lot of important time.

According to our own polls at the time, Pataki had pulled out to a big lead of about three to one. Our fundraising efforts were working though, and Dick Morris decided to take one final poll a week prior to the primary. His theory was that I had a good chance to pull off an upset if the numbers were beginning to implode. Since the poll results, due to that year's calendar, would have to be tabulated the night before the start of the Jewish New Year and since I had to go to temple the next day, I agreed to meet Morris for breakfast at the Marriott Hotel in Penfield, my home town. As soon as Morris entered the restaurant I knew we were in trouble, he didn't look pleased. Sitting down at table, he broke the bad news: based on the poll results, it was clear we could not possibly win. He then made a suggestion so absurd I could not believe my ears. He told me to call all my biggest financial supporters and tell them I was pulling out of the race and throwing my support to Pataki. Clearly

No Room for Democracy

this was impossible; I couldn't make even half of the seven hundred phone calls needed in the few hours remaining.

When I returned home, crestfallen, there was a call from Lisa Linden, my public relations person, telling me that, despite Morris's advice, I should forge ahead. Unfortunately, Morris had begun pulling my ads off the airwaves, a fact picked up by reporters who wrote that I appeared to be pulling out of the race. Returning home after temple services, I talked with my counsel, Frank Penski, who asked me the tough question: did I really want to invest another $50,000 in the race? Morris certainly had discouraged me. Yet almost immediately after my talk with Penski, a call came in from Morris saying that the morning edition of the *New York Times* had a front page article which, he said, "...couldn't have been better if your mother had written it." He urged me to continue to fight, and I agreed. We were back in the race and on TV.

Imagine my shock when Morris called back a few hours later and told me he had called Arnie Burns and another of my strong supporters, Mike Morelli from Westchester County (head of the elite Italian organization Knights of Malta), and told them I had no chance to win. "How could you do such a thing when you're on my payroll?" I demanded. His answer left me even more infuriated; he told me he expected to do business with these men following the campaign and had to ingratiate himself with them. I told him what I thought of him in no uncertain terms and hung up. Morris disappeared after that, showing up only briefly on primary night. By that time, I knew what was meant when I'd been warned to "watch my back" in dealing with Morris.

When the returns began to roll in, it was obvious I was going to lose. Primaries just don't produce voters. Although I carried some towns in my home county and elsewhere, it hurt that voter response that year was very low. We had been hoping for a turnout of around twenty-two percent, but instead we got thirteen percent. When it became clear that the cause was lost, I called Pataki and D'Amato and conceded.

The stress of that campaign really took its toll. For almost a full year after the campaign I had to be treated for stomach pains. As disappointed as I was with the outcome, I still am glad I'd made the effort.

As Teddy Roosevelt pointed out in his "Man in the Arena" speech, it's important for good candidates to enter the political fray, win or lose. I'd made a lot of new friends around the state, and this proved to be of great help a decade later when I worked on my son Matthew's 2005 campaign for New York State Supreme Court. Call me an optimist if you want, but even when the clouds are dark, I can still summon up a silver lining.

The silver lining came in various forms. During the campaign I received the Ellis Island Congressional Medal of Honor for distinguishing myself as an American of Russian-Jewish ancestry and for strengthening ties to my ethnic heritage. Others so honored that year were secretary of state Colin Powell, Gulf War leader Gen. H. Norman Schwarzkopf, and Baseball Hall of Famer Johnny Bench. I admit I had tears in my eyes throughout the ceremony, thinking of my grandparents, whose first steps in America were taken on this island. How I loved them, and how proud they would be.

One of the friendships rekindled during that campaign was with New York City mayor Rudy Giuliani. Rudy and I had known each other for years, probably since I first contributed to his mayoral campaign war chest. In 1988, he came to Rochester at my behest to address a fundraiser for state senate candidate Dale Rath. After his speech, Rudy, his assistant Denny Young and I repaired to a local dairy where we gorged on rum raisin ice cream, and then returned to my house where we stayed up until the wee hours telling stories and laughing.

One night during my campaign I attended a reception for Rudy at the Tavern on the Green in Manhattan. At the conclusion of his speech, Rudy scanned the audience, mentioning some of his well-known supporters in attendance. Bill Weld, then governor of Massachusetts, called out: "Dick Rosenbaum's here!" Rudy responded, "Hi, Dick!" and to the audience he said, "Dick, Denny Young and I got drunk one night in Rochester," to which I yelled back, "Yeah! On rum raisin ice cream!" (This good natured banter with both the governor of Massachusetts and the mayor of New York City certainly didn't hurt my cause.)

Shortly after my campaign ended I received a phone call from Denny who tipped me off that Rudy was going to pressure me to support Mario Cuomo for governor. That signaled trouble. The fact was that Rudy and Senator D'Amato, Governor Pataki's chief fundraiser and supporter, were like oil and water—and I had already publicly endorsed Pataki. Rudy and Al's intense dislike of each other stemmed from an early nasty disagreement regarding who should replace Rudy as U.S. attorney and chief prosecutor for New York's Southern District. Rudy wanted someone in his own incorruptible mold; D'Amato (then known as "the pothole senator") wanted the post filled by someone who wouldn't harass him. (Giuliani, who had often questioned D'Amato's ethics, once told me privately that if Pataki ever was elected governor the Mafia would be running New York State.)

Denny had given me fair warning, because the calls began pouring in. The pressure was intense. Rudy's PR guy, Bill Garth, said my endorsement would be worth four crucial points, enough to ensure a Cuomo win. Randy Levine, president of the New York Yankees, offered to send a plane up to Rochester if I would come to New York for a press conference announcing my support, and shopping center mogul Bob Baker also called to twist my arm. As a last-ditch effort, Rudy called and said, in effect, "I'm out on a limb and I need someone out there with me."

Because I had publicly promised to support Pataki (on the evening I lost the primary) I had to turn Rudy down, even though he has my great respect as a politician—as well as my admiration for his skill and fortitude in keeping the Big Apple together after the 9/11 tragedy. However, as former state GOP chairman I just couldn't go against my own party. I'm glad to say that my friendship with Giuliani remains strong. When our son Matt ran for state supreme court judge, Rudy issued a press release endorsing his candidacy, a kindness for which both Matt and I are grateful.

Two years ago, in a private meeting, I urged Rudy to run for governor in the next election. He refused. It seems he had a bigger target in his sight: the presidency.

Chapter 23

A Change in Employment

When I reached sixty-five in 1998, I knew I was on the slippery retirement slope that comes to all partners at Nixon Peabody. On the occasion of that fateful day you get an unwelcome birthday present: a reminder that on January 1 of the upcoming year partners see a reduction of ten percent in their work "units," the measure that determines your pay. Unit value at Nixon is established each year by a committee of partners and their number fluctuates with the success of the firm; when the firm's annual income is high, unit value rises; if low, it diminishes. At age sixty-six, partners take a fifty percent cut in their units; at the end of the year in which you turn sixty-seven, your units run out.

The prospect of leaving the firm set my superstitious juices boiling. I feared that the day I left the firm and stopped working I'd drop dead, so I began to look for other opportunities. I had already become a member of Judicial Arbitration and Mediation Services, Inc. (JAMS), a national organization. Unfortunately for me, there isn't much demand for JAMS work in upstate New York. The JAMS New York office is in lower Manhattan, and I didn't relish the thought of spending a lot of time running back and forth to New York City where JAMS' real action is. However, I did develop a practice with the firm, work that still continues. I had also become a New York State judicial hearing officer (JHO), a position that can only be filled by someone who has been a judge. JHO cases are assigned by the local administrative supreme court judge.

Diversity makes a law practice interesting. Sometimes it leads to fascinating cases that expand your personal horizons; sometimes it involves you in situations that leave a bad taste. One day shortly after

I'd resumed my career at Nixon, after leaving Integrated, I got a call from Donald Trump, asking me to represent him as a lobbyist. Trump, fearing for his Atlantic City gambling interests, wanted to keep the state legislature from opening up the Catskills to casino developers. I told him I'd be happy to work with him, and flew to Manhattan to work out an arrangement.

When I arrived in his office, "The Donald" told me he was no longer interested in hiring me because his Westchester lawyer Al Pirro (who later went to prison) had told him Governor Pataki and I were on the outs, since I had opposed him in the GOP state primary. I told him that Pirro didn't know what he was talking about, that I had publicly promised to support Pataki after he won the primary, and that he should call Mike Finnegan, the governor's counsel, who would tell him a different story. Trump said he'd made up his mind; it was a no go—and he didn't even offer to pay my traveling expenses. (He later made up for it by contributing to my son's campaign for state supreme court justice.) I think he's a great guy!

I was really bothered by Trump's comments. I'd just renewed my law practice after the disappointing primary and it seemed important for both me and my law firm that my relationship with the governor appear close. As soon as I returned to Rochester after talking with Trump, I made an appointment to meet Pataki in Albany. When I told him what Trump had said, he called in his special assistant, Tom Doherty, and told him to find an appointment for me that would let the world know I was in his good graces. A few days later I learned I was to be appointed chairman of the New York State Fourth Department Judicial Selection Committee. That move would put me on the state judicial executive committee. It also would convey a positive public message and place me in a favorable spot vis-a-vis the governor's operations and my burgeoning law practice at Nixon.

Weeks went by, then months, but no appointment was forthcoming. Finally, about two years later, the appointments were announced: I wasn't even named to the committee, much less its chairman. By that time I didn't need the appointment, but I wanted to know what had

No Room for Democracy

gone wrong. I called Mike Finnegan, who admitted the governor had forgotten his promise; he added, "You know the governor never takes the blame for a mistake." When Mike said, "I'll see that the governor appoints you chairman of the Third Judicial Department's Judicial Selection Committee," I had to advise him this would be illegal; I didn't live in the Third Judicial Department. (Finnegan's ignorance of that law reminded me of the time the state's senate majority leader Warren Anderson appointed me to the New York State Racing Commission, an appointment I had to decline; as a lobbyist I would have been committing a misdemeanor if I'd accepted the post.)

After this fiasco, I resigned myself to the fact that I was out of favor with the state government, but that shadow lasted only a few years. In 1998 Floyd Patterson, the former world heavyweight boxing champion (my former sparring partner!), resigned his post as chairman of the New York State Athletic Commission which oversees sports events, particularly boxing matches. My old friend Ed Musicus, former part-owner of radio stations WHAM and WVOR in Rochester and a great boxing fan, knew that I had been a champion boxer in college and he convinced me to try for the post that Floyd was leaving vacant.

I hesitated, sure that I would be waltzed around again. But Musicus was persistent in his urging, so after a while I let the governor's office know that I was interested. His appointments secretary, Tom Doherty, said he thought my chances were very good and he advised me to come to Albany and meet with Pataki and Bill Powers, then the state GOP chairman. I was dubious about my prospects; during the primary campaign I had angered the chairman by letting it be known that were I to win, he would be fired. However the meeting seemed to go well and I was assured that I had the job. I then met with Zenia Mucha, the governor's press secretary, who told me the appointment would be announced in two weeks. I returned to Rochester filled with enthusiasm, anticipating the prospect of going to all kinds of athletic events all across the country. This was my kind of appointment!

Two weeks later, I had still heard nothing. A month went by (shades of the promised judicial committee appointment) and then I received a phone call from Brad Race, the governor's chief administrator and an old friend, telling me he had good news and bad news. The governor had had to appoint someone else chairman of the three-man commission, but I would be named one of the members. I don't know what possessed me (no doubt it was my extreme disappointment), but I told Race flatly to thank the governor, but to tell him it was the chairmanship or nothing. Race said, "Well, you undoubtedly would be appointed chairman in about a year." "A year is a long time when you're my age," I told him, "so thanks, but no thanks."

About an hour later, Race called back. Doherty had another idea. The Unemployment Insurance Appeal Board (UIAB) was chaired at the time by Michael Cuevas, who was in line to be appointed chairman of the Public Employment Relations Board (PERB), which oversees the state pension system. The senate was in no hurry to confirm the appointment because Joe Bruno, the senate majority leader, and the governor were feuding. Race suggested I call Bruno and ask him to speed up the Cuevas appointment, thus opening up the UIAB chairmanship. Even though Bruno and I had spent many hours playing ping-pong and spar boxing together when I was state chairman and he a legislative staffer, I wasn't sure he would respond to my request after all these years. Was I ever wrong! To my surprise, Joe took my call and immediately agreed to confirm Cuevas. Race called me, astonished at the speed of the transaction, and told me I would soon be chairman of the UIAB by appointment of the governor.

Actually, I wasn't at all sure what I'd got myself into, so I checked the *New York Red Book,* the repository of all facts regarding state commissions and boards, their length of terms, composition, pay scale, and, most important, their duties. I found that the UIAB was a five-member board, with each member and the chairman appointed by the governor for six-year terms.

The board's executive director, Joe Kearney, really knew his stuff, thank God! Kearney had been with the state Department of Labor for more than forty years and he was a real end-issue man. A great reader, he has an extensive library and in another life had been a sailor in the

U.S. Navy. A real Renaissance man, Joe has a thorough understanding of many languages and is a devout Catholic. He'd been with the appeal board for eleven years when I arrived, and without his expertise my first months in the job would have been difficult.

The value of Joe's insights became clear early on when I was asked to decide where I wanted to locate my office. The Department of Labor had generously offered me office space in Rochester, an offer that seemed to me both efficient and expeditious. Joe pointed out that locating my office near one of the sites where the agency holds hearings would be a serious mistake and could lead to unpleasant consequences. (There are eleven such offices sprinkled across the state, all staffed by administrative law judges.) As Joe pointed out, a disgruntled claimant might think he or she could march directly to the chairman's nearby office and challenge the judgment—and in this case, the chairman would be *me*. (Imagine a line of angry claimants pounding on my office door all day long!) I was grateful for Joe's warning and established my office in a building several blocks away from the hearing office. As my assistant, I quickly hired my wonderful former legal secretary, Luann Bauer Holtz, who had worked with me back in the mid-sixties.

I was confronted on my first day at work by a small stack of papers which, on closer examination, turned out to include an order from the attorney general to pay legal fees of about $35,000, relating to UIAB work, to David Raff, a New York City attorney. On inquiry, I learned that the agency had been sued on several occasions for various reasons, including failing to provide translators for Spanish-speaking claimants, failing to issue decisions in a timely manner, failing to give claimants due process by preventing them from adequately presenting their cases, failing to allow cross-examination of opposing witnesses, and so on. Some of the suits went back as far as the 1970s.

Raff had successfully petitioned to have a federal judge appoint him monitor of UIAB's state-wide operation, and one of my predecessors had signed a consent decree agreeing to the monitoring (a lulu of a mistake). As I examined the bills submitted by Raff, I concluded that this monitoring process was in fact an outrageous imposition of federal judicial power on the prerogatives of the state executive branch. The bills were enormous and in my opinion unwarranted in size and frequency. I informed the attorney general that I refused to sign the bill vouchers. Some bureaucrats at the Department of Labor raised specious protests: "Why worry? It isn't our money," and, "If we didn't have Raff to deal with, we'd have to lay off staff, and then we'd have to work harder."

The person on my staff who really knew Raff was chief judge Bob Lorenzo. I sympathized with Bob—his job not only required him to conduct the operations of over a hundred administrative law judges in eleven different offices, but also he dealt with Raff on a daily basis. As chairman, Lorenzo reported directly to me.

The UIAB had set up three-day training sessions that Raff would attend. Afterward, of course, we would get a large bill to cover the fee for his involvement.

Shortly after I became chairman, I met with Raff to see if we might work out a plan to end his monitoring; he readily agreed to meet with me. When he sent a bill for the time spent at the meeting I refused to pay it, and eventually he backed down.

A couple of years ago, I asked the attorney general's office to call a conference with the monitoring judge. I wanted to see whether the original intent of Raff's legal proceedings (ostensibly to improve the UIAB attorneys' performance) had degenerated into the creation of a generous annuity for Raff, with the taxpayers getting hit in the nose. When I resigned on December 31, 2006, we were in the process of perfecting an appeal to the U.S. Court of Appeals for the Second Circuit (which includes New York State), to rid ourselves once and for all of the monitoring imposed on us. We found that the appointing judge (90-year-old judge Robert L. Carter) consistently rules in favor of Raff, awarding him whatever fees he requests.

There is a positive side to the story. During my chairmanship, we managed to vastly improve our operation to such a degree that there is no longer a need for an outside monitor. A capable team, led by chief judge Lorenzo, has made this agency highly efficient. In the meantime, Raff continues to charge about $65,000 a month for his involvement and he has found a way, with the approval of the federal district judge, to increase his bills. I estimate that over the years, UIAB has paid over six million dollars to Raff and his associates. The whole thing stinks. Years ago, the UIAB *did* deserve to be disciplined, but the monitoring has long since outlived its original usefulness.

As angry as I am over the way the system enriches Raff, I am even more dismayed by what I see as the encroachment of the federal judiciary in an area of the law in which it has absolutely no business and through which it is trying to usurp executive powers and run the state government.

Serving as chair of the UIAB was quite a learning experience. When I first took the reins, the board consisted of some talented lawyers, among them 81-year-old Jack Cullen, whose intelligence was exceeded only by his hard work and conscientious attitude. State law requires that there be three members of the governor's party on the board and two members from other parties. The other Republican who served with me and Cullen during my tenure was Lou Zankel, whose father had chaired the UIAB board when I was state chairman. Frank Russo, a Conservative Party member, and Arthur Strauss, a Liberal Party member and a strong contributor to board policy, completed the board membership.

During my eight years as chairman, the board changed rather dramatically. First to leave was Lou Zankel, who had hoped to be chairman, although that was not in the governor's plan. Next Strauss left to fill an appointment in New York City government. Cullen and Russo were simply not reappointed. Mike Greason, a Conservative Party member, was the first non-lawyer to be appointed to the board; he turned out to be an excellent member and has recently been appointed chairman. The other members are all women. Unfortunately, I hear that minor bickering among members has escalated, but as long as the appellate division has the last say on decisions that are appealed, all should be well.

Chapter 24

Another Rosenbaum
Joins the State's High Court

In March 2005, our son Matthew became a New York State Supreme Court Justice. I must have done something right to have a thrill like that visited on me.

Matt, then a lawyer in private practice in Rochester, told me in mid-2004 that he thought there was a real opportunity for him to ascend to the bench. At first I was a bit skeptical, primarily because he was then only thirty-nine. Actually, that was the very age when I became a state supreme court justice, but I had a far longer political pedigree than Matt. At his age, I had been a town justice, member of the county legislature, and Monroe County GOP chairman; I had also wrested control of the city of Rochester from the Democrats and had built a solid reputation as a lawyer, particularly as a litigator.

Matt had been elected twice overwhelmingly as councilman in the town of Penfield, both times leading the ticket. He had also served as the town's deputy supervisor. Matt was enormously popular, not only among his legal colleagues, but among his fellow politicians, and that was important.

It's funny: You always think you know your kids inside and out, but in fact, you don't. Matt and I have always had a very close relationship, but it took a serious election campaign for me to find out not only what a good lawyer he is (very bright, always thorough and well-prepared), but also how highly regarded he is by others, many of whom he met through his years in practice.

It was sometime in the spring of 2004 that I first heard the rumor that Don Wisner was planning to resign his seat on the court and retire in late September. Matt already had his own contacts in high places in Albany—and I had a few myself. We knew that our GOP county chairman Steve Minarik would have a lot to say about who would fill the vacancy, and we also knew that Matt was one of Steve's favorite lieutenants.

Actually, two slots were going to open on the court, Wisner's and the seat left vacant by the retirement of judge Harold Galloway. Tom Cook, chairman of the local Conservative Party, was vigorously supporting John Owens, former clerk to the Monroe County surrogate court judge and for years a card-carrying Conservative, for one of the judgeships. During the campaign, Matt and John ran as a team, but Matt was by far the more popular candidate. He had been endorsed by Rochester's *Democrat and Chronicle* newspaper, which highly praised his character and his work on the court.

The Democrats nominated city court judge Ellen M. Yacknin, who was found not qualified by the bar association poll, and a relatively unknown fellow named Kirk M. Miller. A carpetbagger from New York City, Miller had moved to the Rochester area only a few months before the campaign began, but he had been practicing law for several years and was active in non-profit and charitable work. Still another candidate, Kevin Finnegan, ran on the Working Families party line, but his entry had virtually no effect on the outcome.

New York's Seventh Judicial District is comprised of eight counties, of which Monroe is easily the largest in population. In the summer of 2004, Steve Minarik was visited by Angelo Bianchi, GOP chairman of Seneca County, where voters are a mix of agriculturalists (as in dairy farms and vineyards), restaurateurs, and small businessmen. Minarik asked Bianchi whom he thought should get the early court vacancy and Bianchi's unhesitating answer was "Matt Rosenbaum." Angelo had been a court reporter when I was on the court and was always a loyal friend and supporter, even during my uphill battle for the governorship when he went against the Republican organization which did not surprise me. Once again, Bianchi's support was crucial.

With the Seneca delegation joining the Monroe County bloc, Matt would have a majority of the judicial convention delegates who in

September 2005 at the state judicial nominating convention would nominate the candidates. The six other counties in the district made a lot of noise about a power play which would give Monroe County enough votes to fill both empty court seats, but there wasn't much they could do about it, since the numbers were there. This formula was not unprecedented.

Our next move was to achieve for Matt the appointment to Wisner's soon-to-be-vacant seat. I began systematically to lobby Governor Pataki, Bob Bulman, the governor's head of personnel, and Brooks DeBow, the governor's first assistant counsel. I lobbied Steve Minarik, who by this time had been elevated to state GOP chairman, when he was in Albany, and Matt did the same when Steve was in Rochester. Steve assured both of us that he was pushing for Matt's appointment.

Normally appointments aren't made until at least nine months after the court seat becomes vacant, but in March 2005, about five months after the vacancy, we began to sense that the appointment was imminent. In order to be appointed by the governor to fill a court vacancy, a judicial candidate must pass a poll of members of the bar association and survive a grilling by the state judicial screening committee, which must find the candidate highly qualified. Matt was their unanimous choice.

We were well aware that as soon as the appointment was made, Matt would have to prepare to run in the November election, and in that contest he would have to win his post by popular vote. That meant he had to start raising money for his campaign immediately. We scheduled our first fundraiser for a Monday night in March at a restaurant in Rochester appropriately called "Barristers," and Judy and I left for our winter home in Fort Myers. I was relaxing there in my easy chair after several weeks when my secretary called to say, "The governor wants to talk with you." The governor praised Matt and said this was just the kind of court appointment he enjoyed making; he would send Matt's name over to the state senate the next morning for confirmation. I thanked him profusely, and asked Judy to start packing because we were going home. When we arrived in Rochester, we were informed that Matt had been notified to be in Albany the day after our fundraiser. Pretty tight timing!

The fundraiser proved to be a big success, and that evening a caravan of vehicles headed for Albany to witness Matt's confirmation. The next morning Matt went before the senate judiciary committee, answered lots of questions, and that afternoon was unanimously confirmed. Speeches by Senators Alessi, Robach, and Nozzolio from our district were very supportive. I was moved to tears when I heard the speakers one after the other call up that old phrase, "The apple doesn't fall far from the tree." One week later I swore in my son at the Hall of Justice in downtown Rochester. The next morning's local newspaper carried a photo of Matt and me embracing after the oath-taking, an image that seems to have touched a chord as it was talked about for weeks after and was used in his election campaign.

Our campaign fundraising proved very successful. Eventually our tally reached $200,000, including $100,000 raised in New York City, far outstripping any of the other candidates. Matt's contributors included Henry Kissinger and Donald Trump, along with prominent (and generous) business friends of mine. Toward the end of the campaign, the newspapers announced their endorsements and my buttons really popped when Judge Matthew Rosenbaum was singled out in an editorial as "head and shoulders above the rest."

For me, every day of the campaign was an adventure. I loved it. Matt took me with him to all the outlying counties and we took part in rallies, picnics, barbecues—whatever was going on that might involve voters. We marched in parades, attended band concerts, and met a lot of fine people. I felt like a born-again politician. Wherever I went, old friends remembered me and were eager to help my son.

Most campaigns have an element of fun, and this was no exception. Early on, Matt and I began researching the effectiveness of billboard advertising. We were appalled at the expense involved, but we were afraid that if we didn't contract for the key locations, another candidate might. Eventually we hedged our bets and rented about ten less expensive boards scattered through the outlying counties. (In addition,

No Room for Democracy

Matt hired a giant moving billboard, pulled by a truck, that visited all eight counties and became a noteworthy special attraction, particularly in Monroe County.)

Toward the end of the campaign we got a call from Ontario County judge Craig Doran, an old friend of Matt, who said he had just taken a photo of our billboard at the Mount Morris exit of the New York State Thruway. In big letters, our board said, "Keep Judge Matthew Rosenbaum, Supreme Court." Right next to our billboard was another that read: "Jesus, I trust in you." We laughed and laughed, and I said to Matt, "This just goes to prove what some Christians say: Jews always stick together!"

I will always remember the excitement and fun of my son's campaign. On election night everyone gathered at the Crowne Plaza Hotel in Rochester to count the returns. Matt, who is very devout, had a suite filled with Kosher-only refreshments for his guests. As the returns began to roll in it was obvious that he would lead the ticket.

I never expected at this stage of my life to have had such a great thrill as seeing Matt ascend to the state supreme court, just as I had decades earlier. Matt has been on the bench well over three years now, and the reports out of the courthouse are that he is an extremely able judge and a natural in office. We are indeed very proud.

So that's my story. At the rate that my life's adventures proliferate, who knows what the future holds.

Chapter 25

The Changing Nature of the GOP

When I actively entered politics in 1960, the Republican Party was considered to be a middle-of-the-road party. Then, in response to what was perceived to be the profligate spending of Governor Rockefeller, a branch of the Conservative Party was established in New York State. If you had questioned New York State conservatives at that time about their animus towards Rocky, their first response would be: "He's a big spender."

Rockefeller's name was associated with high taxes, fiscal largesse, handouts to the poor, and costly support for the underdog at the expense of the state's voters (although more money actually went to strengthen New York's education system than any other cause). I found this perception interesting, if not ironic, because Rocky himself was anything but an underdog. The members of the Conservative Party seemed to hate him because they saw him as a liberal, an opinion that was both unfair and untrue.

Over the past twenty years, I've witnessed a metamorphosis in the GOP. I've seen my party move away from its middle-of-the-road position to the right, often the far right, a position that places the GOP in deep ideological opposition to many Democrats. This was not always the case. During the early sixties, the Republican and Democratic parties had more in common than not, and what's wrong with that? The winners were those who could out-strategize, out-work, and out-think their opponents, but there was plenty of goodwill between the parties and their leaders.

Why has the Republican Party changed so much? The answer can be found, I believe, in just two words: zealous ideology. Campaigns were once challenges that entailed both hard work and fun, but now they have become deadly serious struggles for the soul of the electorate. I remember talking to a woman delegate from Georgia about abortion at the Republican national convention in 1992. In order to bring the pro-choice issue to the convention floor according to party rules, it was necessary to have the support of five state delegations. I knew this delegate was personally pro-choice and I wanted her support to bring the measure to the floor. She turned down my appeal by saying that she "didn't dare do it," that she would be considered a pariah in her delegation if she attempted such a maneuver. The pro-life right-wingers had no such hesitation. They had systematically recruited right-wing conservatives and taken over delegation after delegation. Even John Tower, the conservative senator from Texas, told me that in 1976 he was not far enough to the right to qualify for membership in the Texas delegation.

I vividly recall the atmosphere when the Conservative Party was interviewing candidates in the early years of its founding. I was running for a seat on the county legislature and the Conservatives were not sure they wanted to endorse all of our Penfield town candidates for their town offices. I told them that if they wanted me to take their endorsement they would have to endorse our entire town slate, which they finally did. I doubt I could pull off a maneuver like that now.

What has happened over all these years is that the GOP has created a Frankenstein monster; to use a common analogy, it has a tiger by the tail. During my state chairmanship, Nelson Rockefeller told me he'd like to promote legislation abolishing third parties. Although the window of opportunity to do just that was closing rapidly, we could have pulled it off. However, Malcolm Wilson, then lieutenant governor, advised against such a move, saying we might jeopardize some Republican state senate seats. What he meant was that the Conservative Party would refuse to support any senator who voted for the proposed Rockefeller legislation.

Another example of the growing power of the Conservative Party (and there are many) occurred in 1976 when I convened a meeting of the New York delegates to the Republican national convention, in order to determine who was supporting Ford and who was backing Reagan. I had to call the county roll alphabetically, starting with Albany, rather than the usual way, by congressional district, in order to avoid beginning with Suffolk County, normally the first district to be called. I was worried that the Suffolk delegation would abstain and set off other district abstentions. I was aware that the Suffolk delegation knew that the Conservative Party might refuse to endorse Suffolk's local Republican ticket if it supported Ford over Reagan.

I believe that by pulling the GOP further and further to the right, the Conservative Party has made the GOP fair game for the religious right. As a result, the Republican Party is now tied in the public mind to religious issues, a very dangerous state of affairs, and one that threatens the separation of church and state. When someone says to me, "How come you've moved away from the core values of the Republican Party?" I respond by saying, "I never left the party, the current party philosophically has abandoned me." If you doubt my theory, just look at some of the more recently elected members of Congress. In many instances, there is no room for compromise. This is one big reason why the legislative sessions produce very little or nothing—and why the political atmosphere, especially in Washington, has become so acrimonious, personal, and nasty.

I know that in many areas of New York State, Republican county chairmen have deferred to Conservative Party leadership in selecting candidates for local office. I see this as very unhealthy for the future of the Republican Party.

* * *

If the nature of the Republican Party has changed, some of the faces at the national level remain the same. While Don Rumsfeld, former secretary of defense and a longtime GOP power broker, left office in 2006 under a cloud generated by the Iraq war, Dick Cheney and presidential advisor Henry Kissinger obviously are very much with us. I've known both men for forty years.

In the recent Bush administration we have witnessed a powerful ascendancy of the role performed by the vice president. It cannot be denied that Dick Cheney has been a hands-on, highly involved vice president, helping to make vital decisions in practically every aspect of President Bush's national and international policy. This may account for what he said when I visited him in his office at the beginning of W's first term: "I didn't want this job, but I'm very happy now that I have it."

In the past, the vice president worked out of an executive office building across the alley from the White House. I visited Governor Rockefeller there on numerous occasions when he was second in command of the nation. In startling contrast, Vice President Cheney's office is located in close proximity to the Oval Office. In a business where image and perception is everything, this office location adds to the aura of power associated with the vice presidency.

While it may be difficult to get the genie back in the bottle, I believe that the role of the vice president in the future will be—and should be—strictly under the control of the president. Governor Rockefeller insisted that the main job of the vice president was to serve as "standby equipment" and I agree with his position on this. If in the future, a vice presidential candidate insists on assuming inordinate power, using Cheney as a role model, it will be up to the then president to hold firmly onto the levers of his own power, while keeping the vice presidency as a strictly secondary position.

* * *

I consider Dick Cheney to be one of the best and most misunderstood people I've ever met in politics. Not only is he very capable, he is not quite the arch-conservative most people think. I worked with Dick when I represented New York State on the Republican National Committee at a time when he headed the influential Rules Committee. When I repeatedly suggested changes in our by-laws, Dick always entertained my ideas with great equanimity. Our paths also often crossed when he served as chief of staff for President Ford, and before that when he was deputy secretary of defense under Don Rumsfeld.

No Room for Democracy

In 1992, I asked Cheney to host a fundraiser for my gubernatorial effort, a reception on the aircraft carrier *Intrepid*. I knew how busy he was and I was pleased and surprised when he accepted, saying in effect, "When is it? Where is it? I'll be there." Dick stood in the reception line for over an hour that day, shaking hands and exchanging pleasantries. When he told the crowd that I was one of a handful of people in Washington whose word you could count on, I was especially proud.

Cheney used virtually the same words to describe Ariel Sharon, then prime minister of Israel, saying he was the only leader in the Middle East whose word was good. At the time, I was sitting in the very chair occupied by Sharon a month earlier during a White House visit.

Controversial he may be, but I believe that every bit of advice Dick Cheney gives President Bush is based on a deep knowledge of foreign policy gleaned from long years of governmental experience.

Dr. Henry Kissinger, of course, is the other long-standing advisor to Republican presidents and party leaders. I've known Henry for years, and have seen that under that tough exterior he's surprisingly sensitive. He also has a finely-tuned sense of humor, which has created a lot of laughs over the years for both of us.

In 1978, I asked Dr. Kissinger to come to Rochester to preside over the ribbon-cutting at the dedication of a new wing at our municipal museum and science center. I was in Manhattan at the time, so to make the trip easier for both of us I hired a plane from Grumman Aircraft on Long Island. We took off from McArthur Field in Islip and headed west toward Rochester in a bad rainstorm. We'd been in the air only a few minutes when I noticed that Henry was gritting his teeth and holding his armrests in a death grip too obvious to ignore. "Henry," I said, "don't tell me that after all that shuttle diplomacy in the Middle East you're afraid to fly!" He gave me a baleful look and said in his thick German accent, "Deek, dat vas in Air Force Vun and ve vere flying at forty-five thousand feet." Later in the flight, when it seemed we might be late for the celebration, he said, "Deek, vat vill the people of Rochester say if ve are late?" I said, "Henry, the people of Rochester will wait until three in the morning to see you. They think you are God." Quick as a wink, he said, "You mean to imply I'm not?!"

During my gubernatorial campaign in 1992, I decided to ask Henry and David Rockefeller to host a fundraiser for me at the University Club in Manhattan. When I walked into Henry's office to make my request, I found the great diplomat sitting on a couch informally dressed. Greeting me warmly, he said, "Deek, vy aren't there more beautiful vomen in the Republican Party?" He agreed to co-host the event (although he said he hoped he wouldn't alienate Bill Buckley and his conservative friends.).

As soon as I left Henry's office, I realized he'd sparked the idea for a prank I just couldn't resist. Calling a friend, Barry Landau, who is a theatrical agent, I passed on Henry's remark about the absence of beautiful women. The night of the fundraiser two gorgeous blond twins who had graced the centerfold of *Playboy* magazine showed up at the staid University Club; chaperoning them was their mother, who was more gorgeous than they were. Henry was mightily amused when he saw the blond bombshells ("Deek, how did you get zem here?!"), but David Rockefeller wasn't, and insisted that I get Doctor K out of the club "as soon as possible" since David was hosting a dinner to which Henry was invited.

Henry certainly has been a newsmaker for more than a few decades. He once told me that, during his shuttle diplomacy days, newspapers often were full of photographs of him kissing and being kissed by leaders of various Middle Eastern countries, all male, of course. In Israel, on one occasion, it was a different story. As he stepped forward to embrace Golda Meir, then the prime minister, she said quietly and with a smile, "Henry, I thought you only kissed men!" Joking aside, Kissinger said that Mrs. Meir was one of the sharpest, fastest minds he had ever encountered.

*   *   *

I've had a long relationship with the Republican Party and will continue to be a stalwart defender whenever its fight is the same as my fight. Recently I've had a doubt or two about the wisdom of some of its positions, especially its far-right stand on social issues such as stem-cell research and abortion. More than once I've been asked, "How can you

No Room for Democracy

still support the party?" I always answer, "I'm still a Republican. It's the party that's moved away from me."

Chapter 26

Advice from an Old Lion (Who Still Has His Teeth)

In August 2006, my professional life made yet another revolution. After serving for eight years as chairman of New York State's Unemployment Insurance Appeal Board, I became a spokesman for governor George Pataki. Working within New York State's Department of State Office of Regional Affairs, I represented the governor at public events through the last months of his tenure, and responded to citizen inquiries concerning state operations. It's an interesting job, occasionally a challenge, but challenges have always been my meat-and-potatoes.

Now, after fifty years serving the courts, the law, the Republican Party, two governors, and private interests, I am once again back at my old desk at the Nixon Peabody law firm in Rochester, serving as the firm's senior counsel.

***

What I've tried to accomplish with this book is to give interested readers a glimpse of the machinations that are a regular occurrence in politics and government.

It ain't very pretty but that's the way it is! I've also tried to impart some wisdom accumulated over a lifetime to budding politicians in order to help them succeed in the rough and tumble world of politics.

As I approach my eighth decade, I can't say I've become an old graybeard. (The alopecia took care of that!) I'm certainly not Machiavelli, but I have been around—and wisdom accumulates; perhaps the reader will indulge me in sharing a few observations and aphorisms that have meant something to me over the years.

—Never write when a word will suffice. Never speak when a nod will suffice.

—Keep your friends close— and your enemies closer.

—Everyone has friends, even your enemies.

—Give people credit for knowing something.
   They may know more than you, so listen.

—Everyone has an ego, so massage it.

—Don't argue with an institution that buys its ink by the train carload.
   If you do, be sure you're right.

—Yesterday's newspaper is only good for wrapping fish.

—Any story may well be a one-day wonder.

—Never embarrass anyone in public, even in jest.

—Never criticize anyone in the presence of others.

—Always tell reporters the truth.

—Never break a promise.

—Do the onerous jobs first.

—You make your luck.

—Chutzpah: It can be a powerful tool—but use it with care.

—Always be ready to fight.

—A leader must have the guts to lead.

No Room for Democracy

—If you plan to do something risky, be sure to have an escape hatch.

—Primaries were created to give people a say in choosing candidates. What they actually accomplish is to give political bosses cover, since so few people participate.

—Share the good things, so others will help you share the bad.

—Don't blame others for your mistakes.

—Loyalty to your cohorts is worth its weight in gold.

—There is no room for democracy in politics.

—There are no true friends in politics, only shifting alliances.

—If it's your job to choose among candidates for an office who seem equally qualified, make a quick decision. You'll be surprised how quickly the other candidates and their supporters simply fade away.

—Avoid conflicts of interest like the plague.

—Never be afraid to fail.

—Tenacity, persistence, determination, and hard work are an unbeatable combination.

—A sense of humor helps.

—Run through the tape—always. Work as hard at the moment before victory as you did at the beginning of the race.

—If you want to be a player, you have to get into the game.

—If you want to get into politics, make sure you can count.

—Many times throughout your career you will feel the need to consult
with the almighty. That very act can calm your nerves and dampen
pessimism, so don't write him off.

—Preserve idealism in your nature. Trust whomever you encounter.
They will sense it and many will try to meet your expectations.

—Assiduously record the requests and favors you do for people.
At one time or another you may want to call on one for help.

—Respect your religion and others will respect it as well.

—There is nothing you own under the sun nearly as valuable as a good name.

—If people respect you it will be much easier to get them to follow
your leadership.

—Take time to spend with your family. Time well spent with the family
will remind you why you're working so hard in the first place.

—Keep an abundant supply of music, flowers and laughter close by.
Music will soothe you. Flowers will remind you of God's power,
and laughter will buoy your spirits.

—You must guard your reputation like a lioness guards her cubs.
Your reputation will precede and speak for you wherever you go.
Doors will open or close depending on it.

—Be aware that politics can break your heart so prepare yourself
for it to do so.

Nelson Rockefeller, you should have been President.

No Room for Democracy

Afterword

The Democratic presidential primary of 2008 was an epic struggle, and a prototypical fight for power and the ability to impose policy changes, most of which are quite similar in their ultimate impact.

What made the struggle great theatre was not only that one candidate is half-black and the other is a woman, but also the ability of both candidates to maintain a degree of civility toward one another that defies basic human nature.

In this book I discuss the last great political convention of 1976 before the proliferation of primaries to the point that national political conventions have been reduced to cheerleading sessions, PR extravaganzas, if you will, for the eventual presidential nominee. No wonder the media has drastically shortened its participation time.

The Democratic nominee for president was basically selected by so-called superdelegates in the sense that the superdelegate count gave the nominee the necessary votes to win the nomination. And how exactly are superdelegates selected? You guessed it: by the political chairman in recognition of large contributions to the party, or by people who are in a position to do important favors for the chairman. There is no democracy involved—that is to say superdelegates are not elected, they are chosen by just one individual.

The superdelegates include mostly party and elected officials who automatically attend the convention and can support whomever they choose. Normally, the chairman who selects them either exacts a promise or already knows that they will follow instructions.

This is another example of the premise of my book: *No Room for*

Democracy: The Triumph of Ego Over Common Sense.

As I have maintained in my book, the current primary system originally designed to give the voters a say in selecting the nominee, perversely turned out to provide cover for the leaders—the unprecedented voter turnout in the 2008 Democratic primary contest to the contrary notwithstanding.

It is long past time for the complete overhaul of our primary system.

Appendix A. Rockefeller to Rosenbaum Letter, June 10, 1975

THE VICE PRESIDENT
WASHINGTON

June 10, 1975

Dear Dick:

You have told me that the Republican State Committee would like to pass a resolution, at its meeting on Thursday, endorsing the President and me for nomination as the Party's candidates for President and Vice President in 1976.

In endorsing the President for the Presidential nomination, the Committee would be acting in the highest public interest. We have a great President in the White House. As those who are close to him know, and the public is becoming increasingly aware, he stands out above all others on the national scene in the qualities of strength, courage, integrity, perception, balance and leadership that are needed to take us safely through our present troubles.

But the office of the Vice Presidency is something else again. As has been often said, one doesn't run for Vice President. True, the National Convention nominates the Vice President, as it does the President. But, following the nomination of the President, his recommendation to the Convention as to his preference for Vice President has traditionally been decisive.

Whatever others may do, there will be no effort on my part to put the slightest restraint on his complete freedom to make that choice, after he is nominated, in the light of the national interest as he sees it at that time.

- 2 -

        This being my position, I must ask you to
refrain from your proposed action, that might be
construed as putting pressure on the President in
my behalf.

        The President has placed his confidence in
me and I have but one objective -- to do my very best
to help him to the very limit of my abilities in the
great service he is rendering the country.

        With deepest appreciation for your interest
and even more for your understanding, I am,

                        Sincerely,

The Honorable Richard Rosenbaum
Chairman
New York Republican State Committee
315 State Street
Albany, New York   12210

Appendix B. "Toward Regional Presidential Primaries," *New York Times*,
April 19, 1979

Toward Regional Presidential Primaries

To the Editor:

We are fast approaching the season when we will be subjected to a rash of state primaries for Presidential delegates. There were 31 in 1976, and there will be even more in 1980.

For several years now I have been arguing the case for regional primaries to take the place of a primary system that just is not serving the country. In the Northeast, for example, we should have a primary that encompasses the issues common to this region, such as energy needs and loss of commerce and industry.

In regional primaries there would be relatively few contests, the expense to the states would be substantially less than it is now and the great amount of time now wasted in repetitious popularity contests could be used to inform the public about candidates and issues.

The benefits of grouping states which choose to have Presidential primaries in a common geographical area are manifest. Regional primaries could shorten the campaign period and help retain interest in the process. The checkerboard pattern of primaries (remember the Tuesday in 1976 when California, Ohio and New Jersey all voted on the same day?) makes it impossible to use campaign funds efficiently. And candidates should not be subjected to an endurance test by being forced to jet all over the country.

The present system also confuses the public. Citizens unable to keep track of results are impressed and misled by figures on the television screen. Regional primaries would enhance the importance and value of the national party conventions, which not only give the American people a candid view of the political process but also give the parties their only real opportunity to exchange ideas, discuss issues and demonstrate what they stand for nationwide.

I suggest that the regional primary be implemented by the major political party leaders, who should meet with their state legislative leaders to determine date and site. The legislative bodies could then pass the necessary legislation.

The regional primary is an idea whose time has come, and those of us who shoulder the responsibility of party leadership should expend every effort to make this idea a reality in 1980.   RICHARD M. ROSENBAUM
Rochester, April 4, 1979

The writer is a New York State National Republican Committeeman.

Appendix C. Rockefeller to Rosenbaum Support Letter

THE VICE PRESIDENT
WASHINGTON

Dear Dick:

Just a personal note to express my admiration & deep appreciation to you for the job you did, which was largely responsible for nominating the President. It was a super-human effort and you won the respect of everyone

No Room for Democracy

across The country —
and Their affection.

No one but you could
have done it. I'm
proud to know you
and look forward to
working with you in
The future — This time
for you! Very best & again
Thanks — Clinton

DEC 27 1976

30 Rockefeller Plaza
New York, N.Y. 10020

Room 5600

Circle 7-3700

December 23, 1976

Dear Dick:

Enclosed is a letter which I am today
sending to Malcolm Wilson and which I know you
will understand.

As I prepare to leave public office and
return to private life, I want you to know how
deeply I appreciate the unswerving loyalty and
staunch support you have given me over all the
years and, beyond that, the tremendous contribution you have made to the Party and the public
both here in the state and nationally as Chairman
of the New York Republican State Committee during
these last four years.

You have brought to the office of Chairman an
effective leadership that has not been equalled
before in this state nor, as I believe, in any state.
Yours has been a total dedication of the hardest
kind of around the clock and around the week work,
high intelligence, courage and skill in personal
relationships to the Party and its candidates. Your
holding of the state delegation for the President and
your service to his nomination nationally have been
widely recognized as crucial. The positions you
hold as Chairman of both the Northeastern States
Republican Chairmen and of the National Association
of Republican Chairmen reflect the regard which you
have won from your peers in the leadership of the
Republican party across the country.

Judy has played a significant and self-sacrificing
role in all this and I want her to know also how much
she has been appreciated.

I look forward to our continued friendship
and association and to your ongoing strong and
effective leadership of the party in which you
will of course have, as always, my full support.
When you get back from Florida I would like to get
together with you. By any chance would you be
able to sit down with George and me at Pocantico
on Sunday, January 2nd.

With warm appreciation and very best wishes
to you and Judy and the family from Happy and
myself,

Sincerely,

[signature: Nelson]

The Honorable Richard M. Rosenbaum
Chairman
New York Republican State Committee
315 State Street
Albany, New York
12210

30 Rockefeller Plaza
New York, N.Y. 10020

Room 5600   Circle 7 3700

January 18, 1979

Dear Dick:

You have asked for my thoughts on the possibility of restructuring the role of the Vice President of the United States, and I assume that you have a constitutional amendment in mind. My observations are as follows:

1. I think it would be impossible, and

2. I think it would be undesirable.

Inspite of all that has been said about the inadequacies of the present system, on balance I think it was wisely and thoughtfully constructed by the founding fathers.

I have known well all the Vice Presidents since Henry Wallace, and I think it is fair to say that all of them were frustrated. But a Vice President need not be frustrated if he simply accepts, prior to taking the oath of office, that he is assuming a standby position, and that whatever useful purpose he may have will be as a loyal assistant to the President -- without any executive power or responsibility in his own name.

During the period I was chairman of President Eisenhower's Advisory Committee on Government Organization, between 1952 and 1956, we examined ways in which the role of the then Vice President, Richard Nixon, could be expanded and made more important and useful. After an extensive study, we recommended to President Eisenhower that, both Constitutionally and functionally, this was impossible.

A. Under the Constitution, the Vice President is President of the Senate. The functions and duties beyond presiding over the Senate are not definite or prescribed and therefore the present traditional role could be expanded to one of great importance in the Senate except for two reasons:

a) By tradition -- which is very powerful in the

Senate -- the Presidency of the Senate is virtually a cere-
monial job which over the years has been shaped and prescribed as the leadership of the Senate wanted it.

   b) If the Vice President wanted to undertake a more
aggressive and powerful role than acting just as the presiding officer, he is in a very powerful position to do so
and possibly could succeed. However, in doing so he would
arouse the bitter opposition and ire of not only the leadership
but possibly the majority of the members of the Senate.

        This would place the President in a most awkward
position in his relations with the Senate. It would undoubtedly hinder the passage of his legislative programs.
Therefore, this course of action would be politically unrealistic as far as the structure of our present government is
concerned.

   B. Insofar as the Vice President's role in the Executive
Branch of the government is concerned, he is given no constitutional responsibility or authority. He is clearly there as
"standby equipment" in the event of the President's death or
incapacity. If the Congress were to enact or assign, on a
legislative basis, certain responsibilities to the Vice President, whoever was President at that time should veto the
legislation, in my opinion.

        I say this because under the Constitution, the powers
of the Executive Department are concentrated in the hands of
one man -- the elected President of the United States, who is
also the political leader of his party. If a new center of
authority and power, separate from that of the President, were
established in the Executive Branch under the leadership of an
elected Vice President -- who might at any time become President -- this would immediately create the temptation of giving
an ambitious Vice President a platform with separate authority.
This could create a situation in which there would be the
danger of splitting the loyalties of the officers and employees
in the Executive Branch between the President and Vice President,
and some could use this structure to play politics for their
own benefit against the best interests of the Government as a
whole.

        For these reasons we recommended to President Eisenhower
against any constitutional or legislative assignment of inde-

pendent responsibilities and authority to the Vice President.

    C. We recommended that the President could delegate from time to time certain responsibilities and authority to the Vice President -- which he felt could be appropriately and effectively handled by the Vice President.

    This would leave the President free to withdraw those delegations of authority and responsibility at any time if, in his opinion, they were not being properly handled, or if he began to question the support and loyalty of the Vice President.

    If the Vice President is a person of ability, stature and loyalty, there are really unlimited possibilities as to the role he can play in assisting the President.

    D. Of course, the President has a very great responsibility to keep the Vice President broadly informed regarding foreign and domestic affairs and developments as well as to Administration policies. This is vitally important so that if anything happens to the President, the Vice President will be equipped to carry on as President without a period of confusion or hiatus in the stability of the government.

    E. As to the process for the selection of the Vice President, which may well be a subject of discussion at your meeting, I personally favor the present system: namely, that the President make the choice after he is nominated. My reasons for this are:

    1. Assuming the party has selected a man of outstanding competence to be President, he should then be free to choose a Vice President both compatible and loyal to him -- not blindly, but constructively -- and who would assist him in every way the President deems desirable and useful in leading the country.

    2. The President has enough problems to worry about in this really impossible job without having to cope with a recalcitrant or conniving Vice President at his side -- which might be the case if the Vice President were chosen separately by the delegates of the party at the Convention, on the basis of political expediency. This could end up in a disaster.

    Another alternative often discussed would be to have

the President announce prior to the Convention his choice
of a Vice President. In my opinion, this would result in
giving the Vice President a greater political importance
during the election process than he would ultimately have
when he took office, and therefore could only lead to
trouble and furstration for both the President and the
Vice President during the four years that lay ahead.

    I therefore recommend not making any major change in
the traditional role of the Vice President and the original
constitutional concept of the office.

                              Sincerely,

                              Nelson A. Rockefeller

Mr. Richard M. Rosenbaum
c/o Miss Jo Good
The Republican National Committee
310 First Street Southeast
Washington, D. C. 20003

Index

Note: "Plate" indicates references to photographs and captions.

No Room for Democracy

No Room for Democracy

Z

green press
INITIATIVE

RIT Press is committed to preserving ancient forests and natural resources. We elected to print this title on 30% post consumer recycled paper, processed chlorine free. As a result, for this printing, we have saved:

20 Trees (40' tall and 6-8" diameter)
7,371 Gallons of Wastewater
14 million BTU's of Total Energy
947 Pounds of Solid Waste
1,776 Pounds of Greenhouse Gases

RIT Press made this paper choice because our printer, Thomson-Shore, Inc., is a member of Green Press Initiative, a nonprofit program dedicated to supporting authors, publishers, and suppliers in their efforts to reduce their use of fiber obtained from endangered forests.

For more information, visit www.greenpressinitiative.org

Environmental impact estimates were made using the Environmental Defense Paper Calculator. For more information visit: www.papercalculator.org.